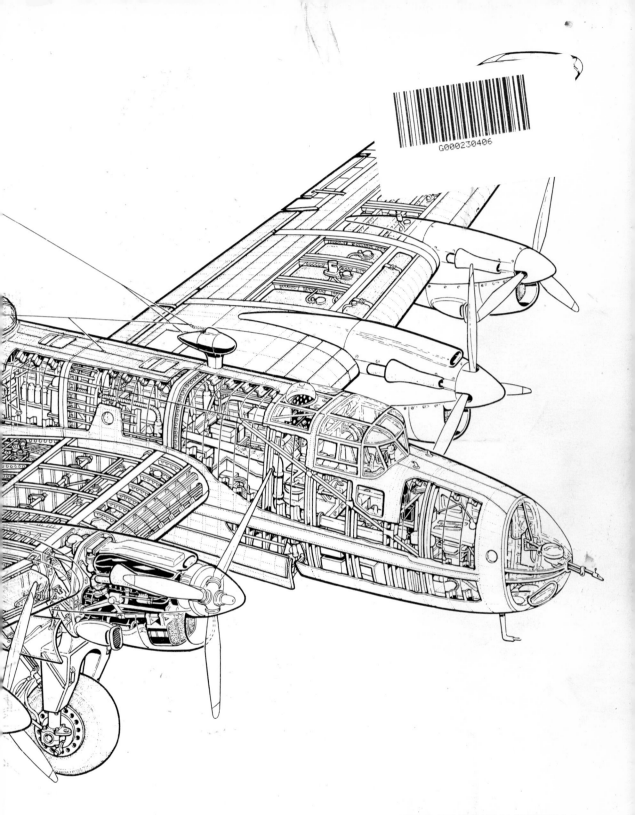

HP 59, HALIFAX 11 SERIES 1A

Halifax
Second to None

The Handley Page Halifax

Victor F. Bingham,
T.Eng. (CEI), AMRAeS, MSLAET

Airlife
England

ISBN 0 906393 66 3

First published 1986
by Airlife Publishing Ltd.

Printed in England by Livesey Ltd., Shrewsbury.

Airlife Publishing Ltd.

7 St. John's Hill, Shrewsbury, England.

Contents

Preface

Some aircraft in wartime are the focus of publicity and propaganda while others soldier on, superb in many roles. The aircraft that is the subject of this book was of the latter type. Her crews were proud of her, glad of her strong construction; built well and well-built, she struck at the German heartland flown by crews handling their first four-engined bomber. Halifax was her name, she was built by Handley Page — and to her crews she was second to none.

From the documents I have read and from correspondence from many people a question arises: Was the Lancaster all that historians say it was, or was the Halifax even better? For, to those of us who flew or worked on the Halifax, it has always been a mystery why historians have ignored its existence for so long. Those of us who have been connected with the Halifax through its design, manufacture, servicing or flying are proud of our connection with the Halifax and her achievements. Wartime propaganda and the media have focused on the Lancaster, and over the past 35 or so years have made it appear to be all things to all men. An out-of-balance picture has been built up; facts and myths have become intermingled.

Propaganda during the war reached the point, in regard to the Lancaster, where No. 4 Group Halifax personnel named it 'The *Daily Mirror* aircraft', for news items invariably began with 'Lancasters and other bombers . . .', irrespective of whether other types of bombers were in the majority. Many people who have contributed to this book, and who flew both the Halifax and the Lancaster, have commented that they could never understand why some pilots rated the Lancaster so highly.

The Halifax was designed and built by a team that had proudly produced superb aircraft for the Royal Air Force for 20 years.

It was designed to a specification that only the Halifax came near to fulfilling. Designed by a team and a firm that was, in later years, shattered and killed by Government intervention, the Halifax survived a change of engines, changes in design, changes in role, to emerge again and again as a great aircraft, an aircraft of all seasons and scenarios, until finally, fitted with Hercules engines she was superb.

Unlike some aircraft which were the darlings of one Command, the Halifax served many Commands, was the master of many roles and many climes. Operating against submarines in the Atlantic, bombing the Ruhr or giving airborne support in Europe, these all came alike to the Halifax and her crews. From the mud and slush of Yorkshire airfields to the hot sands of North Africa, from the cold of Europe to the heat and humidity of the Middle and Far East the Halifax was there — time and again surviving the most severe damage to bring her crews home to fight again. Sometimes we cursed her, many times we were proud of her, but we always admired the strength of the Halifax.

From late 1940, when No. 35 Squadron was equipped with the Halifax, until May 1945 a total of over 50 squadrons had operated or were operating this aeroplane. At the peak of Bomber Command's offensive approximately 35 squadrons were operational in Nos. 4 and 6 Groups, and with all Conversion Unit aircraft included this would give a total figure at any one time in excess of 1500 Halifaxes. The County of Yorkshire was bomber country, Halifax country, and on an operational evening the skies over York and bomb-scarred Hull would be black with the silhouettes of Halifaxes heading towards enemy territory.

This book attempts to chart the Halifax's

history, from the original design concept, through its development and testing and its wartime roles, illustrating how interference from various quarters and insistence on certain specification items affected its performance — interference that Avros did not have to contend with in their production of the Lancaster. With regard to its operations, I have restricted the descriptions to certain particular incidents as the general operational scene is well documented in such books as *Raider, Search and Destroy, Instruments of Darkness, Pathfinder* — and *The Peenemunde Raid.*

Many people have helped me with advice and encouragement, many have sent me information, some supplied their own notes and documents. My thanks go to all. In particular, I am deeply indebted to D. Goode, B. Kerval and staff of the Main Library RAE Farnborough for help in sorting out reports, documents etc; Cedric Vernon (ex-Handley Page) for information on aerodynamics at Handley Page; Alan Dowsett (ex-Handley Page) and the Handley Page Association for obtaining information for me; R. Barker of the RAF Museum; E. Turner of the Air Historical Branch; G. Clout and Mrs H. Roberts of the Imperial War Museum; the staff of the Public Record Office; J. Olsson of the LAP Group; A. W. L. Naylor of the Royal Aeronautical Society; J. Ratcliffe (ex-Handley Page) for information on the background to the Halifax; R. R. Aspden of British Caledonian; E. N. Brailsford (ex-Handley Page) on flight testing; L. Armandias, H. G. Conway and E. Wingrove of British Messier; G. F. Mahony of British Airways for his notes on the Berlin Airlift; Brian Gardner and the Flight Refuelling Archives on flight refuelling involvement, F. S. G. Codling and G. S. Stone of Airtech Ltd. Thanks are also due to K. Atherton, A. Barnard, Ian Burns, P. Caines, G. H. Cunliffe, K. Chapman, 'Nipper' and G. E. Curtis, A. W. Cooper, E. E. Dann, J. R. C. Feardon, Air Commodore P. Gilchrist, K. T. Garnett, J. Cope, D. Hadley, G. P. Hayward, R. Harrington, J. Hampton, E. G. Hardy, R. S. Hogg, Wg Cdr S. Iqbal of the Pakistan Air Force, I. Jenkins, G. Lee, J. McArdle, H. McLean, J. Pierton, R. W. Richardson, H. J. Rix, J. Scott, J. Sheppard, D. Simpkin, D. Sumner, C. Sivyer, T. Thackray, C. W. Walker, R. D. Ward, D. Westbrooke and A. L. Wilson. Finally, my special thanks to Ian Robinson (ex-Handley Page), Fred Gibbons (ex-77 Squadron), Group Capt. Eric Cropper and Derek Reed (both of the Yorkshire Air Museum) for assistance in compiling the book, and to my wife for her tolerance over the period that I was researching and compiling it.

Opinions, where expressed, are my own unless otherwise stated, and although I have tried to cover and record the Halifax's history there are obvious gaps, for the full history would run to many volumes because the Halifax was developed into so many versions and used in so many roles. Whereas the Lancaster was a specialised bomber aircraft, the Halifax had a wider application — versatility was her second name.

V. F. B.

Chapter 1
The Originator and his Team

The aircraft construction firm of Handley Page was named after its first chairman, Frederick Handley Page; it began with him and to all intents and purposes it died with him. Although to some 'HP' appeared penny-conscious and autocratic he was also a father figure. Equally at home on a firm's outing or in the design office, he knew his staff by name and spent many hours each week in the Works right up to the later years when he became seriously ill.

He was born in Cheltenham on 15 November 1885, and his parents were of the Plymouth Brethren faith. After a three-year course in electrical engineering at Finsbury Technical College he went to work for Johnson & Phillips Ltd, who were electrical machinery manufacturers. While gaining experience and promotion with this firm he became interested in aeronautics and by 1907 had become a member of the Aeronautical Society of Great Britain. In 1911 he became the aeronautical engineering lecturer at Northampton Institute, having by then become involved in the construction of aircraft. For in the year 1909 he had registered himself as a private limited company, named Handley Page Ltd, to engage in aeronautical engineering, the first such company registered in Great Britain.

Both his knowledge and his autocratic manner were part of the firm of Handley Page and no doubt account for a part of the history of the Halifax — in modern jargon no doubt he would be termed the kingpin of Handley Page — for his decisions and opinions were

A Halifax Mk.III.

voiced regardless of a person's rank in the Service or the Government. His penny-conscious manner may have come from his family background, but in any case it was a necessary qualification in the tight financial climate between 1918 and 1939, which affected both the Royal Air Force and the aircraft industry.

In spite — or because — of his manner, he had many friends, and he was also generous enough during the war years to have paintings commissioned for squadrons who operated his aircraft. Many Service and civilian acquaintances communicated items of intelligence to him, both in regard to foreign aircraft and factories and methods, and also other manufacturers. He was made fully aware of the dispersal of aircraft manufacturing facilities in Germany and was fully in agreement with a similar dispersal being carried out in Great Britain — although later disagreeing with the Shadow Factory Scheme, as it meant the placing of aircraft factories away from the London area.

His office was basically the drawing offices; much time was spent there with the draughtsmen at their boards, though his 'inner sanctum' was more like a drawing-room and was furnished that way. Though trained as an electrical engineer it was in aeronautical engineering that he made his mark, for the name of Handley Page has been synonymous with large aircraft and heavy bombers since 1914, when Rear Admiral Sir Murray Sueter demanded a 'Bloody Paralyser' and Handley Page designed and built the 0/100 for the Royal Naval Air Service. The Halifax followed on in a long pedigree of large bombers from the Handley Page stable, such as the 0/400, V1500, Hyderabad, Heyford, Hampden and Harrow, and added another success to the name of Handley Page.

In later years 'HP' was knighted as Sir Frederick Handley Page, but this appears not to have diminished his interest in the firm that bore his name, and which was recognised throughout the aircraft industry by its winged HP emblem. He chose his top staff wisely, and all were experts in their own fields and in the art of aeronautics generally. In 1912, 'HP' took on G. R. Volkert and in 1914 appointed him Chief Designer. Volkert had been educated at Northampton Institute where 'HP' was a lecturer and had gained his Engineering Diploma with Honours; he remained the Chief Designer up until his retirement in 1945, except for two years when he was a member of the British Air Mission to Japan. The Halifax was designed under Volkert's control.

By 1921, Dr. G. V. Lachmann had come into the 'HP' orbit following a meeting in Berlin. Educated at Darmstadt and Göttingen, he served in the German Flying Corps in 1917-18 as a pilot and in 1929 joined Handley Page full time, covering aerodynamics, stressing and slot development. With Volkert, J. Ratcliffe and R. S. Stafford he was responsible for the design and development of the Halifax.

J. Ratcliffe joined Handley Page in 1933 as Chief Draughtsman and was responsible for the HP56/57 drawings. In 1939 he was appointed by 'HP' to control the Outside Production Office, being responsible for Halifax production and development.

J. S. Stafford joined Handley Page in 1926 as a technical assistant in the Aerodynamics Department, followed that with some flying as test observer, and then became Chief Aerodynamicist in 1933, finally taking over the job of Chief Designer at the end of the 1939-45 war.

Both Ratcliffe and Lachmann considered 'HP' frugal and inclined to be a bit of a martinet. He allowed no executive office to be heavily carpeted, for instance, and his influence on design did not always benefit the final product. This influence, when it differed from their own opinion, was quite often deflected by Lachmann or Volkert if they felt that it adversely affected the design — although 'HP' early on did sense the coming change from biplanes to monoplanes.

Handley Page and 'HP' were one; he was a total autocrat and proud of his firm and their products. If it was his refusal to join the two main manufacturing groups that was the cause of the end of Handley Page, then similarly it was the fault of the government of the day that gave Handley Page no further contracts that caused that end. Maybe he was right in his refusal, for those two main manufacturing groups did not afterwards produce one new design of their own. While the two groups eventually became British Aerospace, Handley Page had in the meantime gone into liquidation and a superb design and manufacturing team was scattered, a team whose loyalty Sir Frederick Handley Page valued highly, a team he had fought to retain in the face of Government machinations, a team that produced the Victor — the last Handley Page bomber and the last and best of the bombers, and in truly Handley Page tradition, well designed and built.

Chapter 2
Specification, Design and Development

The specification

The Handley Page Halifax really began at the start of 1935, when a heavy bomber specification which had not been fulfilled was updated and issued as Air Ministry Specification B1/35, with a limit on wingspan of 100 ft and, if possible, the all-up weight to be no greater than 20,000 lb. Handley Page's design study to Spec. B1/35, the HP55, of which a prototype was ordered on contract 441975/35, was a mid-wing monoplane of 95 ft wingspan, and these characteristics:

    Tare weight of 16,221 lb
    Normal loaded weight of 26,326 lb
    Wing area of 1070 square feet
    Wing loading of 24.6 lb/sq ft
    Bomb load of 2000 lb for 1500 miles
    cruising at 224 mph

It was planned to be powered by two Bristol Hercules HE1SM engines.

By the start of 1936 the B1/35 was in the design stage and a one-twentieth scale model of the aircraft was produced for wind tunnel tests. By July 1936 the Air Ministry was asking Handley Page's how soon before the B1/35 (HP55) was to be in production, and were even considering it without a prototype. But, as 'HP' pointed out, the HP55 could not fly before the autumn of 1937 as the Bristol Hercules engine delivery date was not until August of that year, providing there was no delay in the engine's production.

On 24 August 1936 Air Ministry Specification P13/36 for a twin-engined all-metal medium bomber was issued, and also Specification B12/36 for a four-engined heavy bomber was sent out to a number of companies in the aircraft industry. The requirements of Spec. P13/36 were of a wide and conflicting nature and began as follows:

The Air Staff require a twin-engined medium bomber for worldwide use. It should be an aircraft that can exploit the alternatives between long range and very heavy bomb load which are made possible by catapult launching in a heavily loaded condition . . . During all operations it is necessary to reduce time spent over enemy territory to a minimum. Therefore the highest possible cruising speed is necessary . . .
In order to ensure that the all-round defence is adequate, power operated gun turrets are to be located in the nose and tail. The aircraft must be suitable for operation by day or night at home and abroad.

The specification also mentioned the possibility of combining the medium bomber, general reconnaissance and general purpose classes in one basic design, which could be adapted at some stage in construction to each specific role. Consideration was also being given to the possibility of carrying two torpedoes.

From this it appears that the general purpose role that had bedevilled so many aircraft designs in the 'twenties and 'thirties was still raising its head, in spite of experience proving how inefficient a GP design could be — apart from the saving of Government money, that is.

The performance requirements of Specification P13/36 were:
A speed not less than 275 mph at 15,000 ft at two-thirds maximum engine power at maximum cruising rpm.

The maximum load at accelerated take-off (catapult launch) to be not less than 4000 lb bomb-load with a range not less than 3000 miles at 15,000 ft at two-thirds maximum engine power.

Under maximum load conditions it was hoped that a range of at least 2000 miles would be obtained when carrying the maximum possible bomb-load of 8000 lb. Maximum range to be not less than 3000 miles.

Service ceiling to be not less than 28,000 ft at normal loading.

Specific items mentioned in the specification were:

(a) Variable pitch airscrews, or some similar device, to be fitted.
(b) Armament: Front turret to mount two Browning 0.303 inch guns and the rear turret to mount four Browning 0.303 inch Browning guns, with a proviso that any alternative scheme for the remote control of the guns would be considered.
(c) Attention to the design to provide easier maintenance in the field.

The engines available for the P13/36 designs were the Vulture by Rolls-Royce, the Napier Sabre and the Bristol Centaurus. With the Vulture being the most advanced in its development, this was the engine chosen for both Handley Page's and Avro's designs to the P13/36.

During the decision-making of the Operational Requirements Committee prior to the issue of Specification P13/36 a number of points was raised regarding the armament — one of which was the total elimination of the nose gun turret, though this consideration was dropped. But one point which was actioned — though not fulfilled in any design or derivative of Specification P13/36 — was the raising of the cruising speed requirement from 220 mph to 275 mph. Consideration was also given to the fitment of beam-mounted Vickers K guns, something that did not appear on the Mk. 1 Halifax until it entered service.

A further limitation, which was part of both the B12/36 and P13/36 Specifications, related to the size of main components, the reason behind this being the transportation of these main components by normal RAF MT — without the use of special transport for different types of damaged aircraft or replacement components. These limits were as follows:

(i) Centre fuselage not to exceed 35 ft long, 9 ft 6 in high and 8 ft wide.
(ii) The remainder of the fuselage components not to exceed 22 ft long, 9 ft high and 7 ft wide.

A.M. SPECIFICATIONS B.1/35 and P.13/36 COMPARATIVE WEIGHT AND PERFORMANCE TABLE			
	B1/35 'Hercules' HE.1.SM	P13/36 'Hercules' HE.1.SM	P13/36 'Vulture' FS
Wing area	1070 sq ft	970 sq ft	975 sq ft
Span	95 ft	90 ft	90 ft
Structure weight	9647 lb	9900 lb	9900 lb
Tare weight	16221 lb	16769 lb	17955 lb
Total weight, normal load	26326 lb	26840 lb	25376 lb
Wing loading, normal	24.6 lb	27.5 lb	26.0 lb
Bomb load, normal	2000 lb	2000 lb	1000 lb
Range, normal	1500 miles	1500 miles	1000 miles
Range, with 4000 lb bombs without overload	900 miles	900 miles	—
Speed, cruising	222 mph	230 mph	275 mph

Figure 1. Comparative table from 'HP'.

After careful consideration at Handley Page's it was found that an aircraft built to meet the P13/36 specification would be similar in general arrangement and overall dimensions to the B1/35. Further investigations were then pursued to determine whether an aircraft built to the P13/36 specification could fulfil the requirements of the B1/35 specification; it was found that all the requirements could be met with the exception of the mid-upper gun turret, which was offset to some extent because the P13/36 had a four-gun tail turret as against the B1/35's two-gun tail turret. Using the same engines as the B1/35 the performance of the P13/36 was calculated to be slightly better than that of the B1/35.

Although Handley Page's were by then in the design stage of the B1/35 aircraft, on 22 September 1936 'HP' wrote to the Air Member for Research and Development pointing out these similarities and enclosing a Comparative Table of the B1/35 with Hercules and the P13/36 with Hercules and with Vultures (see Fig. 1).

Obviously 'HP' did not share the Air Ministry's optimism over the Vulture and felt it would not be available in time, for in his letter he suggested that Bristol Hercules engines be fitted in the first aircraft until the Vulture became available; then, if a second P13/36 was ordered at the same time, the first Vulture engines could be fitted in this one, allowing the first machine to be used for trials and production mock-up purposes.

During September 1936 Handley Page's tendered for the P13/36 aircraft, quoting a price of £50,000 each prototype. It was decided at Handley Page's that to obtain the increased cruising speed of the P13/36 specification the wing span could be reduced to 90 ft, the wing area being reduced from 1070 sq ft to 975 sq ft, and the wing loading at normal load increased from 24.6 lb/sq ft to 27.5 lb/sq ft.

After a series of exchanges of correspondence between 'HP' and the Air Ministry regarding a decision on the B1/35 or the P13/36, in January 1937 the Air Ministry cancelled the Handley Page version of the B1/35 in favour of the P13/36. On 3 February 1937 'HP' was again writing to the Air Member for R & D suggesting that two machines to P13/36 should be built simultaneously, so that one would be available for flight trials and the other for armament equipment layout and the study of production problems, and again stating that the necessary data was available to use the Hercules engines if the Vulture engines did not mature in time.

In April 1937 the Air Ministry ordered two prototypes of the Handley Page HP56 to Specification P13/36, as well as two of the Avro type 679 to the same specification, all to be powered by the Rolls-Royce Vulture engine. In July 1937 'HP' called for tests on the HP56 one-sixteenth scale model to be expedited.

The design of the Vulture had begun in September 1935, conceived as a quick means of obtaining a 2000 hp engine by combining two Kestrel engines on a single crankshaft to form a 24-cylinder 21-litre engine of 'X' formation. It was type-tested in August 1939 at 1800 hp, for take-off using 87 octane fuel, and production began in January 1940 with the power being gradually increased to 2010 hp in March 1941. Unfortunately, further running after the type-test revealed serious problems — connecting rod failures and installation trouble being just two. These problems, coupled with the problem of producing both the Vulture and Merlin engines in only three factories, created an overload on Rolls-Royce.

The man-hours required to produce a Vulture engine were 50 per cent greater than for the Merlin engine, and the greater potential for development of the Merlin as against the Vulture were just two more considerations when it came the time for the decision to re-engine the HP56 with four Merlins in place of the two Vultures.

During the time that the twin-engined Vulture-powered P13/36 HP56 was crystallising in design, alternative schemes were being considered at the Air Ministry, for it was becoming evident that insufficient production of the Vulture engine would make it impossible to power both the HP56 and the Avro 679. So, in July 1937, the Air Member for R & D requested drawings from Handley Page's that represented the twin-engined P13/36 and also a four-engined machine to be based on the same specification. On 20 July 1937 'HP' forwarded copies of two drawings to the Air Ministry, one being No. 5601/A representing the P13/36 aircraft, while the second represented the same machine with four Taurus engines installed. In the letter accompanying the drawings 'HP' pointed out the difficulties of making the P13/36 a four-engined machine, whether powered by Merlin or Taurus, and that the change in design from the present twin to a four-engined design would be neither P13/36 nor B12/36; the extra weight and space that would be required for tanks, controls and engine installations would be out of proportion to the rest of the design. He completed his letter with a request that Handley Page's be allowed to proceed with the design as a twin-engined machine. (see Fig. 2).

Figure 2
Handley Page HP56 to Specification P13/36.

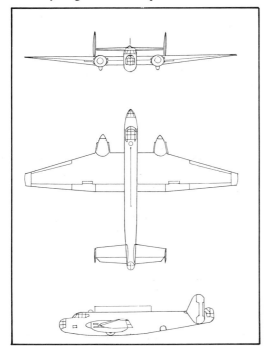

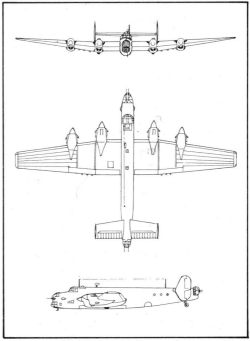

Figure 3 — Handley Page HP57.

From correspondence that ensued over this period it is obvious that the change from two to four engines at this stage of the design was not palatable to 'HP'. The points he made regarding the fitting of four engines into a twin-engined design were legitimate, and when the final design with four engines did emerge it was a different aircraft in looks and size (see Fig. 3) from the P13/36. Its all-up weight had then increased to 55,000 lb with an empty weight of 23,000 lb. As 'HP' pointed out to the Director-General of Production on 21 December 1938, the change in design to accommodate the four Merlins finally resulted in a delay of six months in producing the aircraft.

Design and development

Tenders for the medium bomber specification P13/36 were originally asked to be returned by 7 January 1937, but it was March before Handley Page's tender was submitted. 'HP' himself objected to the four-gun tail turret requirement, as his preference in rear armament was for an upper and lower gun turret amidships.

By March 1937 the Handley Page Aerodynamics Section was laying out a Model Test Policy for the P13/36, with an order for one-tenth scale models for the NPL and the RAE and a one-sixteenth scale model for Handley Page tests. In April 1937 the same section had obtained a comparison of the features of the Avro and Handley Page tenders, which were:

and to man the front turret), one wireless operator and one rear gunner. The specification required that the nose turret mounted two Browning 0.303 inch machine-guns with not less than 1000 rounds per gun and arc of fire in azimuth not less than 180 degrees, and the tail turret four Browning 0.303 inch machine-guns with 1000 rounds of ammunition per gun with a reserve of 6000 rounds (or 4000 rounds if 1500 were provided per gun) and a similar arc of fire in azimuth.

	HP	Avro
Wing area	975 sq ft	850 sq ft
Span	88 ft	80 ft (probably)
Petrol for long range	1650 IG	1600 IG
Top speed	320 mph	328 mph
Take-off	Satisfactory	Unsatisfactory
Wing loading (lb/sq ft)	27.0	30.0
Wing thickness	21%	20%

Volkert's design for the P13/36 specification was a mid-wing monoplane having a thick aerofoil section. The wing shape was similar to that chosen for the HP55 (B1/35), having a strongly swept-back leading edge on the outer span, reminiscent of the Douglas DC2/3 series of aircraft, which it has been said that Volkert admired. The wing was to be of two-spar construction and the fuel cells integral to the wing. The two pilots were housed in a glazed cabin whose top was level with the top surface of the fuselage.

On 5 April 1937 Volkert was spelling out to the various departmental heads the experimental features of the HP56, namely the proposed integral wing/tank construction, the fully stressed skin type wing employing corrugated and flat sheet in combination, the stainless steel exhaust system, the sliding bomb-door scheme, the introduction of the Messier hydraulic undercarriage system and the catapulting requirement.

On 30 April 1937 Contract No. 624972/37 was placed for two prototypes of the HP56, serial-numbered L7244 and 7245, specifying the Vulture engine as the power unit to be used. A crew of four was also specified — two pilots (one to act as bomb aimer/navigator

Other requirements were oxygen equipment, crew compartment heating, a parachute hatch aft of the bomb bay capable of being used for supply dropping, a message pick-up hook, autopilot, complete radio and blind landing equipment, camera, flare tubes, and a method of carrying and dropping either two 18-inch torpedoes, or four 2000 lb AP bombs or sixteen 500 lb bombs or sixteen 250 lb bombs.

It was intended that parts such as the fuselage monocoque, the tailplane, flaps and ailerons were to follow Handley Page recent design practice, but the proposed integral wing/fuel tanks and the combined flat sheet/corrugated stressed skin were a complete break with any standard design feature. The wide use of corrugated sheet in combination with flat sheet in highly stressed areas called for accurately produced corrugations, for which at that time there was no capability. Another innovation was the sliding bomb-door scheme, which was still to be made and tested, the actual method of power operation being considered of secondary importance.

The undercarriage proposed for use by Volkert was the Messier, which conflicted with the ADM. Nevertheless, Handley Page's were prepared to consider this system and

Halifax prototype, L7244, at Boscombe Down 1940, without turrets. (IWM)

seek Air Ministry approval, with the intention of designing the whole of the mechanical gear themselves and only putting out to contract the hydraulic components.

Of all these innovations only the Messier hydraulic system and undercarriage went into full-scale production on the Halifax aircraft, for although the two prototype aircraft had integral fuel tanks the production Mk.1 aircraft utilised the self-sealing type tank, which was by then an operational necessity. Due to shortage in Messier undercarriage production, and at DTD's insistence, the Dowty system was fitted as a substitute and the aircraft called a Halifax Mk.5, until the castings used on the undercarriage entailed a reduction in landing weight, when a reversion was made to the Messier. The combined corrugated/flat sheet stressed skin was never used on the Halifax and only appeared with the arrival of the Victor.

The next problem to be considered was the type of dive brake that would be required to satisfy the 70 degree dive-bombing requirement of P13/36, especially as there had been recent experience of failures of elevators during dives. In May 1937 the Aerodynamics Section were considering both the slotted flap and the Shrenk flap, an approach being made to the Air Ministry with a view to conducting full-scale research. On 15 June the Air Ministry notified Handley Page that the angle of dive requirement had been altered from 70 degrees to 25 degrees and to simplify bomb stowage the maximum number of bombs could be reduced from 16 to 15.

In July 1937 a mock-up conference was called and a preliminary mock-up of the pilot's cabin made ready for Air Ministry inspection; but on a preview inspection by the Flying Department, Major Cordes the Chief Test Pilot raised objections both to the rudder bar, which he considered too narrow and not parallel to the centreline of the aircraft, and also to the position of the undercarriage and flap gate, which had levers operating horizontally. After the Air Ministry representatives had viewed the mock-up and reacted favourably to the gate set-up, Major Cordes made an even stronger protest, disagreeing emphatically with their decision and pointing out that they would not be the ones using it, and that the gate should be in a vertical position, so that the levers moved in the same sense as the undercarriage and flaps.

9

The gate was then re-positioned where he wanted it and in the correct operating plane. This was followed in August by the beginning of the drawings for the HP57 and, by November, information had been received from Rolls-Royce on the Merlin installation, so the design team began to proceed with the design of the engine mountings and installation, which resulted in July 1938 in an order being placed on Rolls-Royce for power-plant equipment for one aircraft only.

Some relief was given to the design team by the Air Ministry's decision to drop the requirement for the carrying of torpedoes, and 'HP' pressed for the dropping of the catapult requirement — for investigation by the Aerodynamics Section on data supplied had determined that with the four Merlin engines at take-off rpm of 2850 the take-off run to clear a 50 ft screen was 760 yards. With Rolls-Royce contemplating a take-off rpm of 3000 then the take-off run would be reduced to 710 yards for the same conditions — sufficient to make catapulting unnecessary. Further relief from the varied requirements of the specification came with the DTD's decision to delete the 25 degree dive-bombing requirement, this being due to an uncertainty that large aircraft could be dived safely with dive brake flaps. That and the catapulting requirement had put heavy demands on the stressing and had serious effects on the design; but at the same time Handley Page were asked to provide as large a diving angle as possible without causing undue structural and weight increase.

From the above it will be seen that the specification had been over-ambitious and completely out of touch with reality. That the Handley Page design and production staff managed to produce an aircraft in 38 months that mainly met the requirements was beyond expectations, yet they did, and that was to Handley Page's credit and not the Air Ministry's.

No requirement for fuel jettisoning had been called for by the Air Ministry, but the Handley Page Production Engineer considered that the weight of fuel in the maximum load case would make the aircraft too heavily loaded to land if an emergency occurred within the first two or three hours after take-off, so it was proposed to develop a suitable flush fitting jettison valve for fitting

Halifax Mk.2 R9430 being flown on one engine to determine the rate of sink for emergency flights on one engine. (IWM)

to the two outermost sections of the wing tanks. To improve take-off lift and handling, leading-edge auto slots had been considered for fitment to the HP56 and these were carried over to the HP57 design.

At this stage in design the HP57 was emerging as a conventional mid-wing monoplane with a slab-sided fuselage for ease of production, but due to the decision to repower the HP56 design with four Merlin engines it had been necessary to alter the mainplane plan outboard of the inner engines, so that the HP57 had a straight spar and taper on leading and trailing edges — whereas the HP56 had been similar to the HP55 in having leading-edge sweepback only. The inner engine nacelle fairings terminated at the leading edge of the flaps and the engine nacelle positions were mid-slung, this position giving lowest drag at low incidence — which corresponds to high speed. Unfortunately, in practice this did not occur. Instead, higher drag resulted, which entailed further investigation and an extension of the inner nacelle fairings to the trailing edge of the main flaps, but this did not occur until flight testing of the prototypes had begun. The mid-slung nacelle position was maintained and, apart from the underslung positions on the Mk.2 Series 2 trial aircraft, was continued

Catalina-type flame damper fitted to Hercules 16 engines of Halifax B3 HX229 for tests at Boscombe Down. (RAE)

until the installation of the Hercules engines, when it proved ideal for the radial engine.

The Air Ministry made known to Handley Page their interest in alternative engine installations for the Halifax and the consequent performance figures, the engines suggested being four Napier Dagger, Bristol Taurus or Hercules. The Aerodynamics Section considered the Dagger and Taurus engine installations to be so inferior in their performance to that of the Merlin that they did not include them in their comparative

Handley Page-designed venturi-type exhaust for Halifax Merlin engines (RAE)

performance data. This is hardly surprising in the case of the Dagger, after Handley Page's experience with it installed in the HP52 Hampden airframe.

With the Hercules a different picture emerged. The increase in power-plant weight with the Hercules was about 1500 lb. The Hercules HE-1SM engine using 87 octane fuel was the one chosen for comparison, although the Hercules HE-6SM requiring 100 octane fuel would give 1500 bhp for level flight at 15,000 ft but would require certain airframe strengthening:

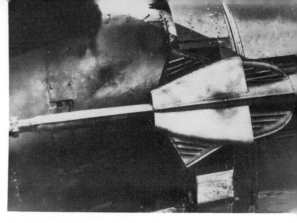

Catalina-type flame damper fitted to Hercules 16 engines of Halifax B3 HX229 for tests at Boscombe Down. (RAE)

	Merlin 10 87 octane	Hercules HE-1SM 87 octane
Max level bhp	1025	1275
Max level height	17,500 ft	13,500 ft
Cruising bhp at 15,000 ft	670	810
Take-off bhp	1075	1330
Take-off rpm	3000	2800
Total weight for 1000 yd take-off	51,000 lb	60,000 lb
Tare weight	29,900 lb	31,440 lb
Range with 3500 lb bomb-load	2530 miles	1900 miles
Range with 11,000 lb bomb-load	1100 miles	600 miles
Range with full tanks (1880 gallons)	2830 miles	2400 miles
Maximum speed	320 mph	325 mph
Cruising speed at 15,000 ft	272 mph	280 mph

The decision on the Merlin installation was a sore point with Handley Page's and aircrew for many years. Coolant leaks, radiator failures and flame damping of the exhaust were three of many faults with the Merlin, and even during the development stage doubts were being expressed about Rolls-Royce's performance in producing an acceptable liquid-cooled installation for the Halifax. On 28 March 1939 there were discussions taking place within Handley Page's management with a view to pressing the Air Ministry for instructions to design alternative air-cooled engine mountings as the design and development staff at Handley Page were increasingly disappointed with their experience in working with Rolls-Royce on the Merlin installation. Every single item in the cooling system, for example, had been

changed not once but many times, with the result that Drawing Office charges on the engine installation were far higher than necessary due to the duplicated work resulting from Rolls-Royce alterations.

In a letter from Handley Page's Production Engineer to the Managing Director and other management on 29 March referring to their discussions, Volkert not only spelt out the above points but also mentioned that practically the entire engine cowlings were double curvature and therefore necessarily costly, even with large quantity production. Further to this, he wrote that the liquid-cooled nacelle seemed to have only one advantage — reduced drag — and it was even questionable whether this could be achieved in the case of the inner nacelles, the fairing section being determined by the undercarriage wheels. Liquid-cooled engines in front of thick wings involve serious problems in regard to exhaust outlets and the cooling system is not only elaborate but also costly and heavy. What was not mentioned was that the liquid-cooled engine and its components such as radiators are highly vulnerable in battle. Incidentally, at this date the latest dry weight was no less than 1430 lb.

In October 1939 Farren of DTD suggested to Volkert that Handley Page's should consider alternative American engines of similar power to the Merlin, so 'HP' agreed to investigate the Cyclone G200 and the Pratt & Whitney 'Twins', although by this time the design and development teams were already investigating the Bristol Hercules, which developed 1330 bhp at 2800 rpm at take-off against the Merlin's 1075 bhp at 3000 rpm.

Meanwhile a choice in armament and turret position and types was being considered, which was eventually decided in favour of the Boulton & Paul type. Tests were therefore carried out by the Aerodynamics Section in their wind tunnel on a one-sixteenth scale model to check on drag, and the effects on directional trim and aircraft loads. The results were considered to be satisfactory with nose and tail turrets, although 'HP' and Volkert would have preferred a mid-upper and a mid-under turret as opposed to the tail turret demanded by the specifications and insisted upon by the Air Ministry.

It will have been noted by now that Avro were given priority over Handley Page regarding the Vulture engines; it was Handley Page's who were required to fit Merlins, but it was still Handley Page's who were being asked to consider alternative engines. The same was true of the turrets, for it appeared that the Frazer-Nash production of turrets would not be sufficient for both aircraft types, so it was Handley Page's who had to consider alternatives.

Returning to 1938, drawings were still being prepared of the various details and layout of the HP57, and by 27 October the drawings for the integral fuel tanks had been completed. A decision was required on the drawings for the centre section fitted with

independent tanks. In the HP57 the new intermediate wing section between the inboard and outboard engine nacelles was designed with an integral fuel tank between the spars, which gave the necessary torsion and stiffness without incurring too great a structural penalty. At this stage the total fuel capacity was 1980 imperial gallons. During the mock-up stage, in a conference on fuel jettisoning, a problem originally not considered by the Air Ministry in the P13/36 discussions, no agreement could be reached. Thus it was solved by adding three external jettison pipes under each intermediate wing, so arranged that they deflected with the flaps to ensure that the jettisoned fuel was clear of the tail unit and any static discharge.

In the meantime work had commenced on the two HP57 prototypes at the Cricklewood works, where the factory layout was revised by the Works Superintendent, J. Hamilton, to utilise the split assembly principle that Handley Page's had introduced on the HP52.

By January 1939 the production drawings had commenced issue and the material required had been ordered, and the Merlin 10 power-plant installation had been approved by the Air Ministry after flight trials in the Whitley, although Volkert was not very happy with the cabin heating system. The Messier hydraulic system was also considered acceptable for use on the Halifax by DTD, although Messier had yet to get into production.

During 1939 occurred the first of many requests, variations and alterations that were to affect the Halifax and its developments throughout its life. For in February in an interview that 'HP' had with the Chief of Air Staff, Air Chief Marshal Newall, he was informed that a variant of the HP57 fitted with a 20mm cannon was being considered, and for this purpose an underslung cannon-type gun turret would be tried. This did not reach fruition, like many other schemes, but badly-needed drawing office and experimental time was wasted on many of these projects. In June Major Cordes, in a letter to the Production Engineer, stated that he considered the pilot's forward exit through the roof was too small, a point he had raised in previous reports, and concluded by stating that the Flying Department would carry out no dives or manoeuvres likely to impose severe stress until the exits were deemed satisfactory by the Flying Department. This accent by the Flying Department on exits, controls and control positions reflects great credit on them for determining that the aircraft was satisfactory for Service operation; that the aircraft had a deficiency in directional control under certain extreme conditions during its operational service, which was also not picked up by A&AEE at Martlesham Heath, was not in any way due to lack of thorough testing on the part of either establishment.

The first prototype HP57, numbered L7244, was completed at Cricklewood prior to the declaration of war in 1939. No turrets were fitted, because they were still not available, the wing had HP automatic leading edge slats and therefore no barrage balloon cable cutters, and the Merlin 10s drove DH two-position variable pitch propellers with duralumin blades. Because the integral fuel tanks between the inboard and outboard nacelles were to be used for the carriage of water ballast for the full load and overload tests, the fuselage bomb-bay had temporary fuel tanks installed in it. As Radlett airfield at that time had an operating length that was considered unsatisfactory in case of emergency, the aircraft was dismantled and taken by road to 13 OTU at Bicester for re-erection and testing, the re-erection being carried out by a picked team from the Radlett Flight Shed. When it appeared, the HP57 was now seen to be a conventional aircraft with a rather angular, deep, slab-sided fuselage having a mid-mounted wing with taper and dihedral on the outer panels and square-cut wing tips. The high set tailplane had twin fins and rudders mounted as end plates. During the initial taxying trials Major Cordes expressed dissatisfaction with the hydraulic brakes then fitted, and eventually refused to carry out further testing until the Dunlop pneumatic brakes were installed.

On 25 October Major Cordes, with E. A. Wright as flight observer, took off on the Halifax's first flight. Preliminary handling flights were carried out by the same crew and were generally satisfactory, although during these early flights the complaint arose of fuselage oscillation. During the early part of 1940, experiments were carried out on the prototype to cure this problem. These included improved wing/fuselage fillets and the lengthening of the inner nacelle fairings, which resulted in the Chief Designer issuing a memo on 4 June 1940 to the effect that experiments were still continuing to find a final solution to the fuselage oscillation trouble, but meanwhile production aircraft would be modified to have the tailplane set at an increased angle of incidence and that the first ten production aircraft would have the inner engine nacelle fairings of intermediate length, which at that time was the type fitted to the first and second prototypes. Larger fairings, which had a portion attached to the flaps, were then going into production. The change in tailplane incidence was simply to optimise longitudinal trim to reduce the maximum 'up' tab travel required.

Apart from the advanced features originally considered for the HP56-57 design, research was pursued throughout the life of the Halifax to improve its performance and efficiency. One of the Handley Page team originally involved in this research was Dr G. V. Lachmann, a German national who had never bothered to become a naturalised British subject. Upon the outbreak of war Dr Lachmann, like many other foreigners, was interned under Defence Regulations 18B. 'HP' made many written and personal appeals to the authorities for the release of Dr Lachmann, but these had no effect and he remained interned, although he was allowed to work on basic aerodynamic and structural problems for Handley Page, being kept in touch with this through his assistant, G. Lee. It is in no way to the credit of the authorities that a scientist of Dr. Lachmann's ability, who had been involved with the design of British military aircraft, should have been kept interned — rules were meant to be guidelines, yet many officials used them so rigidly that they indicated the officials' own ineffectiveness and stupidity.

From being Dr. Lachmann's assistant, G. Lee progressed through the firm to become Stafford's assistant on the Victor. His forte was research — mainly on tailless projects during the war — but that is another story.

Technical policy regarding the Halifax was discussed in a meeting between Air Commodore A. Mansell and 'HP'. They covered the development of the Halifax, not only the carriage of a heavier armament of 0.5 inch machine-guns in mid-upper and rear turrets but also consideration of the fitting of Griffon or Sabre engines. To consider either the Sabre or Griffon engines in 1940 was a little premature, for while at Rolls-Royce development of the Merlin was being given prominence the Napier Sabre engine was not satisfactory until the MAP had called in Bristols to machine and supply sleeve valves to Napiers for the Sabre — which was two or three years later.

Handley Page's had started the development of the Halifax with the HP56 powered by the Vulture. This had progressed to the HP57 when the Air Ministry had insisted on the fitment of four Merlins, then Farren had suggested fitting American engines — even Dagger, Kestrel and Taurus engines had been suggested — but the Halifax went into service with Merlins and the design was only fully exploited when Bristol Hercules engines were fitted — the same engines that Handley Page wanted to fit into the HP56 prototype as an expedient while waiting delivery of the Vultures. This entailed much development and research, not to mention financial and time expenditure on modifications to satisfy the Ministry and Service requirements. 'To satisfy requirements completely one either had to be a genius or a miracle had to occur' is how one design staff member described it.

The flight testing of the prototype was carried out by Major Cordes and E. A. 'Ginger' Wright. Major J. L. Cordes had joined Handley Page Ltd as an assistant test pilot in 1928 and was responsible for the development flying of the slotted wing. Later

on it was his recommendation to 'HP' that resulted in the purchase of the field that became Radlett airfield. And it was through Major Cordes that the Halifax, as well as other previous aircraft from Handley Page's, were so well developed from the flight controls and handling points of view.

In June 1940 the flight experiments with L7244 resulted in the rudder remaining 'as flown', the elevators to continue in production with the original 'pointed' nose while further experiments were made to L7244 to obtain the best compromise in nose thickness, and the aileron tab to be of increased area. This was accepted as standard for production. A meeting was held on the 22nd between the firm and the Aeroplane & Armament Experimental Establishment (A&AEE) when the flight tests were discussed. The DTO of A&AEE stated that the longitudinal stability was sufficient for their requirements and that the aircraft should have no snags in dive conditions.

When the second prototype, L7245, took to the air for the first time at Radlett on 17 August 1940, flown by Major Cordes, it was seen to have been painted yellow underneath and was complete with turrets. The Merlins drove Rotol constant speed propellers; these, though not fully feathering at that time, were chosen for the production aircraft.

By October the Halifax was involved in a wide range of tests at A&AEE and, during a visit there by Handley Page's Assistant Chief Designer, the CTO summarised the tests so far carried out. He said that the handling at the stall was very good and no wing dropping

K. Chapman and crew at HCU Riccall, Yorkshire. Halifax Mk.2 Series 1 (Special). Note mix of 3- and 4-blade props. (G. P. G. Hayward)

occurred during take-off or landing, and it was agreed that the flying characteristics of the aircraft at 50,000 lb were such that the wing slots should be deleted in production. All this was borne out by the A&AEE report dated 21 December 1940, in which it was stated that the flying characteristics were quite satisfactory with the slots locked in. The remainder of the report was reasonably satisfactory, for it was found on take-off that the aircraft had a medium tendency to swing to the left which could be corrected by a light touch of the brakes and full rudder to approximately 40 mph; otherwise the take-off was normal and straightforward and the aircraft needed no helping into the air. The stall was straightforward, with no wing dropping, the control column required pulling back about three-quarters of its travel from the mid-position to stall the aircraft, and the aircraft was stable.

The rear turret was tested satisfactorily in a dive up to 295 mph, but while the front turret was being traversed it tended to stick in various beam positions at aircraft speeds above 260 mph IAS. Access and exit to both turrets was easy, and accessibility for maintenance and re-arming was satisfactory. However, complaints were made about the fuel jettisoning, rear turret ammunition feed drums, draughts and flare fittings.

Aircraft L9485 arrived at Boscombe Down also in October and Sqn Ldr Maguire of A & AEE criticised Handley Page's for the condition in which it had been delivered. This criticism was quickly put to rest by a letter from Major Cordes who explained that the aircraft had been evacuated from Radlett on account of enemy action and it was Handley Page's intention to complete the work at A&AEE prior to handing it over.

The handling of the Halifax is best illustrated by Air Commodore P. A. Gilchrist RAF (Retd) who was a Flight Commander when No. 35 Squadron received the Halifax, flew the prototype at Boscome Down and flew on the first Halifax raid. In a letter to the author he remembers the prototype L7244 well; in his words, 'petrol tanks in the bomb-bay, no turrets and it would leap off the

ground in about 300 yards'. In a further letter regarding squadron aircraft and training he recalls 'that the Halifax handled so well that I would land it hands off the control column by using the fore and aft trim wheel only — for the benefit of new pilots'.

Prior to this period the Avro Manchester had arrived at A&AEE Boscombe Down and had created a good impression by carrying out steep turns around the airfield. Its good all-round view from the cockpit received favourable comment, but also noted was the difficulty in climbing over the spars in the fuselage — the space left was much less than on the Halifax — and the addition of a central fin suggested a lack of directional stability. When the aircraft was weighed it substantially exceeded the figure quoted by Avro's. The Halifax was never catapult-launched at Boscombe Down, even though in the design stage it had been stressed for this, but the Avro Manchester was catapult-launched during its stay there and got airborne satisfactorily.

Meanwhile, Handley Page's had been considering a more heavily armed version of the Halifax, because they felt that there were doubts about the ability of the new heavy bombers to defend themselves satisfactorily against cannon-armed fighters, and had proposed to the Air Ministry the HP58, to be known as the Mk.2, which was intended to be defended by a Boulton & Paul 'H' dorsal turret and a Type 'O' ventral turret, each mounting two 20mm cannon. The rear fuselage tapered to the rear and had no rear turret. The mock-up was prepared at Cricklewood, a contract issued in July 1939 to convert L7244 after its flight trials to the HP58 Standard, and by 15 December 1939 the mock-up had been officially inspected and approved. Unfortunately, wartime delays caused continual hold-ups with production of these turrets so that in September 1940 Mr Rowe of MAP agreed that work on the HP58 (Mk.2) should be suspended. So the HP58 was still-born and the Mk.2 was, when produced, a logical development of the Mk.1 and still defended by rifle calibre machine-guns.

It must be emphasised that Handley Page's

were disappointed with the performance of the Halifax, for it was below their calculations in many respects. Yet Avro's were in a worse predicament: their Type 679 Manchester with its wingspan of 80 ft 2 inches and Vulture engines was far from satisfactory. The prototype L7246 had carried out a forced landing with total fuel failure after only a few flights at A&AEE and then Air Marshal Tedder (Director-General of Scientific Research) flew on the second prototype L7247 and expressed his dissatisfaction with it.

The Vultures were neither reliable nor up to power and the wing area was insufficient, as was the tailplane. This resulted in the wingspan being given a temporary increase to 90 ft 1 inch, and then a final wing span of 95 ft and a tailplane span increase from 22 ft to 33 ft. Even then Avro's problems were not over, for Hives of Rolls-Royce had informed the MAP that he did not intend to develop the Vulture as more active development of the Merlin would yield better results. As a result of this the Manchester was ordered to be droppped and, worst of all for Avro's, the Halifax was to be substituted.

So, by the middle of 1940, Dobson and Chadwick were faced with the fact that they had an airframe without an engine, and a decision was taken to redesign the Manchester to take four Merlins. At a meeting at Avro's with Air Marshal Tedder and Air Chief Marshal Freeman, Dobson (with Hives' agreement) displayed a model of the Manchester with a four-Merlin wing. This Freeman agreed to, provisionally, so no steps were taken to insert the Halifax in place of the Manchester and MAP also provisionally agreed to the four-engined Manchester on condition that the aircraft was produced by the end of December 1940. Lt.-Col. L. R. Fell of Rolls-Royce undertook the design and supply of the power-plants and, as the Merlin power-plant for the Beaufighter was already in production at Rolls-Royce Hucknall, this became a straightforward adaptation to fit into the four-engined Manchester (provisionally known as the Mk.3). The redesign of the outer wing was started by Avro's and the wingspan increased to 102 ft (ignoring the 100 ft limitation that both Short's and Handley Page's had had to conform to).

The Mk.3 Manchester — now renamed Lancaster — made its first flight on 9 January 1941 and the second prototype was under way. Chadwick had by now taken a design

Halifax Mk.2. Series 2 HR756 with Merlin 65s, used for trial installations at Hucknall (Rolls-Royce), 1943 (IWM).

team to Woodford and proceeded to lighten and redesign the airframe inherited from the Manchester. What was apparent to the unbiased onlooker was that the close cowled Merlin ex-Beaufighter power-plant would be unable to cope with hot tropical conditions, again ignoring the P13/36 requirements. So, while Handley Page's were not only attempting to conform to the requirements but also a host of modifications for extra equipment for various roles, Avro's were building their aircraft as a bomber for the European theatre of operations.

The undercarriage was by now causing delays on the Halifax line, because British Messier were just getting into quantity production. Buchanan of MAP felt that there should be an alternative source of supply so he took the decision to get Dowty to proceed with an alternative design to the Messier, one which would pick up on the same bearing forgings. Dowty, having spare work capacity, felt they could adapt the Manchester undercarriage to suit the Halifax. 'HP's' reply to this proposal was not totally in agreement and concluded with: 'Now that we have the same engines and possibly the same undercarriage for Lancaster and Halifax, someone may one day have a bright idea and ask why not use the same aircraft structure and greatly simplify the present material difficulties?'

This remark no doubt referred to the material shortages that Handley Page's were experiencing and reporting — the steel required for jigs and tools being considered by some civil servant to have no bearing on aircraft manufacture. Nevertheless, by January 1941 a visit had been paid to Dowty at Cheltenham to check on both undercarriage and hydraulic equipment. After an internal discussion at Handley Page's and a phone call to Dowty it was ascertained that Dowty could not supply off-the-shelf shock absorbers to satisfy the 12 inch stroke required for the levered suspension Dowty undercarriage for the Halifax. Also considered was a complete change-over from the Messier hydraulic system to the Dowty, but it became obvious

that an alteration of such magnitude would affect the production of the aircraft. Even so, considerable drawing office time was expended, with subsequent increase in financial expenditure, though this was possibly recuperated when the Mk.5 Halifax was eventually produced.

In April, Mr Farren of DTD and Mr Rowe visited 'HP' to discuss future development of the Halifax. Under consideration was the use of the Griffon engine, but with the increase in engine power came an increase in engine weight and fuel consumption, so it was finally agreed that Handley Page should stick with the Merlin 20 and gain a small increase in the all-up weight. It was also agreed that the present 13,000 lb maximum bomb-load capacity was itself generous and sufficient for the Halifax. The Chief Designer showed the arrangements for carrying two 4000 lb bombs or one 8000 lb bomb in the fuselage and it was pointed out that for short range it appeared possible to carry four 4000 lb bombs under the fuselage if the bomb-doors were left off, though R. S. Stafford made the point that this latter arrangement might entail spar strengthening for such a load concentration. Further suggestions concerned the carriage of 1000 lb GP bombs in the wing bomb-bays and whether it was permissible to sling bombs on racks under the wings. Farren stated that the Halifax was on the whole already an efficient design, so that any improvement of one item would not make any appreciable difference, but he liked Handley Page's proposals for Beaufighter or Mosquito nacelles and the scheme for utilising lowered nacelles with the outer engines positioned a foot further forward, enclosed main wheels, a new single leg undercarriage and a retractable tailwheel. Handley Page's undertook to obtain particulars of the Merlin 60 Series engines and let DTD know what they could offer with a Halifax powered by these engines.

An estimation by Handley Page design staff for a production Mk.1 aircraft with a fuel capacity of 1360 imperial gallons gave the following data:

	50,000 lb	55,000 lb
Maximum cruising speed at 15,000 ft	265 mph	263 mph
Range with 8000 lb bomb-load	1000 miles	1970 miles
Range with 11,000 lb bomb-load	390 miles	1360 miles
Bomb-load with full tanks	3000 lb	8000 lb
Range with full tanks	1980 miles	1970 miles

These estimates were based on the original drag estimates, which were later found to be too optimistic. Quite a large proportion of the performance fall-off was due to three main factors.

First, it must be appreciated that the science of nacelle design, drag estimation, thickness/chord ratio and flow was not as advanced as it is now. The NPL had circulated new information on 18 per cent, 21 per cent and 25 per cent thick wings during the period of HP56/57 design, so, partly for structural reasons and also to accommodate some bombs in the wing centre section, a 21 per cent thick wing was chosen, and also an aerofoil section of NACA 23021 for the intermediate and centre section wings. This unfortunately created greater wing drag than the 18 per cent wing — which could have been used, but to achieve the same strength it would have been heavier.

Secondly, the mid-slung nacelles were hardly the best choice for the Merlin engine for, while mid-slung nacelles give lowest drag at low incidence (high speed), at any increase in the angle of attack the drag also increases, and as the Halifax obviously did not fly at high speed continuously to and from the target, then the drag was higher than with an under-slung nacelle. Thirdly, the engine nacelle frontal area was large to accommodate sufficient radiator area to allow proper engine cooling for the aircraft to perform in either temperate or tropical climates, as required by the P13/36 specification.

A further problem that manifested itself during flight testing and development — and at other times, as will be related later — was aileron snatch, which usually occurred at low speed on the climb, particularly with full power. The Frize-type ailerons had rather sharp noses and, with the bottom of the nose radius only about 0.05 inch in-set from the wing contour, any rigging that was not fairly correct and allowed the aileron nose to protrude slightly resulted in aileron snatch. This was solved by rigging the ailerons so that the noses were always slightly in-set with the control wheel neutral.

By August 1941 the Technical Department were engaged on the introduction of Hercules engines on the Halifax, an increase in span to 104 ft by the increase of span to the outer wings, and a decreased undercarriage retraction time. The Hercules-powered Halifax was designated the Mk.3 and in a letter to the MAP it was stated that this aircraft could be made utilising the same jigs and, apart from the engine nacelles, with very little alteration. It was suggested that if any new orders were to be placed then this should be the aircraft ordered, as by the time things were ready the Mk.3 would be flying and any technical difficulties ironed out.

So up to now we have the following Marks produced or proposed:

Mk.1 Series 1 — First 50 production aircraft: maximum all-up weight 55,000 lb. No mid-upper turret or beam guns. 24 volt generators were mounted on inboard engines only. The aileron mass balance was below the wing.

Mk.1 Series 2 — Next 25 production aircraft: structural alterations permitting all-up weight increase to 60,000 lb. 24 volt generators mounted on inboard engines only. No mid-upper turret but Vickers 'K' guns in beam hatches. Aileron mass balance repositioned above the wing. (Fig. 4 gives range and bomb-load variations).

Mk.1 Series 3 — Halifax aircraft from L9600: 24 volt generators mounted on engines numbers 2, 3 and 4. Larger oil coolers were fitted for the installation of Merlin Mk.20s and the fuel capacity increased to 1636 gallons.

While the Mk.1 Series 3 was getting into production, the Mk.2 with its Merlin 20 or 22s was following along the production lines. The all-up weight was still 60,000 lb but the fuel capacity had been increased to 1882 gallons by the addition of No. 6 tanks. Performance was no better as the beam guns had been replaced by a type 'C' mid-upper turret and

the tare weight was now 34,980 lb as against the Mk.1 Series 1 of 33,860 lb.

Further progress was being made on the Hercules-powered Halifax and a new project and development, provisionally called the Mk.4, was being given a semblance of form. It would use a strengthened fuselage with a stronger floor and larger fuselage bomb compartment, its power would be a choice of a more powerful Hercules or a Griffon, and it would have a single-leg two-wheel

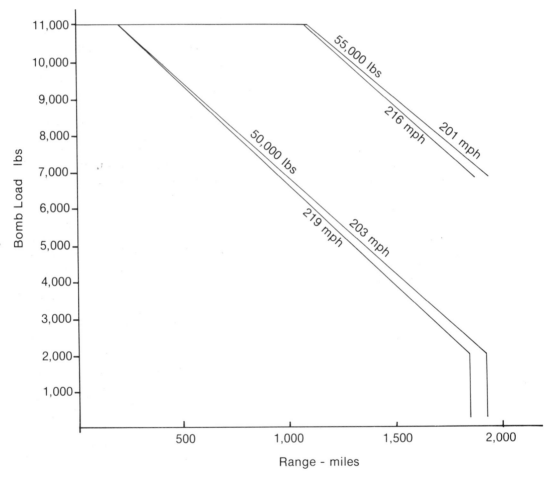

Figure 4 — Halifax Mk. 1 Series 2, range and bomb-load (with beam guns). Based on weighed tare weight and full-scale cruising speed and fuel consumption. The graph shows range and bomb-load for maximum weak mixture power at 15,000 ft and at economical speed at 2400 rpm. Tare weight 32,863 lb; load (without bombs) 3813 lb; empty weight 36,676 lb; normal fuel capacity 1392 gallons.

Halifax Mk.2 Series 1A HR679 with extended nacelles. A trials aircraft with Type A turret installed in place of Type C and mod. 452 nose fitted. (IWM).

undercarriage each side with a redesign of the tail unit to reduce drag. In October it was agreed with the MAP that the Hercules-powered Halifax would be called the Mk.3 and be powered by the Hercules Mk.6 engines, while the new project would be designated the Mk.4. A number of the Mk.4 features were meanwhile at the testing stage and it was decided to set aside a B2, Serial HR756, as the prototype for the HP60 Mk.4. The airframe was modified to have engine nacelles in the lowered position, similar to the Lancaster, with the inner nacelles projecting aft of the wing trailing edge. Also into being came the Mk.5, having Merlin 22s, Dowty hydraulics and undercarriage.

Even with all these developments under way the Research Department had not been coasting along, for Mr Haynes of that department had reported to 'HP' by memo of their investigations into various types of undercarriage and retraction, ways of reducing the ground angle of the Halifax, and attempts to clean up the present undercarriage to reduce retraction times and drag. Among the types of undercarriage investigated were the single-leg sideways retracting, single-leg with aft retraction and wheel twisting to the horizontal plane, as on the Junkers 88, and also a tricycle undercarriage.

By November the MAP were saying that they would want as many of the Mk.4 improvements incorporated on the standard Halifax production aircraft as soon as possible. In the same month L9520 was fitted with a Lancaster tailwheel to try and eliminate the 'shimmy' experienced with the Messier tailwheel. This 'shimmy' was to plague the Halifax for a long while, caused in some cases on 'rogue' aircraft by incorrect setting up by maintenance personnel, but it was a fault to be experienced by the Halifax to the end of its days with the slightest fall-off in maintenance standards or the wear of tailwheel assembly components.

With the Mk.2 Series 1, it was found on operations that the front turret was rarely used, and this was almost the same with the mid-upper turret. Furthermore, it was determined that with an engine out it was hard to come back on three engines without casting everything overboard, due primarily to the extra drag of the Type C turret in the mid-upper position. 'HP' was always in favour of reduced armament in night bombers, and in a letter to Air Marshal Linnell at the MAP in December made the point that a night bomber did not require the same amount of armour or armament as a day bomber. He further stated that with the removal of the front and mid-upper turrets and the gaps covered with fairings a saving in weight of 1450 lb could be made, with an increase in performance of about 16 mph. In early 1942 the SOE made known that their requirement was for a fast, long-range penetration aircraft and so five Halifax B2 Series 1 aircraft were modified against Works Order No. 228 to have their front and mid-upper turrets removed and the apertures faired in, long-range tanks fitted in the fuselage, external fuel jettison pipes removed and the fitting of paratroop cover and fairing.

21

These aircraft went to No. 138 Squadron at Tempsford and the type was designated the Mk.2 Series 1 (Special). The type of nose was known as the 'Tempsford' both at the Works and generally in the RAF. When the performance of this aircraft became known at No. 4 Group there was a clamour to have the front and mid-upper turrets removed and, although this clamour was not unanimous, the manufacture of the nose was carried out for No. 4 Group by Tollerton Aircraft Services. Sometimes this nose was known as the Tollerton nose, sometimes as the 'Z' nose, or 'Z' aircraft.

In a letter on the 26 March 1942 'HP' suggested the removal of mid-upper turret, jettison pipes and navigation blisters from the side of the fuselage, but by then the SOE aircraft were being prepared and No. 4 Group was following suit. Also in the letter was a number of complaints referring to the continual increase in fixed equipment and protection equipment, etc:

	1941	1942
Total fixed equipment	2851 lb	3599 lb
Protection equipment	1739 lb	2574 lb

Although the Halifax structural weight to maximum weight ratio had not been greatly affected and was still 30 per cent, at the rate of increase of equipment and modifications he pointed out that there would be no effective bomb-load at all by the end of the year. Some of the modifications and trials installation on the aircraft were target towing, a paratroop installation, a heavy gauge protective engine cowling, an under-turret installation, arrester gear for landing, and rocket apparatus for take-off.

So once again we have the inevitable — the manufacturer continually attempting to improve the performance and uprate the engines for more power, while the Air Staff continually increase the equipment carried. Unfortunately for the Halifax, it was an aircraft considered suitable for so many roles that it was built with basic fixtures to allow the fitment of the equipment for the role. It is obvious that if the Halifax had been built for one role only and with no restriction on wingspan the RAF would have received an aircraft of the Mk.3's performance much sooner. That the arrester gear, for example, was not required at squadron level is proved by the fact that in May 1942, during a visit by Major Nicoll of Handley Page's to No. 4 Group, the AOC requested that Handley Page's kill off the proposal for fitment of the arrester gear. How many more fittings were not operationally required? A further example is the fitment of 'Monica' fighter warning radar. In operational use it was found to be more trouble than help because it could not distinguish between friend and foe, with the result that if it was left switched on in a bomber stream the crew became a bundle of nerves from false warnings. Why wasn't this considered before fitment?

The 31st production B1 aircraft from Cricklewood was L9515 and it was selected as a development aircraft for the improvement of both range and performance. During this development programme the No.6 tanks were installed, the engine cowlings were modified to a reduced cowling frontal area, and the engines were replaced with Merlin 10s. With these various modifications L9515 was the subject of many A&AEE reports. In 1942 L9515 was further modified with a metal mock-up nose of streamlined form and the engines replaced with Merlin 22s. Upon completion of the tests, approval was given to the introduction (mod.452) of a Perspex nose of similar shape. About the same time L9515 acquired inboard nacelles, which were extended aft of the wing trailing edge to ease the turbulent airflow over the inboard wing section, and a type A Mk.8 (mod.451) turret was also fitted. After this HR679 was then modified to become the first Mk.2 Series 1A with the lengthened nose section and mod.452 Perspex nose, which increased the total overall length to 71 ft 7 ins. The Merlin 20s were then replaced with Mk.22s, and the Gallay radiators and oil coolers with Morris single-block radiators. The Perspex nose was first made in one piece but MAP objected to this practice on the grounds that damage done to the nose by shrapnel would not be localised.

B2 HR756 was now acquiring its various features but as no Merlin 65s were available — these were all destined for fighters — Mk.22s were fitted. HR756 was now designated a Mk.2 Series 2 and considered for production to follow the Series 1A, but Volkert pointed out to DTD that the production departments would have very little enthusiasm to tool-up for the Series 1A and, after a short run, tool-up for the Series 2 and suggested that the Series 2 should disappear in favour of the Mk.4 with Merlin 61s. Thurstan James of DTD asked why Handley Page did not use the standard Lancaster engine nacelles complete, to which Volkert replied that the Lancaster nacelles had a very small margin of cooling and required a higher climbing speed than the Halifax. So the Series 1A was authorised for production but with the proviso that the flame damping problem of the Merlin must be solved.

Now the flame damping problem had been

Carriage of two 4000 lb bombs for take-off tests at Boscombe Down on Halifax B1 L9485. (RAE).

at the centre of investigations at the A & AEE as well as at Rolls-Royce and Handley Page's for a long time — and would continue for a long time. In hindsight, it would appear to have been a problem over-emphasised on the Halifax by the authorities, for biographies of German airmen since 1945 have mentioned picking up *Lancaster* exhaust flames at 100 - 200 yards, yet the Halifax continued to be the subject of flame damping trials even after the fitting of Hercules engines. A flame damping trial on Halifax W1008 with Merlin 22s carried out in 1942 indicated a small glow directly behind and from the side at 175 yards. This aircraft had engines fitted with ram's horn type exhausts with anti-glow shrouds; other aircraft had saxophone type exhausts with flame damp shrouds and were considered by A&AEE to be satisfactory.

In May, in a letter to Volkert 'HP' referred to new design work on the Halifax in regard to future policy and development. The five projects covered were:

(a) Large diameter fuselage (at least 9 ft).
(b) Pressurised fuselage (at least 9 ft).
(c) Large diameter fuselage as in (a), but adaptable as ordinary commercial freight or mail carrier.
(d) Large diameter fuselage as above, adapatable as a high-speed troop transport or passenger carrier.
(e) Following the fuselage development, the wing to be replaced by a laminar flow wing.

In 1942 came an increase in incidents and accidents to Halifax aircraft resulting from pilots getting into difficulties under conditions of excessive sideslip. This had been produced when violent use was made of the rudder and rudder overbalance had occurred. Flight trials of the Halifax had found that rudder control was good for normal manoeuvres and it was thought both by Handley Page's and A&AEE that the overbalancing tendency was not so important — straight sideslips and engine cutting at low speeds was not part of the testing procedure earlier on. In fact, in Part 3 of A & AEE/760a the rudders were stated to have little response

Prototype Halifax Mk.2 L9515 fitted with Handley Page-designed metal mockup of Series 1A nose. Aircraft has extended inner nacelles and the leading edge slats locked in and sealed, fitted with BP Type A turret. (Business Press International Ltd.)

below 120 mph but to be effective at higher speeds. At speeds below 150 mph there was a tendency for the rudders to overbalance — this was to be investigated. Then came complaints from the Service of rudder over-balance when carrying out evasive manoeuvres or engine cutting at low speeds. Some accidents could not be explained — nor could the crews complain, for the aircraft were splattered across the countryside — but from results obtained from aircraft investigation teams, and from reports from crews who were high enough to get out of trouble, the cause was pinpointed as insufficient fin area and resultant overbalance of the rudder.

This directional instabliity under certain conditions with the Halifax is well known to most aviation enthusiasts, yet the fact that the Lancaster suffered from longitudinal instability was, and is, a nicely kept secret by authors covering the Lancaster. To quote RAE Report R & M 2300: 'For instance on the Lancaster longitudinal stability and control deteriorated with speed, so that having reached a fast diving speed, great difficulty

was experienced in recovery; some aircraft dived into the ground or disintegrated'. Against this, the Halifax's stability and control were so good that, if trimmed level and forced into a dive, it had to be eased out of the dive; for if left alone it would rapidly pull out with possible failure of the wings under load. On the Lancaster, fast diving was due to its known tendency to nose over at high speeds; and in earlier Lancasters structural failures were attributed to fin failures, so modifications were made to strengthen the fins and attachments. Alterations were also made to the evasive manoeuvres.

To return to the rudder overbalance problem, a continual programme of development flying was carried out by both Handley Page's, A&AEE and the RAE to improve the Halifax. Various rudder variations and areas were experimented with until eventually the type 'D' fin and rudder was standardised.

At this point it may be interesting to compare the Halifax and Lancaster basic details and performance:

	Halifax 2 Series 1A	Lancaster 1
Wingspan	98 ft 8 in	102 ft 0 in
Wing area	1250.0 sq ft	1297.0 sq ft
Length	70 ft 1 in	69 ft 6 in
Max weight at take-off	60,000 lb	61,500 lb
Engine	Merlin 22	Merlin 22
Maximum speed,		
mph in 'M' gear	262 at 11,600 ft	261 at 12,800 ft
mph in 'S' gear	261 at 18,500 ft	260 at 19,500 ft
Cruising speed,		
'M' gear	229 at 14,500 ft	239 at 14,700 ft
'S' gear	215 at 20,000 ft	233 at 20,000 ft

As will be seen from this there was very little to choose in top speed between the Halifax and Lancaster, but the Lancaster's top speed was obtained about 1000 feet higher while the cruising speed of the Lancaster was noticeably ahead of the Halifax. From this we can assume that that extra 47 sq ft of wing area and the slimmer nacelles of the Lancaster made that difference.

By now Handley Page's had tested a metal aileron trim tab to replace the wooden ones originally used; Morris single-block radiators and oil coolers were being introduced to overcome complaints of inadequate cooling during hot summer months, and the following propellers were approved for use on the Halifax in combinations, symmetrical if possible (the only four-engined British bomber approved to fly with combinations of three- and four-blade propellers):

RXF 5/1, RXF 5/3, RXF 5/4, RS 5/5, RS 5/14, RS 5/16, RS 5/17, RS 5/18, RS 5/18A. What was more important was that Handley Page's were at last ignoring the 100 ft wingspan restriction, and an increase in wing span to 103 ft 8 ins was being investigated.

Early in 1942, after complaints from squadrons about lack of performance, a Mk.2 (DG221) of No. 10 Squadron was used for flight testing for an official investigation. The investigation found that small additional equipment items were fitted, workmanship was generally bad and the aircraft was camouflaged with a rough night finish. At approximately the same time A&AEE were carrying out further tests on that old favourite L9515 to determine consumption, range and

operation of the Mk.2. These tests determined that the Halifax Mk.2 was a remarkably easy aircraft to operate, although there were difficulties arising out of the critical flight conditions when heavily overloaded. It was found that the precise power conditions used for climbing had very little effect upon the range and that it was possible to cruise over a wide range of air speeds without materially altering the range per gallon obtained; but the use of hot air intakes was found to reduce the range by the order of 16 per cent, a similar effect being confirmed on the A&AEE Lancaster.

The original bomb doors were metal skinned and could only completely enclose 2000 lb bombs; the 4000 lb and 8000 lb bombs could be carried but the doors could not be completely closed. Trials at Boscombe Down determined that there was no deterioration in take-off performance with the bomb-doors in this position but it did restrict the range. This was borne out in the operations against *Tirpitz* in April 1942 when 45 Halifax aircraft took part and, according to eye-witness accounts, the Halifax take-offs were superior to those of the Lancaster. On that operation 11 Lancasters took off with full tanks and 6000 lb bomb-load, being followed by 11 Halifaxes, each with full tanks and 5500 lb bomb-load. The Halifaxes carried modified RN Mk.19N mines, which made it impossible to close the bomb-doors fully.

To make the fuselage accommodate the larger bombs of the 4000/8000 lb type, agreement was reached with MAP that Phillips and Powis Ltd be given design and

Halifax B1 L9608, having been Christened *Halifax* by Lord Halifax on 12 September 1941, prepares to taxi out for take-off. (IWM).

final assembly approval of a set of doors to Mod.289. These were termed Type B doors and were fitted to V9985 for trials but were not acceptable to AM/DTD. For the Halifax Mk.3, Type C doors were manufactured by Evans Bellhouse but these were not interchangeable with those fitted to the Halifax Mks.2 and 5.

1942 was turning out to be a busy year for all departments, for, as well as all the previously mentioned work, the Halifax Mk.3 with Hercules 6 engines was started in the experimental shop. Works Order 228 covering the conversion of aircraft for SOE operations was issued, the H2S blister installed on W7823 for speed trials was ready, W7801 was modified and delivered to Netheravon for glider towing duties, and the fitting and flight testing of various rudder/fin combinations was carried out. The Mk.4 project was held in abeyance and an interest was shown in the conversion of the Halifax Mk.3 for Coastal Command use.

The last proposal was because German U-boats in the North Atlantic were by 1942 able to operate outside the range of the RAF land planes then in use by Coastal Command, and a suitable aircraft to fill this gap was being sought. During the last week in November a group of Coastal Command officers led by Wing Commander Melroy Hayes paid a visit to Handley Page's to discuss the Mk.3 with Stafford, their insistence on the Mk.3 powered by the Hercules 7 or 17 stemming from reports of Merlin unreliability received by Coastal Command from Bomber Command. This visit was reciprocated by a visit by Major Nicoll of Sales on 4 December to discuss the operational requirements. Briefly, Coastal Command's aim was to have the Halifax Mk.3 carry four 18 inch torpedoes or two 21-inch naval aircraft type torpedoes together with six depth charges. On the basis of this, Projects provided an outline of the proposed Coastal Command aircraft based on the assurances given by Bristol's regarding the engines:

Fuel total of	1882 gallons
less reserve of	142 gallons
	1740 gallons
Consumption	168 gph
Estimated endurance	10.3 hours
Mean cruising speed	178 mph
Range	1600 nautical miles

With a load totalling 8220 lb this would allow for an operational endurance of 8.5 hours, giving a range of 1280 nautical miles.

It was intended that the torpedoes should be stowed in the main bomb-bay and the depth charges in the wing bomb cells, the 0.303 inch Vickers K gun in the nose being replaced with a 0.5in. Browning or 20 mm cannon.

By 10 December a general requirement for Coastal Command was received and two alternatives were considered, but initially it was decided to proceed with a scheme employing the Mk.2 fuselage with new bomb-doors hinged on the fuselage skin as the original hinges prevented the carriage of the two torpedoes. This was followed on the 11th by General Arrangement drawings, giving the rough layout of the Mk.3 adapted for torpedo carrying, which were delivered personally by Stafford to Wg Cdr Melroy Hayes. Stafford also discussed with him the Mk.2 Series 1A and Handley Page's efforts at cleaning the aircraft up and improving the reliability of the Merlin. It was also pointed out that Coastal Command would get their aircraft more quickly if they accepted the Mk.2 Series 1A as it was already in production. The Mk.2 Series 1A was in fact the aircraft eventually modified and accepted into service with Coastal Command although Mk.5 Series 1A were also employed; both were eventually replaced by the Mk.3.

The choice of the Halifax for this long-range overseas type of work in preference to the Lancaster was in no small measure due to its more capacious fuselage, availability and better ditching record. From reports it appears that the Merlins did not like the long-endurance, low-speed flying carried out by Coastal Command, although a flight was made in 1943 in a Mk.2 (HR815) by a Coastal Command crew with an A&AEE observer that lasted 14.5 hours and covered 2132 nautical miles without any failure, and operational flights of 13 hours were commonplace. Most of these aircraft were equipped with ASV Mk.3 radar, were fitted with three 230 gallon tanks in the bomb-bay and carried depth charges in the wing cells.

Before leaving 1942 we can record three further events in the Halifax calendar. First was the carriage and dropping of the first 8000 lb bomb in action, carried out by a No. 76 Squadron Halifax in April, with Essen as the target. The second event was the assignment of two Halifax aircraft to the Telecommunications Research Establishment (TRE) for the installation of H2S and its development as an operational route and

Halifax B2 Series 1 aircraft. Note fuel jettison pipes and heavily shrouded exhausts on the Merlins. (IWM).

First production Halifax Mk.1. L9485. Retained as a trials aircraft and later used at A&AEE as an armament trials aircraft — here fitted with Type C turrets in nose and mid-upper positions, E Type rear turret and Boulton & Paul K ventral turret; the side gun hatches are also retained. (RAF Museum)

bombing aid, the scanner for the H2S being fitted under the fuselage aft of the bomb-doors in a streamlined Perspex cover. The choice of the Halifax was again because of the capacious fuselage and the choice of stations for the scanner. The first Halifax so modified unfortunately crashed when carrying the first airborne experimental magnetron valve and all on board were killed, including a number of scientists involved in developing the H2S. Fortunately the other Halifax was being prepared and with increased priority was carrying out the first trials with the Bombing Development Unit before the end of 1942.

The third and last event was to kill off any chance of Halifax production in Canada. With the tailing-off of production of the Hampden in Canada, a Mk.5 was despatched as a pattern aircraft but, unfortunately, the failings of the Dowty undercarriage became apparent and that put an end to the idea. The Mk.5 was the HP63 and differed from all other Halifax versions in utilising a Dowty levered-suspension type undercarriage and a revised hydraulic system, also by Dowty, which utilised DTD 44 fluid. The undercarriage used the same pickup points as the Messier but unfortunately, in the interests of speedy production, castings were used in place of forgings and stress failures occurred in service. This restricted the maximum landing weight to 40,000 lb. By the end of 1943 the production of the Mk.5 in the UK was completed and most of the Mk.5s were either converted for Coastal Command or other types of duty.

Returning to the Merlin failures and defects, a meeting was convened with the MAP in January 1943 to try and to overcome the excessive number of failures that were

28

being experienced. Not much appears to have resulted immediately from this except for a general observation that all components such as header tanks, radiators, etc must be flexibly mounted. 'HP' brought this matter of failed components to the attention of Major Nicoll of Sales who pointed out to him that it was the Rolls-Royce components that were failing — so why not ask Rolls-Royce?

HP61 Hercules Halifax versions

The first Hercules-powered variant was the Mk.3. The prototype Mk.3 was a converted Mk.2 Series 1 (Special) (R9534), which was first flown in October 1942 and which was fitted with a Type C turret and Type A fins and rudders. Early trials with the Mk.3 prototype showed that Type A rudder power was inadequate to deal with two-engine asymmetric flight with Hercules engines fitted, so a design was evolved consisting of upper and lower fins and rudders of equal area (Type E). With this tail, although rudder power was adequate, rudder overbalance was experienced at large deflections. This rudder overbalance problem has been mentioned previously, and the modifications which were raised in 1942-43 were important in improving the directional stability of the Halifax. To explain the rudder/fin combinations, alterations and their effects, the following table sets out the different types, areas and descriptions:

Type	Description	Fin (sq ft)	Rudder (sq ft)	Total (sq ft)
A	Standard fin/rudder on Mks. 1, 2, and 5 aircraft	28.95	29.85	58.8
B	Bulbous nose to Type A (Mod 413), caused 'hunting', trailing	28.95	29.85	58.8
C	Rudder as A with cut-back nose balance but without bulbous nose*	30.15	28.65	58.8
D	Type C rudder but fin area increased by about 50% (Mod 814)	44.05	28.65	72.7
E	Symmetrical fin and rudder with upper and lower fins of equal area. Rudder proved adequate but overbalance at large deflections	31.25	33.25	64.5
F	Similar to Type E but 2 ins. cut-back nose of rudder. Overcame normal overbalance but trailing effect exaggerated	32.65	31.85	64.5
G	Similar to Type F but unbalanced part of rudder removed and corresponding area added to fin	35.63	28.87	64.5

*Mod 670 introduced to limit rudder maximum travel by 3 degrees.

Type D was accepted by A & AEE as the final solution and was incorporated immediately into Mk.3 production, and also fitted retrospectively to all Halifax Mks.2 and 5. Meanwhile Stafford had RDT issue a warning to all Halifax squadrons to: (a) avoid excessive yaw at slow speeds; (b) with one or more engines out maintain the airspeed as high as possible, and always above 120 mph IAS.

The Mk.3 Halifax was originally intended to be one of many variants — an interim model, pending development of the high-altitude Hercules and while development of the Halifax Mk.4 took place. Unfortunately the high-altitude Hercules engine never proved reliable or satisfactory and, due to extensive development commitments, the building of the Mk.4 prototype was abandoned, so the Mk.3 became the next main Service type and the most mass-produced version of the Halifax.

In May 1943 R9534 was being fitted with Type D fins and rudders and flight trials had already been carried out with Beaufighter type air intakes to improve performance. By now the decision had been made to incorporate into the Mk.3 production aircraft a number of the aerodynamic and structural improvements of the cancelled Mk.4. Some of these were the local doubling of spar webs, an increase in some bolt sizes, some tubes of the Messier undercarriage to be improved in strength, the introduction of the Mk.4 floor and the re-introduction of the retractable tailwheel assembly. MAP also ruled that the Mk.3 was to be tropicalised from the outset of production. With this marriage of airframe and Hercules engine the Halifax was second to none; with further development and powered by a more powerful Hercules we considered the Halifax superior to all.

With the introduction of the Hercules engines no further Merlin-powered versions were introduced and the Hercules versions went from strength to strength, covering many roles at home and overseas. To return briefly to the Mk.2 Series 2, when HR679 was flown at Handley Page's and at A&AEE it was powered by the Merlin 22 and differed from the Series 1A in the following respects:

1. Engine nacelles were lowered relative to the wing and Beaufighter-type spinners were fitted to the propellers.
2. Main landing gear and wheels were completely enclosed within the nacelles when the undercarriage was retracted.
3. Cabin heating air scoops were removed from above the inboard engine nacelles and placed in a new position below the wing near the root.
4. Six-way ejector exhausts without shrouds were fitted to the engines.

The improvement in cruising speed from these differences over the performance of the Series 1A was only 9 mph, with both aircraft at all-up weights of 57,000 lb. The cruise ceiling was 19,000 ft under temperate summer conditions. The Series 2 was not considered a sufficient advance on the Series 1A to warrant further development, especially with the Mk.3 accepted for production, so after the tests the aircraft was transferred as a trials aircraft to Rolls-Royce flight test establishment at Hucknall.

The above was of passing interest only, as by then the Hercules-Halifax combination was proven and already established for production — the first production Mk.3 was to fly on 29 August 1943 at Radlett. Further developments of the Halifax were also in the project and design programme — further development of the Mk.3, a Mk.6 powered by Hercules 10 SM engines, the HP64, HP65 and HP66.

The HP64 was a transport version of the Halifax utilising Halifax wings, tail, undercarriage and power-plants with a new circular section pressurised fuselage, but the MAP would not allow Handley Page's to undertake such design work because it would interfere with their bomber production. As at that time Flight Refuelling Ltd had spare design office and workshop capacity available they were asked to design and produce a rear fuselage for testing.

The HP65 was to be the logical step up — improvement of the proven Halifax airframe, which would give a greater bomb-load, longer range, and better operational height and cruising speed than the existing Halifax. In August a Drawing Office Memo had been issued regarding the HP65 design policy and broadly laid out the main features. Volkert requested that a model wing section of laminar flow type be constructed so that the design and workshop problems of attaining the requisite degree of smoothness could be solved, the model wing to be capable of undergoing both load and aerodynamic tests. It is not generally realised that Handley Page's were the first in Great Britain to introduce this type of aerodynamic model. The HP65 project proposal was to utilise the standard Mk.3 fuselage modified to accept a stronger bomb-beam and larger bomb-doors, to be married to a wing of a NACA 66 series laminar flow aerofoil section with a wingspan of 113 ft and a 11 : 1 aspect ratio, tapering uniformly from centreline to tip and constructed around a single spar at 40 per cent wing chord. The wing structure incorporated integral tank bays to house bag-type fuel tanks and had leading edge de-icing by hot air from the engines. The engines were the turbo-supercharged Hercules 38s, which were still under development, and the four power-plants were housed in the 55 ft centre section. The undercarriage intended for use was to be of the single-leg type with twin wheels and was to be fully enclosed in the nacelle when retracted. With its fuel capacity of 2500 gallons it was estimated that the HP65 would cruise at 20,000 ft at 240 mph with a range of 3170 miles and with a maximum speed of 350 mph at 27,000 ft.

It was normal practice for Major Nicoll of Handley Page Sales Department and 'HP' to keep in personal touch with the squadrons operating Handley Page aircraft. One visit by Sir Frederick Handley Page in 1943 was to Nos 4 and 6 Groups, which gave both satisfaction and food for thought. The satisfaction was in the form of general comment that the outstanding feature of the Halifax was its robustness and strength, summed up by the AOC No. 4 Group who said 'there was one point on which no complaint had ever been made, and that was

as to the lack of strength of the Halifax'. Food for thought was the fact that, though generally speaking No. 4 Group were happy with the Halifax, they would like an improvement in its general handling characteristics, which they felt were inferior to the Lancaster. This was more than any aircrew had dared say in 'Betty's Bar' in York!

Sir Frederick was given to understand that neither Bomber Command nor the Air Staff would agree to the removal of the mid-upper turret to improve the performance of the Halifax, and it was not until the AOC 4 Group gave orders for its removal and for sorties to be carried out in this configuration that it was done. The improvement in performance without the turret was such that 4 Group intended to keep the turrets off.

Back at the works, it was decided in March 1943 to modify R9534 to take the turbo-blown Hercules engine for trials, although Handley Page's considered that the engine in its present form was not a satisfactory design. By October it was apparent that the Hercules 38 engines was not good enough to reach production status within the foreseeable future. Furthermore, the problems involved in achieving a manufacturing process and tooling for the laminar flow wing resulted in N. E. Rowe of DTD suggesting to Handley Page's that they abandon the HP65 project and concentrate on a conventional two spar wing but utilising the 55 ft wing centre section. On 27 November the discussion on the project with DTD and DOR resulted in a new design being registered as the HP66, covered by Specification B27/43. Against this specification two prototypes were ordered, powered by Hercules 100 engines, and also a third prototype, designated HP69, and powered by Hercules HE 15MT. This was followed in December by J. S. Sorley of the MAP confirming to Major Nicoll that the two prototypes were required and that standard bomb-doors were to be fitted as the Air Staff had ruled that they did not require the carriage of 4000 and 8000 lb bombs. It was also planned to move the H2S scanner forward to a place under the nose. But the month before, in a meeting with DOR and

DTD, it had been stated that bombs not larger than 4000 lb would be required, yet even so, the new nose was to be designed to suit the large bomb-doors! Obviously decisions changed as frequently as the month.

In January 1944, Stafford (Handley Page's Assistant Chief Designer) wrote to 'HP' referring to a discussion on the performance and load capacity of the HP66 powered by either the Hercules 100, Hercules 100MT or Merlin RM14 SM engines, and brought to his notice that calculations indicated that at the same all-up weight the bomb-load for the turbo-supercharged engine would be 2500 lb less than with the Hercules 100 engine but, if ceiling performance was the criterion, then there was still a case for turbo-supercharger development. As an insurance against any failure in the engine projects, Handley Page's had made provision for Merlin 65s in RAE idealised powerplants to be interchangeable with the Hercules, and to this end trials had already been flown in Halifax Mk.2 DG296 and Halifax Mk.3 LV795.

Returning now to the standard production Mk.3, at the beginning of production certain wing strengthening was introduced to make the aircraft suitable for all-up weight of 65,000 lb, but this was initially limited to 63,000 lb until the introduction of strengthened sliding tubes in the undercarriage and the strengthened tailwheel assembly, which were expected to be introduced before the twentieth aircraft. Meanwhile, two sets of strengthened wings with extended wingtips were being test flown on R9534 and HR845. The additional weight involved in strengthening the wings, increasing the skin gauge from 24 to 22 gauge, plus the new wingtips, amounted to 60 lbs, and with the addition of the strengthened tubes and tailwheel assembly the total increase rose to 110 lbs. The aircraft would only then be cleared for an all-up weight of 65,000 lb.

The Halifax Mk.3 was a formidable operational machine, embodying the proven strength of the basic Halifax airframe with new improved equipment and aerodynamic refinements, yet still retaining the Halifax

safety features. It was to be produced in greater numbers than any other Mark and was to give to Halifax crews the satisfaction of having a superb proven aircraft, second to none. Between 14 September and 22 October 1943 a Halifax Mk.3 (HX227) carried out a 150-hour intensive flying trial at Boscombe Down and received an assessment on maintenance and reliability that stated: 'Altogether the aircraft was far better as regards maintenance and reliability than was expected of four-engined aircraft and the intensive flying was completed in less time than has been taken for any other four-engined aircraft'.

On receiving the report from their representatives at A&AEE Boscombe Down Handley Page's were more critical of some items that had become defective or had failed, and action was immediately taken to rectify these and carry out modifications.

Boscome Down and Handley Page's both carried out trials on the extended wingtips of a Mk.2 (HR845), the intention being to incorporate this as a modification on later production Mk.3 aircraft and also on aircraft returned for major repair. The A&AEE assessment was that the rate of climb increased by 70 - 120 ft/min, service ceiling increased by 800 ft, maximum weak mixture cruise increased by 7 - 10 mph and cruising ceiling increased by 1700 ft.

When Handley Page tested the aircraft at Tempsford against a standard Mk.2 (HR679) they found that the rate of climb increased by 70 - 120 ft/min, service ceiling increased by 1000 ft, maximum weak mixture cruise increased by 8 mph, and cruising ceiling increased by 1700 ft.

With the entry into production and service of the Mk.3 a further version of the HP61 was being finalised. Like the Mk.3 this version was also tropicalised from the word go. The introduction of this version was because of the development by Bristols of the Hercules 100 in a self-contained power-plant and with an RAE-Hobson injection carburettor. As operations in tropical zones had indicated that a fuel system would operate better if it was permanently pressurised, Handley Page

L9485 on the ground. (RAF Museum)

introduced this with a pressure transfer system and a grouped fuel-tank layout. This refinement (and others) was introduced into the Mk. 3 airframe. The fuel tankage was increased to 2190 gallons, a nitrogen protection system was provided for the fuel tanks, the wingspan became 103 ft 8 ins and the H2S blister became a permanent feature. This new variant was designated the Mk.6. The nitrogen system for the fuel tanks was schemed by Flight Refuelling Ltd, was flight tested on HR875 and approved for production at the start of November.

Although initially the Mk.6 was planned to have a wingspan of 103 ft 8 ins and an all-up weight of 68,000 lb, Stafford in a letter to 'HP' on 28 January 1944 proposed that the Mk.6s at present on the production line should have the 98 ft 8 ins wingspan and only be cleared for 65,000 lb until VG recorders were available. Unfortunately all the VG recorders were in use on Lancaster and Stirling aircraft, and without VG recorder information clearance could not be obtained for the Mk.3 all-up weight of 65,000 lb and the Mk.6 all-up

weight of 68,000 lb. Eventually, VG recorders were obtained and then the two marks were cleared to their new all-up weights.

Mark 6 airframes then began to get ahead of Hercules 100 engine production and Hercules 16s were substituted. With this engine the designation became the Mk.7 and the all-up weight was reduced to 65,000 lb. This was the last bomber mark to be introduced and the great majority went to the RCAF squadrons of No. 6 Group and the Free French squadrons of No. 4 Group — Nos 346 and 347 — although some Mk.7s became A7s and served with No. 38 Group both at home and overseas. The Mk.6 and Mk.7 were similar in improvements and only differed in engines and all-up weight.

By the end of 1943 the Air Staff had made the decision to concentrate on the Merlin-Lancaster and the Hercules-Halifax, and started to phase out the Stirlings and Hercules-Lancasters from the operational units. At this stage it may be useful to compare the improved Halifax with the improved Lancaster.

33

	Halifax 3	Lancaster 1
Wingspan	103 ft 8 ins	102 ft
Wing area, sq ft	1275	1297
Empty weight in lb	37,900	37,000
All-up weight in lb	65,000	65,000
Maximum speed, mph	282 at 13,500 ft	278 at 13,000 ft
Cruising speed, mph	241 at 11,800 ft	239 at 14,700 ft
Time to 20,000 ft	42 minutes	44 minutes
Service ceiling	20,000 ft	23,000 ft
Engine and hp at take-off	Hercules 16, 1580 hp	Merlin 24, 1470 hp

From this it will be seen the both the Halifax and the Lancaster had improved but that the Halifax had made the greatest progress. But whereas Handley Page's gave a different mark number for each development, Avro's maintained the Lancaster at Mk.1[1], apart from the Mk.2 with Hercules engines. Even when improved from the prototype, improved to carry the 8000 lb and the 12,000 lb bomb, and even when the rear Frazer-Nash turret was replaced with the Rose turret it still stayed a Mk.1; they only added 'Special' to the B1 after a stripping operation to increase the bomb-load to 22,000 lbs. This in no way implies criticism of Avro's but does illustrate Handley Page's different approach; by the termination of the Halifax production line 27 distinct types of Halifax had been produced and all-up weight had increased from 50,000 lb to 68,000 lb.

During 1943 Cunliffe-Owen at Eastleigh had been modifying Halifax aircraft for Coastal Command, for both maritime reconnaissance and met. duty roles, in both of which the Halifax excelled. At the end of August a Mk.2 (JD212) had a trial installation of rocket projectiles fitted, outboard of the fuselage but under the centre-section. The aircraft proved a satisfactory armament platform and the handling was not affected, but the installation was not adopted as standard.

Although DTD and DOR had determined that there was no need for the Halifax or the HP66 to carry bombs larger than 4000 lb, the opposite was true of the Lancaster. Probably because of its longer bomb-bay, it was developed to carry the 12,000 lb bomb, the 12,000 lb 'Tallboy' and the 22,000 lb bomb.

Its all-up weight went up to 68,000 lb, as on the Halifax Mk.6, and then on the B1 'Special' to 72,000 lb. This development of the Lancaster did not really reflect on the Halifax and owed more to the machinations of top authority who had very little liking for 'HP's direct approach. Bomber Command's Chief was not above pointing out in letters to 'HP' that, on certain raids, the Halifax loss rate was higher than the Lancaster — yet he never mentioned when the reverse was true.

For all that, the Halifax was in great demand both at home and overseas, and in many roles: No. 38 Group required them for glider towing, SOE drops and airborne support; Coastal Command wanted them for maritime reconnaissance and met. duties; No. 100 Group wanted them for radio/radar surveillance and countermeasures; Transport Command required them for high-speed transport of men and equipment. In fact the only Command that did not require them was Fighter Command — although in 1945 squadrons of No. 38 Group did for a period come under the operational control of 2nd TAF, Europe. Their Halifaxes did well when giving close support bombing to the troops advancing into Germany. On 7 January 1944 Halifax LL186, Rootes 399th production aircraft, was allocated as the trials aircraft for Modification 1020, which was the conversion to Coastal Command met. duties. By 29 January it was agreed that met. conversion kits should be manufactured by Cunliffe Owen to the same standard as LL186. These

[1] I am aware that Mks. 1, 2, 3, 7 and 10 Lancasters were produced. I am emphasising that Avro did not change their mark number with change of equipment, as Handley Page did.

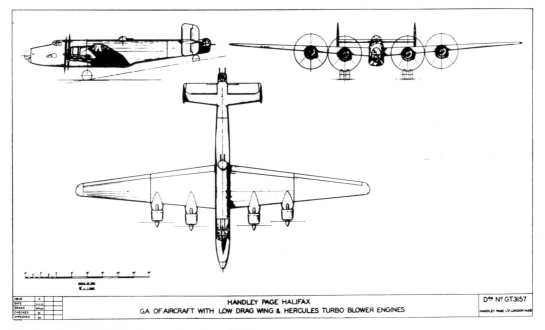

Handley Page HP65 Bomber project, June 1943. (RAF Museum).

meteorological duty aircraft were equipped with a separate met. observer's station having a fair degree of comfort (!) and were fitted out with radio altimeter, air position indicator, *Gee* and *Loran*. Like Coastal Command's other Halifax aircraft, these Mk.5s were flown by ATA from their parent factory to Marwell Hall for Cunliffe-Owen to convert. Approximately two weeks later they were collected and flown to St Athan for the fitting of ASV Mk.2. Being Mk.5 aircraft they were fitted with Merlins, and the long-endurance flights on meteorological duties with these engines were not always happy ones; the Merlins still had a distaste for long-range, slow-speed sorties and engine failures frequently occurred.

The Halifax in most respects was easy to handle. Both the A&AEE and Handley Page's had reported slight swing on take-off, which could easily be held and the aircraft needed no helping into the air, but it was generally accepted as being not so easy to land as a Lancaster, which conversely took a longer time getting into the air. On the Halifax Mk.6 a geared rudder tab was

introduced to eliminate a further irritation — the violent swing that occurred on engine failure. With this mod. fitted the footload compared with that of the Lancaster. The prototype Mk.6 was a converted Mk.3 (LV776) which first flew on 19 December 1943, and was on its flight trials in January 1944. Due to Hercules 100 engine production delays the first production Mk.6 (NP715) did not fly until 10 October 1944, with Mk.6 aircraft being issued to No. 4 Group squadrons in 1945. The performance was excellent — and superior to any mark of Lancaster or previous Halifax:

Weight empty	39,000 lb
Max all-up weight	68,000 lb
Max cruising speed	272 mph at 22,500 ft
Max speed	312 mph at 22,000 ft
Climb	45 minutes to 20,000 ft
Service ceiling	24,000 ft
Max bomb load	14,500 lb
Max range with max bomb-load	1260 miles
Max range with reduced bomb-load	2400 miles

35

To be totally unbiased one must accept the fact that the Halifax and the Lancaster were not two of a kind; they were totally different in design concept. The Lancaster was a superb bomb-carrier but the Halifax a superb all-rounder; the Lancaster was a relatively quick conversion of the Manchester to fill the production void left by that aircraft, while the Halifax was the designers' response to the tight corset of the specifications.

The origins of the Halifax as a transport aircraft began positively in 1943 when DTD and DOR decided, on the basis of the use of Halifax aircraft as glider tugs and paratroop aircraft, that a Halifax stripped of its offensive and defensive gear would fulfil the role of transport aircraft. For this duty a number of Mk.3 aircraft were stripped of everything but the rear turret, fitted with a pannier to fit into the bomb-bay, and the aircraft was designated the C3. It was DTD's idea that with the cessation of hostilities all Halifax aircraft could then be quickly converted into troop and equipment transports. With the success of this conversion, plans were put in hand to develop a transport aircraft to be based on DTD's Type B transport. From this eventually emerged the Mk.C8, which had no military or defensive equipment at all, used the same pannier as was developed for the C3 and had the fuselage fitted with a streamlined cone in place of the rear turret.

After the formation of the Airborne Forces in the UK a number of obsolescent aircraft were used as glider tugs and paratroop trainers, but with the growth and expansion of specialisation and the introduction of larger gliders more powerful tug aircraft were required and 'clapped-out' operationally time-expired Halifax and Stirling aircraft were acquired. With the introduction of the Hamilcar it became necessary to introduce more powerful tugs. In co-operation with No. 38 Group the Halifax was developed into a successful Hamilcar tug, first as the Mk.A5, then later the Mk.A3 and Mk.A7.

The development of the Airborne Support squadron variants really began with SOE's request for a fast long-range penetration aircraft, and from this was developed a similar aircraft having towing equipment. The aircraft had no front or mid-upper turret, the ammo tracks for the Type E rear turret were shortened in length and the ammo boxes placed further to the rear nearer to the turret, equipment for 12 paratroops was fitted with exit cone and a glider towing hook fitted aft of the tailwheel. These Halifax A5s first entered squadron service in February 1943 when No. 295 Squadron started to re-equip, but the first variant specifically developed for the Airborne Forces was the Mk.A3. This version did not enter service until 1944, so that the A5 was the version used in most of the Airborne Support operations. Seeing that so much publicity has been made of the Lancaster's lifting power it might be interesting to show a comparison between the Halifax Mk.3 and the Lancaster Mks.1 and 3 when tested as tugs for the Hamilcar.

These are official AFEE test figures and indicate the terrific potential of the Halifax for many roles. Meantime, the Halifax A5 and A3 had been cleared for Hamilcar towing, these aircraft — like all No. 38 Wing (later No. 38 Group) aircraft — having the SOE modifications with top turret removed, no H2S scanner and no Tricell flare chutes, but they were fitted with *Rebecca* and *Gee* as standard.

	Halifax 3	Lancaster 1 & 3
Tug weight	59,400 lb	49,500 lb
Glider weight	37,500 lb	36,000 lb
Take-off distance to 50 ft screen	2,400 yds	2,600 yds
Cruising speed	130/135 mph	135 mph
Climbing speed	135 mph	130 mph
Still air range	1,270 miles	540 miles

No. 100 Group was formed in November 1943 to give back-up support to Bomber Command by the use of electronics and spoof bombing raids using 'window' and bombs. Its contribution to the bomber offensive was out of all proportion to the number of aircraft used, not only in diverting Luftwaffe night-fighters away from the main streams but also in the airborne data collection of enemy radio and radar transmissions. By March 1945 No. 100 Group had decided to standardise on two aircraft, the Halifax and the Boeing B17. The Halifax B3 was chosen because of its performance, capacious fuselage (once again) and ready availability, but unfortunately only the B17 could accommodate the *Jostle 4* device. The airframe itself was standard B3; no alterations were made to it by Handley Page's, the secret equipment being installed at RAF MUs.

The final Airborne Forces Halifax was the A9, designated the HP71, which ultimately replaced all previous Halifax marks and which was powered by Hercules 16 engines. Its tare weight in service was 37,830 lb although Handley Page originally quoted a figure of 39,750 lb. The rear turret was the Boulton & Paul Type D with 0.5 in. twin Brownings and the fuel capacity was 2070 gallons in a grouped system similar to the A7. Boulton & Paul were designated the subcontractors for the detail design on the A9 and 145 aircraft were produced by Handley Page.

The A9 did not go into service with the RAF until 1946, when Nos 47 and 113 Squadrons were re-equipped with them. By this time Handley Page's had schemed the A10, which differed from the A9 in being fitted with Hercules 100 engines. The production of this version was cancelled along with the production of other Halifax aircraft listed in the next chapter.

Early in 1945 flight trials were carried out on a Mk.3 (HX229) to test the effects of the pannier on performance, which was especially significant with peace fast approaching and the possible use of the Halifax in civil aviation. By June 1945 BOAC were requiring the loan of three Halifax C8 aircraft for use on development flights on the West Coast of Africa from London to Lagos. BOAC's

Handley Page HP65 Bomber project, June 1943. (RAF Museum).

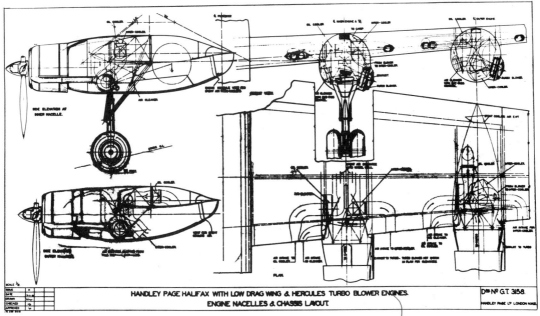

HANDLEY PAGE HALIFAX WITH LOW DRAG WING & HERCULES TURBO BLOWER ENGINES.
ENGINE NACELLES & CHASSIS LAYOUT

intention was to fly the aircraft intensively, carrying out all the inspections and overhauls at night at the terminal points — this is more fully dealt with in Chapter 7.

When the B1/39 specification was issued one of the requirements was for the provision of refuelling in flight, but with the withdrawal of the specification no further RAF interest was shown in flight refuelling until VE day approached and the Pacific became a possible area of operations for Bomber Command. This idea was pigeon-holed with the approach of VJ day and the use of B29s by the USAAF, but in 1946 Coastal Command became interested in the flight refuelling of Halifax Met. 6 aircraft and meetings took place between Handley Page's, Flight Refuelling Ltd and the Ministry of Supply to discuss the project and contracts.

The meetings with the M of S took place at Thames House, London, and discussed the increase of the Halifax GR6's fuel capacity from 2880 gallons to 3840 gallons. This Coastal Command did not want; their desire was for refuelling in flight to increase the range without losing any fuselage or bomb cell capacity, as three 230-gallon bomb-bay tanks were already in use. It was finally agreed that arrangements be made to refuel these three tanks and, if practicable, the No. 2 tanks

as well. The tail turret was to be removed and replaced by a fairing with ballast. Small windows were to be fitted to enable the operator to see the refuelling pipe as the winch pulled it towards the 'receiver' aircraft. The winch was hydraulically operated and would require the installation of two pumps fitted to the power-plants, the decision on which power-plants to fit the pumps being left to Handley Page.

At the 2 April 1946 meeting it was determined that ten Halifax 'receiver' aircraft and three Lancaster 'tankers' should be converted for Meteorological duties in Coastal Command. The trial installation Halifax was already at Flight Refuelling Ltd at Staverton airfield and the conversion would be completed by November. It was decided no further conversions would be carried out until the trial installation aircraft had flown and proved satisfactory. If satisfactory, Flight Refuelling Ltd would manufacture and assemble the parts and Y.A.R.D. would cover the fitting of the assemblies to the other nine Halifax aircraft. However, during the trials of the aircraft Coastal Command lost interest in flight refuelling, partly due to retrenchment but also because a new replacement aircraft was being manufactured.

Chapter 3
Production

Preparation

As the years progressed after 1933 it was becoming more and more obvious that the new Germany was again Great Britain's enemy and that time was short to produce a modern bomber force. By March 1934 the Defence Requirements Sub-Committee (DRC) of the Committee of Imperial Defence (CID) had produced a report which concluded that Germany was the main potential enemy against which long-term defence had to be prepared. A second DRC report resulted in July 1935 with a decision by the main Committee that, as it was impossible to guarantee peace beyond January 1939, the DRC must produce a defence programme providing for a state of readiness by the end of the fiscal year 1938-39. This decision was reflected in the various Air Staff Schemes that appeared; for instance, the Air Staff Scheme C of 1935 called for 68 bomber squadrons. This was superseded in February 1936 with Scheme F which, although still calling for the same number of squadrons, required a heavier type of bomber carrying twice the load.

Also in 1936 the specifications B12/36 and P13/36 were issued, the latter being amended on 3 September 1937 in the case of Handley Page's tender to the use of four Merlin engines. The HP57 that was produced under this amended specification was still to use the serial numbers allocated to the HP56. With

Production of pilot's compartment. Top portion of Halifax Mk.2 front fuselage at Duple Bodies and Motors Ltd. (J. Olsson).

these decisions made, Handley Page at Cricklewood began the job of estimating the cost of jigs and tools and setting up a production line.

The Air Ministry required that the two HP57 prototypes should be hand-built while the production of production jigs and tools proceeded. The first prototype was to be completed sufficiently for it to be used as a trials aircraft at Martlesham Heath while the second prototype would be fully equipped for Service use. So as to prevent any delay the Air Ministry insisted that this aircraft must not be used to check the jigs — the whole emphasis being on getting the two prototypes finished and into the air, where tests and trials could eradicate or highlight any faults found in the new bomber.

The drawings for the HP57 started in mid-August 1937, and the production drawings started to be issued in December 1938 with the jig and tool design and production commencing at approximately the same time.

To be suitable for production and to satisfy the Service, an aircraft's performance is not the only criterion — the aircraft must also be capable of being produced simply, quickly and cheaply, it must be easy to maintain and require as little maintenance as possible. Two processes in the Handley Page production set-up were to satisfy a proportion of these; both were to speed up production and both were to make the Halifax an acceptable production aircraft as well as a cheap aircraft to produce. The first of these processes was Photo-lofting, which Volkert had seen being used in Naval architecture while he was visiting the USA. With the approval of 'HP', Volkert adapted and pioneered this method for aircraft use in Great Britain. Using the method, components are accurately drawn on specially prepared metal sheets, these are then photographed and the drawings are then reproduced photographically on sensitised metal sheet, which can then be circulated to subcontractors or put on to the jigs. The other production innovation was the split-construction method, which Volkert had pioneered and introduced for the HP54 Harrow. The improvement of this and a

revision to the production workshop layout was the responsibility of the Production Manager, J. Hamilton, who had joined Handley Page from Beardmore's in 1929.

To digress a moment from production it must be said that the various Air Ministry schemes for expansion of the RAF, and insufficient funds, not only retarded development of the bomber force but also placed constraints on the manufacture of the new four-engined bombers.

First, the operational requirements of the RAF and the German Luftwaffe were totally different. Whereas the Luftwaffe's aim was a tactical force of fighters and bombers to support the German Wehrmacht, the RAF had to maintain a fighter defence of the United Kingdom and also forces for strategic purposes — not least of which should have been protection of the sea lanes.

For the RAF these schemes were:

Scheme H (Early 1937)
Increase of the RAF's United Kingdom first-line force to nearly 2,500 aircraft at the earliest date after April 1939, and was to include 1659 bombers.
Scheme J
Bomber Command's strength to be increased to 90 squadrons with 1442 aircraft. This scheme was intended to reach completion by the beginning of 1943 and would cover the introduction of the new, large four-engined bombers.
Scheme K (Late 1937)
Increase of fighter strength while cutting down the number of first-line bomber squadrons and reserves.
Scheme L (March 1938)
This provided for the rapid expansion to 12,000 aircraft over a period of two years. The emphasis was on fighter production with no increase in bomber aircraft.

From this it will be seen that a long production run of large bomber aircraft could hardly be planned — either by the Air Ministry or by the aircraft manufacturer. And without a long production run the aircraft would not be cheap nor would there be sufficient squadrons with up-to-date aircraft.

Manufacture and assembly of centre section of Halifax Mk.2 at LPTB Aldenham. (J. Olsson).

New bomber aircraft required new equipment and new engines. Production of the Vulture was giving trouble, production of turrets was insufficient, the requirements were being changed, engine manufacturers' delivery dates were not dependable — these were problems that the airframe manufacturer had to take in his stride. And on top of that a squadron of Halifax aircraft was expected to be in service by the summer of 1940. So every process to speed production was considered by Handley Page's. English Electric, who were manufacturing Hampdens, were also brought into the Halifax set-up. Scheme L did improve things, for it doubled the production target for the Halifax while at the same time calling for the production of 1500 Manchesters and 1500 Stirlings. Now production lines could be set up, with new subcontractors for parts and subcontractors for jigs and tools, but two more problems still had to be solved: production of the Messier undercarriage and hydraulics, and the supply of Boulton & Paul turrets.

In March 1938 Lt.-Col. Disney, the Director of Aeroplane Production, asked 'HP' for information regarding workforce and tools required if production was to be increased, to which 'HP' replied that the need was to double the amount of existing machine tools and that approximately 2000 more semi-skilled workers would be required. At this particular time the Machine Shop was the only area at Cricklewood on double time, and 'HP' considered that by March 1939 twice the present output could be obtained if his requirements of machine tools and semi-skilled workers could be met, for he felt that the subcontractors who produced his jigs could quickly produce more when required.

By 6 October 1938 'HP' was writing to the Director-General of Production pointing out that if production of 1000 aircraft to HP57 was required then a peak delivery rate of 50 to 60 aircraft per month would be necessary, which would require manufacturing space three times that of Cricklewood, and that the jigs for this production would cost about £750,000. Following this up, on 10 November 'HP' wrote to Air Marshal Freeman, Director of Production at the Air Ministry, pointing out that if the policy of big machines was to be carried out than the number produced must be 1000 of type — otherwise, at the production rate and with the methods then in use, the aircraft would be out of date before they entered the Service in larger numbers. This continual prompting by 'HP' was not just that of a business man but the thoughts of a man and his staff who recognised that the day was fast approaching when the numbers required to satisfy the needs of the RAF could not be produced by one factory alone, and that more jigs, more tools, other factories and new dispersal units would be the key to production and survival. This was borne out by 'HP's proposal to organise jig manufacture so that extra jigs were built and kept in reserve against an emergency.

During November 1938 Handley Page's also proposed a high-speed development of the Hampden which would have a wider fuselage, be powered by Merlin engines, have a 2000 lb load of bombs and a maximum speed of 315 mph. Tedder was interested in the proposal but only if available immediately; he concluded his reply with 'What we want is Halifaxes, and plenty of them, early.'

The production order for 100 Halifax aircraft given on 7 January 1938 against Specification 32/37 meant for Handley Pages more jigs, more work, more staff, jobs to be revised. . . in fact the whole factory to be geared up for a long production run of a new bomber. A look at this production specification shows that the maximum bomb-load was still the same at 8000 lb, but the crew had now increased to five. Four Merlin engines with two-speed blowers provided the power, but mention was now made of flotation gear by the fitting of four metal containers — the General Reconnaissance version? In December it was estimated that the jigs to produce 50 to 60 aircraft per month would approximately cost between £1m and £1.25m and a proposal for the stages of work was laid out as follows:

January to June 1939:
    Halifax master jigs under construction. Textile machinery makers labour force on Halifax templates and jigs to be increased.

June to December 1939:
    Main Halifax jig production at the textile machinery makers.

January to December 1940:
    Building up Halifax production.

Also mentioned was that by June 1940 delivery would be made of the first Halifax from the works of English Electric. This was because the increase in orders for the Halifax would make it impossible for Handley Page's at Cricklewood to cover it on their own, and English Electric were the logical constructor as they were already producing the Hampden. Full sets of jigs were sent by Cricklewood to the English Electric Preston assembly lines and co-operation between English Electric and Handley Page was so good that on 8 September 1939 'HP' commented in a memo on the valuable co-operation from English Electric — praise indeed!

The Air Ministry Supply Committee were, by November 1939, planning the provision of tools on the basis of 500 Halifax aircraft being produced at a rate of 22 per month, which was to be the total of Handley Page's and English Electric's production. The Handley Page programme was at this time already three to four months in arrears due to shortage of materials, which the Ministry concerned did not seem able to rectify — in fact correspondence over the matter at this time appeared to be getting acrimonious. Austin and Armstrong Whitworth were not now considered for the Halifax production scheme as the maximum required production rate would be about 100 aircraft per month. These would be constructed at Cricklewood, a new shadow factory at Speke, the English Electric factory and the Nuffield factory, as confirmed by Air Ministry letter S49637/S8 of 9 November 1939. For this, 24 sets of jigs were required and by 14 November 'HP' was able to confirm to the Under-Secretary of State that 80-85 per cent of prototype jigging and tooling was already complete and 60 per cent of main and sub-assembly jigs were completed. Handley Page had taken over the old Nieuport Aircraft works at Cricklewood, which added a further 70,000 square feet of floor area.

As we know, at the outbreak of war the Government brought into use the Shadow Factory scheme and the Ministry envisaged a much larger programme for the Halifax, so that three more manufacturing units were brought into the picture: the London Aircraft Production Group, Rootes Securities and Fairey Aviation. The London Aircraft Production Group consisted of the London Passenger Transport Board (LPTB), Duple Bodies and Motors Ltd, Chrysler Motors Ltd, Park Royal Coachworks, and Express Motor & Body Works Ltd; these were initially the responsibility of the parent Company but eventually the LPTB took over the management though Handley Page still remained responsible for imparting the necessary information to the firms concerned.

On 24 October the prototype flew, and as the flight tests continued so did the changes. This had been foreseen, as had the production by subcontractors, and the necessary planning for such an emergency had been carried out. 'HP' had at this critical time also determined his staff and their responsibilities: Volkert was in charge of design and production; Lachmann was in charge of research and development, and continued to contribute even during his period of internment; Major Cordes was the Chief Test Pilot; J. W. Ratcliffe was Chief Draughtsman, and was placed in charge of the Outside Production Office; Stafford was head of the Aerodynamics Section and eventually took over as Assistant Chief Designer; J. Hamilton was Production Manager at Cricklewood; H. W. Smith was Works Superintendent at Cricklewood; D. Robinson was the Assistant Works Superintendent at Cricklewood; W. Robinson was the Chief Inspector; McKenna became during the war the Chief Draughtsman; Salmson was the Superintendent of the Experimental Shop; and MacRostie was the Works Superintendent at Radlett.

The first two years of war, like the years of expansion, were fraught with shortages and complications, due to a number of factors:

(a) Management pre-occupied with organising subcontracts and programmes.

(b) Training of more personnel with the increase in factory area and subcontractors.

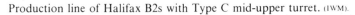

Production line of Halifax B2s with Type C mid-upper turret. (IWM).

(c) Shortages of certain materials such as extrusions.

(d) Controls and priorities laid down by the Ministries.

(e) Modifications to the aircraft brought about by testing.

(f) Incorporation of the modifications into the production line.

Regarding priorities, it must be realised that in 1940 top priority for everything was given by Beaverbrook to the Hurricane, Spitfire, Blenheim, Wellington and Whitley, and it was not until the end of 1941 that the War Cabinet made the decision to enlarge the heavy bomber programme and thus give greater priority to the large bombers.

Contract 692649/3/C4(e) covered the supply of 100 HP57 Halifax aircraft to take Merlin engines in accordance with Specification 32/37 and the serial numbers allocated were: L9485 to L9534; L9560 to L9584; and L9600 to L9608. This contract and specification stated: 'Production of Halifax 1 aircraft to be constructed fully representative of Halifax L7245'.

By 1 January 1940 the Air Council was considering whether the Halifax should have a higher priority regarding material delivery — at that time only fighters had top priority — and had placed orders for 100 more aircraft from Handley Page's on top of those already ordered, 300 Halifaxes from the new Speke factory and a further 100 aircraft from English Electric. Yet by the 18th 'HP' was writing to the Under-Secretary of State at the Air Ministry complaining of the non-delivery of certain essential extrusions and forgings and expressing his opinion that the provision of a squadron of Halifaxes by the summer was now impossible (it was unrealistic from the start). It was by now obvious that the provisioning of materials, or lack of it, was prejudicing the manufacture of aircraft. In the meantime Handley Page's and their outside suppliers had by the end of November 1939 produced 9024 drawings for aircraft and 400 jig and tool drawings to satisfy production. Again, on 7 February 1940 at a meeting at the Air Ministry it was stated that ordered fabricated light alloy parts were overdue on delivery and Cricklewood was working without overtime and many new tools were lying idle.

The output of production aircraft detail assemblies began in January and it was planned that the final assembly of the first production aircraft would start in August. Also started in January was the setting up of the Outside Production Office, which had to deal with the expansion of production of the Halifax and which was headed by J. Ratcliffe assisted by Trapmore of the Contracts Office. Some of the functions of the Outside Production Office were to: arrange the training of key workers; supply technical information and copies of drawings; arrange for supply of templates, sample parts, etc; supply information and drawings for jigs and tools; assist 'daughter' firms on selection of tools, buildings, etc; answer queries from 'daughter' firms; render advice and give technical approval; and deal with allocation of spares for AOGs and NIVs.

A Co-ordinating Committee was also set up, chaired by Thurstan James, who was Director-General of Halifax Production at the MAP, and including J. Ratcliffe representing Handley Page Ltd, and F. D. Crowe (HP Resident Engineer at Preston). The committee met monthly at the Central Hotel, Birmingham, to co-ordinate the supplies from factories manufacturing Halifax aircraft and parts. Ratcliffe considered that these meetings were not only essential from the supplies point of view but also allowed all parties to see all problems.

A Group Materials Committee was formed from representatives of each firm, under a neutral Chairman elected by the Ministry of Aircraft Production; a representative of the Outside Production Office acted as technical consultant to the Committee. This committee met once a month to discuss material shortages, etc.

The first production aircraft (L9485) flew on 11 October 1940 and was powered by four 1280 hp Merlin 10s; like the two prototypes it had leading edge slots and was flown to

A&AEE Boscombe Down for completion and testing.

The various members of the Halifax production group were called 'daughter' firms and each firm had 'dominion' status. Thus the five companies in the group had equal status from a manufacturing point of view, and common problems in administration and material supply procedure. The parent company meantime had the responsibility of supplying drawings, technical advice and approval and the proving of the jigs. In order to maintain a high standard of interchangeability, components were to be cross-checked on the jigs of similar components, while to maintain the high standard of production aircraft one aircraft per hundred from each 'daughter' firm was to be flown to Radlett and tested by the parent company's pilots; any discrepancies or adjustments were reported to the daughter firm concerned.

By June 1940 it had been decided to extend the inner nacelle fairings to the trailing edge of the flaps to reduce drag, but the first ten production aircraft were accepted with the fairings of intermediate length. It was also decided that on production aircraft the slots would be locked in — in fact the first 75 production aircraft were fitted with this type of wing. A new set of outer wings was by now under way, with the leading edge redesigned to have slots deleted and the leading edge profile skinned over; a date remained to be determined for the introduction of this type of wing into production. This was followed by an internal memo at the end of 1940 from 'HP' suggesting that tests be conducted to 'clean up' the Halifax, one idea being the closing of the locked-in slot and the mainplane. In regard to the nacelles, a 35 inch extension aft of the mainplane trailing edge would make an appreciable improvement in drag reduction, it was suggested.

By this time further properties had been taken over for the production of the Halifax airframe and components: Kenneth Hill Sandblasting Co at Letchworth; E. Beckett & Son at Willesden; Car Mart Ltd, Boundary Road, NW8; Armstrong Siddeley Service

Construction of Halifax outer mainplanes at Park Royal Coach Works. (J. Olsson).

Station, Colindale; Daimler Co Ltd, The Hyde, Hendon; Elstree Film Studios; Godfrey Davis, Neasden Lane, NW10.

This was followed by the take-over of the MGM film studies at Boreham Wood, where rubber press tools were installed. The Cricklewood factory had meantime been extended to take over the buildings there which included the Smiths Crisps factory and that housing Armstrong Siddeley Cars. It was also proposed that the London Passenger Transport Board car sheds at Aldenham should be allowed to be completed and taken over by the London Aircraft Production Group for aircraft assembly.

By late 1940 the MAP were wishing to establish a repair organisation in the York area for the repair and overhaul of Halifax aircraft. This was eventually set up in the shadow factory complex at Clifton aerodrome, and is more fully described later. Handley Page were responsible for the administration of the York Aircraft Repair Depot complex and also for the technical assistance and information to the LAP Group. They were prepared to accept this extra load and leave the decision regarding the fees to the MAP — it was felt that the main thing was to get on with the job.

Arrangements had been made in late 1939 for distribution of jigs and tools to four locations, each site to contain one complete set for each main component. This was proceeded with at speed, jigs and tools being produced by Handley Page's and subcontractors, and small tools being made by the factories involved in aircraft production. By mid-1941 three sets of assembly jigs were at Cricklewood and one set at dispersal units. It was intended that as soon as the first set at the dispersal unit achieved working capacity a further set of jigs from Cricklewood would be transferred to the dispersal unit. During this time Buchanan of the MAP suggested to 'HP' that visits be arranged between Handley Page and English Electric for each to see how the other was working; there could be some production fixture one was using to accelerate production that the other might copy — especially so if it was suitable for unskilled labour.

With jigs and tools distributed, production drawings ready, English Electric set up and the L.A.P. Group being organised, full production was ready to roll.

Full production

Handley Page's produced their first Mk.1 Series 1 aircraft (L9485) and flew it on 11 October 1940. Production was exceptionally slow at first, in spite of all the production processes evolved by Handley Page's to speed it up. Some of this was due to changes to the airframe brought about by operational needs and some by the lack of certain materials such as extrusions.

English Electric produced their first Halifax (V9976) and it was flown from Samlesbury airfield on 15 August 1941. It was the first of their contract for 200 Mk.2s. This was followed in September by Handley Page's flying their first Mk.2 (L9609).

As has been explained previously, the Halifax, like the HP52 Hampden and HP54 Harrow before it, was designed from the start to utilise Handley Page's various methods for speeding production. The biggest aids were of course the split construction and sub-assembly methods. The fuselage and mainplane was constructed around the centre fuselage, which was integral to the centre mainplane. The front fuselage housed the crew and was bolted on to the centre fuselage, and aft of the centre fuselage was the rear fuselage, which at its rearmost end was bolted on the rear section housing the rear gun turret.

The centre section wing was extended to, and included, the inner engine nacelles. To this was bolted the intermediate wing, which extended to, but did not include, the outer engine nacelles. The outboard engine nacelle was part of the outer mainplane and the whole of this was bolted with special bolts to the intermediate wing — see diagrams of Mk.1 and Mk.3 layouts.

R9540 was sent as a pattern aircraft to LAPG and at the start of 1942 production started on their first contract for 200 aircraft of the B2 series. They eventually produced 450 of them, delivering their first B2 (BB189) on 10 January. The LAP Group assembled their aircraft at Leavesden (London Passenger Transport Board) from parts and sections manufactured at the other plants of the LAP Group: Chrysler Motors at Kew produced rear fuselages; Park Royal at White City produced outer wings, nacelles and engine cowlings; Express Motors at Enfield produced tail units, flaps and intermediate wings; Duple Bodies & Motors at Hendon produced front fuselage shells; LPTB Aldenham produced centre fuselage and power units, fitting out components prior to delivery to Leavesden.

In their setting up for production LAP Group suffered the usual pangs; for instance, initially each plant was to fit out each component, but then this was changed to full fitting out at Aldenham and Leavesden. Also, later, at Duple Bodies the toolmakers had constructed one large drilling jig rather than a number of smaller ones to drill all the holes in the nose for the turret fitment. Just as it was completed the mod. 452 nose was introduced, the front turret deleted, and so the drilling jig was obsolete before it could be used.

Another company starting production of the Halifax in 1942 was Rootes at the new factory at Speke, who delivered their first

Completing the assembly of a Mk.2 Halifax at LTPB Leavesden with the outer wings being lifted into position. (J. Olsson).

LPTB Leavesden: final assembly of Halifax B2 from components and assemblies of the London Aircraft Production Group. (J. Olsson)

aircraft, a B2 (DG219), on 1 April; only 12 of the B2 aircraft were produced before production was turned over to the Mk.5s, the first one (DG231) being delivered on 12 August 1942.

Fairey Aviation at Stockport began their production of the Halifax by producing the Mk.5, their first production aircraft being DJ980, delivered on 27 October 1942. Altogether 246 Mk.5 aircraft were produced by Fairey before changing over to the production of the Mk.3s. The production of the Mk.5 was due to the desire by the MAP to have an alternative undercarriage to the Messier, which was in short supply, and also due to a change in the Messier system with the introduction of the Lockheed pump.

The total Halifax production group comprised 41 factories and dispersal units of $7\frac{1}{2}$ million square feet, 600 subcontractors and 51,000 employees. This set-up produced one complete Halifax each working hour, which involved 30,000 different components. In one hour of production: 256,000 airframe parts (excluding rivets) were made, fitted and inspected; two-thirds of an acre (7 tons) of light alloy sheet was cut, formed and fitted; 70,000 rivets were closed; 3 to 4 miles of electrical cable were fitted; 1 mile of piping was fitted; 3 miles of sheet metal were rolled or drawn into sections.

In 1941 Handley Page's were complaining of the shortage of Merlin 10s and 20s. With this, and the shortage of Messier undercarriages and the troubles being experienced with the Messier hydraulic pump, the Halifax production line was experiencing difficulties. The Merlin shortage could not totally be blamed on Rolls-Royce for, in addition to supplying Merlin engines for Battle of Britain aircraft, they were developing and/or producing the Griffon, Peregrine and Vulture engines, as well as providing assistance at the start of the war to Fordair in France for the production there of Merlin engines — all this from the three factories at Derby, Crewe and Glasgow, There was often a wide discrepancy between programme and performance, as well as a shortage of the latest marks of Merlin and a surplus of the older marks.

Also in 1941, Parliament had made the decision to enlarge the heavy bomber programme and, as most of the fighters as well as the Halifax and Lancaster were powered by the Merlin, it was obvious that the Rolls-Royce Group alone could not undertake the supply of all the engines required. It was considered that no more than a 20 per cent increase from this group could be attained, so a further source of supply would have to be considered. Unfortunately for the Halifax, once the Lancaster was established in service Rolls-Royce leaned towards development of the Merlin and its installation to improve it for the Lancaster.

Bristol's development and production of the Hercules was still behind schedule, priority on the Hercules being given to the Beaufighter night-fighter. Trouble was still being experienced with sleeve and reduction gear, so although Handley Page's were interested in the installation of the Hercules they would still have to continue using the Merlin 20 and 22. However, when the Hercules did appear it was producing greater power than the Merlin and was satisfactory for operation under temperate or tropical conditions.

After production and acceptance aircraft were usually flown away, most often to Maintenance Units. When the aircraft were required by the squadrons they were delivered by Air Transport Auxiliary crews, amongst whom were female pilots like Lettice Curtis — she was responsible for over 200 Halifax delivery flights. Aircraft required overseas were sometimes delivered by crews posted overseas or, in the early years, by a Ferry Transport Unit. This job was later carried out by Ferry Command, who were responsible for delivery flights world-wide.

When the ATA pilot arrived at the factory he (or she) presented a delivery chit to the AID representative. This was in three parts, one for presenting to the AID on collection, one for receipting by the person receiving the aircraft when delivered, and the third part a signal to No.41 Group RAF, the Group responsible for delivery or collection of

Halifax Mk.IIs straight from the production line at English Electric factory, Samlesbury near Preston, April 1943. (British Aerospace).

aircraft. In return for their copy of the delivery chit AID collected the ATA pilot's signature on the receipt form, and this was followed by the handing over by AID of the airframe, engine and propeller logbooks and the 'travelling Form 700'.

At Handley Page's Cricklewood was situated the main factory with the offices facing on to Claremont Road. Cricklewood assembled the details and up to sub-assembly of main components, with the detail work being carried out in the 'Armstrong' shop. The main factory housed the assembly of the fuselage, wings, centre-section, fins and tailplanes; accommodation was also provided for the machine-shop, toolroom and sheet metal workers.

Separate from the main factory, and to the left of it from Claremont Road, were the drawing office and experimental shop. The sub-assemblies and main components were transferred to Radlett for final assembly, Radlett also being the testing site and providing accommodation for the Flight Test Section.

In 1952-53 Sir Frederick Handley Page gave evidence to the Select Committee on Estimates (Re-armament) and stated that the first prototype HP57 cost his firm £85,000-

£90,000 (the tender for the P13/36 in HP56 form in 1936 was £50,000). Sir Frederick had a favourite saying: 'To the victor the spoils'; it would be fair to say that the Halifax was a winner and that Handley Page's contribution to victory more than repaid the British Government's investment. Production models of the Halifax were reputed to cost £12,500 each.

Unfortunately for posterity, the records of many firms involved in the production of aircraft, including the Halifax, have been lost or destroyed; and their older employees are no longer with us, therefore much has been lost that cannot be replaced. But some facts are still available; for instance, during the peak production of the Halifax, one complete Halifax was produced each working hour, and, out of 10,018 British-built heavy bombers produced between 1940 and mid-1944, 4,046 were Halifaxes — 40 per cent of the total. The total production of the Halifax was 6176 when the last one (Mk.A9) was delivered to the RAF in 1946. More could have been produced but for changes in role and requirements and interference by bureaucracy.

In talks with pilots of No.4 Group in 1943 it was found that squadron pilots' preference

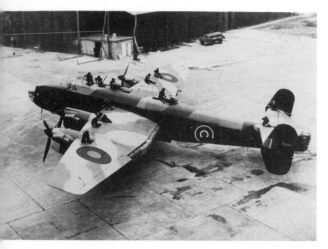

Final preparation and inspection of a Halifax Mk.2 at Leavesden after manufacture at the London Aircraft Production Group. (J. Olsson)

was in general for aircraft manufactured by English Electric, closely followed by Handley Page. The preference for English Electric aircraft was said to be because they had a lower empty weight, were lighter to handle and performed better. Aircraft manufactured by the London Aircraft Production Group were referred to as the 'London Bus' aircraft in the squadrons and were not generally the favourites, but even some of their aircraft had lower empty weights than the Cricklewood machines. So Sir Frederick asked for an investigation to ensure that all manufacturing processes and variations of design were being strictly controlled to prevent 'heavy' aircraft and to ensure good and light handling characteristics.

The English Electric Co at Preston had the reputation of being one of the best of the aircraft companies producing the Halifax, and were to confirm this when they later designed and produced their own aircraft, even winning recognition from 'HP' for this. The English Electric Works were at Strand Road, Preston and RAF vehicles leaving there would drive down Strand Road to the Grand Junction — five roads in the centre of which was set a pill-box gun post with concrete-filled oil barrels. Presumably the object was to deter any German troops who had had the audacity

to come so far. It has been said that the first time a 'Queen Mary' aircraft transporter tried to negotiate this series of obstacles it first knocked over some of the concrete barrels and then burst the main water pipe which at that point ran above ground.

A firm which received very little publicity for its wartime production efforts was Cunliffe-Owen of Eastleigh. In 1943 they received a contract for the conversion of Mk.5 Halifax aircraft for Coastal Command, the ATA delivering the aircraft from the factory to the Cunliffe-Owen dispersed site at Marwell Hall, where the conversion work was carried out. Upon completion the aircraft were then flown by service personnel to St. Athan for the fitting of ASV radar. They were also responsible for the production of conversion kits for Coastal Command met. aircraft and, with the introduction of the mod.814 Type D fins, they obtained a contract for the production of 10 aircraft sets per week.

Another company to produce this type of fin was the Heston Aircraft Co who quickly produced 30 hand-made sets. These were allocated for fitment to Nos 35 and 405 Squadrons by working parties. No.41 Group supplied 90 aircraftmen, split into working parties, who along with aircraftmen at the squadrons fitted the fins and rudders on site.

Bombing could be, and was in some places, an interference to production. Handley Page's at Cricklewood was never embarrassed by enemy action, although obviously air raid warnings did slow down production, and being in the London area did not help in that respect. Duple Bodies of the London Aircraft Production Group was once badly damaged by enemy bombs and numerous near misses occurred, one of which demolished a nearby block of flats.

As the tempo of production increased, night shifts were being worked, conventions and practices had to be revised, and unskilled as well as semi-skilled labour was drafted in, with experience varying from garagehands to housemaids. The dilution in some work areas was two skilled men to 16 or 18 personnel of doubtful ability. As the work progressed, so the teams at the various factories built up experience and unsuitable personnel were weeded out, the ones remaining being welded into a team under the guidance of the skilled men. Female operatives became adept at marking out and some were trained locally as riveters or drilling operators. The more adept ones were sent on basic engineering courses by the MAP to acquire a higher skill and thus contribute more.

By mid-1943 the MAP had issued their programme to cover aircraft production from July to the end of 1943. This determined that one-third of the total Halifax production was to have H2S equipment and standard bomb doors, with the remainder having large bomb-doors without the H2S. Stafford had to explain to the MAP meeting that the large bomb-doors had been struck off charge (SOC), only 50 sets having been ordered, so that steps would have to be taken to get orders for large bomb-doors increased. It was noted that the production of the large doors was hardly likely to start until July. The bomb-doors were not the only things in short supply, for the Halifax Material Committee was still reporting shortages of materials such as steel forgings, aluminium alloy forgings and stampings.

When Ratcliffe was promoted from his position as Chief Draughtsman to take charge of the Outside Production Office and to sit on the Group Materials Committee, his position as Chief Draughtsman was taken by J. McKenna, who then was responsible for the Halifax design drawings — and later others right up to the Victor. Even at the height of production and development there were never more than 90 draughtsmen employed, and of course, they were also responsible for passing drawings to the daughter firms.

The final production line was naturally at Radlett — and Cricklewood — with the introduction of the Mk.A9, where 145 of this type were produced. It can be said that the Halifax — from Mk.1 to A9 — was strong and well produced. To those who produced her and those of us who flew her, she was second to none.

* * * * *

Halifax Mk.IIIs under manufacture by the English Electric Company at Samlesbury, circa 1944. (British Aerospace)

York Aircraft Repair Depot (48 MU)

With the introduction of the Halifax to Nos 4 and 6 Groups in the period 1940-42 the Air Ministry allocated most of the existing Yorkshire aerodromes to these Groups. The Headquarters of No. 4 Group was at Heslington Hall, one mile South East of York.

In February 1941 the Ministry of Aircraft Production made it known that they wished to set up a repair organisation in the York area. This was formed later in the year at Clifton aerodrome, York, in a shadow factory complex. The management was provided by Handley Page Ltd, who eventually employed about 2500 civilians of which a large proportion was female. The organisation was known as the York Aircraft Repair Depot (Y.A.R.D)

Contractors started work on three runways and the construction of two sites for the repair of Halifax aircraft. Initially four hangars were constructed on the north-west side of the airfield. This site, known as Rawcliffe, ultimately finished up with five hangars. During the latter part of 1942 the third runway was completed and during the same year the second repair depot, known as Water Lane, was completed. Altogether 16 hangars were built at both depots. (At Water Lane in 1943 a Halifax caught fire during maintenance work and three hangars and nine Halifaxes were destroyed).

The Handley Page manager throughout its seven-year life was Eric W. Pickston, the Chief Inspector's post was filled by Larry Gain and AID was represented by G. Middle. Much of the labour force was recruited from the local LNER carriage works at York and thus the initial output of repaired aircraft from Y.A.R.D was slow, while aircraft repair experience was built up. The first aircraft completed was Halifax L9510, which was tested by an all-RAF crew, checked and cleared by AID and collected by an ATA crew.

Most of the Halifaxes handled by Y.A.R.D. were Category B damaged aircraft, meaning that extensive damage had occurred which warranted dismantling the aircraft and despatching it to Y.A.R.D. by the RAF salvage unit, No.60 MU. Most common Cat. Bs involved wheels-up landings, or under and overshoot crashes, which caused damage to front fuselage, lower half frames, inboard nacelle and undercarriage doors, bomb-doors, rear fuselage, etc.

The Depot also handled Cat.AC aircraft — extensively damaged but repairable on site — and also Halifaxes which had suffered severe damage to airframe or main spars by flak or fighters. Also serviced were Middle East based aircraft, which were flown in for 240 hour inspections, and aircraft which had been subject to violent evasive action (one particular Halifax had been looped).

Initially the aircraft returned to Clifton were repaired and reassembled using the original airframe units but with new engines and propellers. It was soon realised, however, that one particular aircraft might have suffered severe front fuselage damage, while another might have been returned because of flak damage to its wings and tailplane. A system of major unit interchange was therefore instigated, which resulted in a dramatic increase in the numbers of repaired and rebuilt Halifaxes.

There were considerable technical problems to the system of major unit interchange as some 2000 modifications were carried out from 1941-43. Detailed modification checks had to be carried out before substitution of major sections could take place. Once structural repairs were completed and the aircraft reassembled the aircraft was subjected to the same rigorous inspection as a production line aircraft.

A new department controlled by G. W. Schuler (Works Manager) was established, and, upon receipt of a crash report, a 'made up' aircraft was planned from substitute units. For instance, upon notification of a Cat.B crash the procedure would be:

(a) Notification of Category B and location.
(b) Visit by Works Site Inspector for damage assessment.

(c) Report with aircraft serial number, mark, etc, to Planning Department at Rawcliffe, specifying crash damage.

(d) List of anticipated replacement parts submitted to stores for preparation of parts, new engines, propellers, etc.

Output of aircraft from Y.A.R.D. Clifton during 1944 averaged approximately 15 per month with pre-flight preparation and re-flight tests being the responsibility of C. Carpenter. Re-flight tests were very few and no flight accidents occurred during the life of the Depot, though there were several incidents involving three-engined landings.

The test personnel, once the procedure was consolidated, were Handley Page's Radlett-based pilots, who visited Clifton on monthly tours. They were J. Talbot, T. V. Mitchell, J. Marsh, and W. G. Sanders. During the 1947-48 period T. G. Hazelden took over as Chief Pilot after the death of J. Talbot and visited Clifton as part of the flying. Flight observers at Clifton, who acted as second pilots, were R. Baines, J. Harding and I. Robinson and they were based at York; their duties also included visits to Nos 4 and 6 Groups and the sorting out of rogue aircraft.

No. 60 MU was situated about nine miles north of York and was responsible for the salvage and transport of crashed Halifax aircraft to Y.A.R.D. Equipment for the salvage usually consisted of several 'Queen Marys', tripod jacks and a five-ton Coles crane. RAF Linton-on-Ouse was the site for its first experience of salvaging a crashed aircraft and, obviously, problems were experienced due to the lack of correct lifting gear. In fact a fatal incident did once occur when the aircraft slid sideways as lifting started, trapping an airman between the jack and the inboard nacelle.

Approximately 2000 Halifax aircraft were repaired at Clifton or on site by Y.A.R.D. personnel. Components damaged beyond repair were 'reduced to produce' by Pilkington Bros of Doncaster and all serviceable detail parts recovered from these components were serviced and used again for repair or production.

Each aircraft was flight tested to the precise procedure adopted for new production aircraft and took, on average, 45 minutes. The test procedure comprised a visual ground check, a wheel brake test, straight and level flight with a check on trim and control heaviness/lightness, a stall with wheels and flaps up, a dive to maximum speed, and a check on fuel consumption. Each propeller was feathered in turn, with a check on three-engined flying.

With the completion of the Halifax programme and the production of the Halifax A9 restricted to Cricklewood, the York Aircraft Repair Depot was closed in 1948. With its high standard of repair and liaison with Nos. 4 and 6 Bomber Groups it had contributed enormously to the bomber offensive, and had helped in the production and improvement of the Halifax.

Handley Page Drawing System

From the beginning of the Halifax design Handley Page's own drawing system was utilised. The Halifax drawings started with the numbers 57, although as production of new Marks began some detail parts peculiar to a specific Mark started with the type number instead; e.g. Mk.2 = 59, Mk.3 = 61, Mk.5 = 63. Also, where a part was an alternative, an 'A' prefix was added. The Handley Page system was thus:

Type No.	Number	System	Detail
57	0000	L	000

The system used a letter for each section as follows:

A = General Arrangements
B = Wings
C = Fuselage
D = Hydraulics
E = Flying controls
F = Tail unit
K = Equipment
[1]L = Electrics
P = Ground equipment
S = Standard parts

[1]originally covered both electrics and equipment.

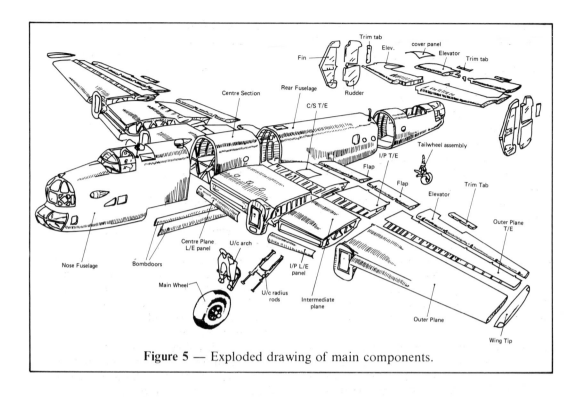

Figure 5 — Exploded drawing of main components.

New Halifax Mk.IIIs manufactured by English Electric at Samlesbury, circa 1944, waiting for disposal. The nearest Halifax NR 134 operated with the following RCAF Squadrons: No.434 Squadron at Croft, No.426 Squadron at Linton-on-Ouse and No.425 Squadron at Tholthorpe. She was eventually struck off charge on the 2 November 1945. (British Aerospace)

Once the design of the aircraft was completed an exploded drawing of the components was made (Figure 5), for it formed the basis of the design and the datum point from which the jigs for production originated. 'HP' himself made it mandatory that both his drawing office and the design department start their layouts with an exploded drawing of components — with the split into sub-assemblies being part of the design work. Further to this. 'HP' was most keen that the design should include as many sub-assemblies as possible, both to facilitate manufacture and transportation about the factory and to help in the provisioning of spares. 'HP' thought that if these things were firmly laid down at the beginning it would save trouble in the long run.

The scheduling and planning at Handley Page's were broadly standard practice, with the Drawing Office compiling the schedule of materials and sending these to the order department. The material schedule with drawings was then sent to the production department, where it was perused, summarised and requisition chits written out for the material. These chits and drawings then went to the rate fixing department, where a check was made for jigs and tools, with an estimate of the time that each job would take.

After this, charts would be raised covering the time schedule, progress of parts and individual airframe assemblies, These charts were then made available to the Production Manager, Works Superintendent, etc. Stores Control maintained a record of subcontract items and a record of embodiment loan items in stock.

When modifications were introduced, the main modifications were made by the Drawing Office, although later on towards the end of the Halifax production, the Modifications Office was set up separately from the Drawing Office.

* * * * *

Production figures

This is a synopsis of the total production of the Halifax, but it is not intended in any way to be detailed or explanatory. As has been stated previously there were five major manufacturers in the Halifax Production Group, which were fed by 41 subcontractors. From 1939 to 1946 these five manufacturers produced 6176 Halifax aircraft of eight different marks, as well as the two prototypes manufactured by Handley Page.

The English Electric Co produced a total of 2145 Halifaxes, the largest number by any manufacturer in the Halifax Production Group. The grand total of production was 6176, comprised of:

84	Mk.1s
1976	Mk.2s
2091	Mk.3s
904	Mk.5s
467	Mk.6s
413	Mk.7s
96	Mk.C8s
145	Mk.A9s

These were split up among the five manufacturers as follows:

	Mk.1	Mk.2	Mk.3	Mk.5	Mk.6	Mk.7	C8	A9	Total
Handley Page	84	614	326	—	142	182	96	145	1589
English Electric	—	900	900	—	325	20	—	—	2145
Fairey Aviation	—	—	326	246	—	90	—	—	662
Rootes Securities	—	12	279	658	—	121	—	—	1070
London A/C Prod	—	450	260	—	—	—	—	—	710
	84	1976	2091	904	467	413	96	145	6176

From these eight marks were developed 27 sub-types, which in 1945 were catalogued by J. Ratcliffe together with brief details of each:

13 Bomber versions
Mk.1 Srs 1,2,3; Mk.2 Srs 1, 1 (Spec); 1A, 2. Mk.3; Mk.5 Srs 1,1 (Spec); 1A; Mk.6; Mk.7.

4 Transports
Mk.C3, Mk.C6, Mk.C7, Mk.C8.

4 Airborne Support
Mk.A3, Mk.A7, Mk.9, Mk.A10.

Coastal Command
Mk.GR2, Mk.Gr Srs 1A, Mk.GR3, Mk.Met 2 Srs 1a. Mk.Met 5 Srs 1A, Mk.Met 3.

These were the types as produced by the manufacturer, though there were interim types that were conversions after leaving the factories, e.g. A5 Srs 1A.

When Contract 692649/37 was issued to Handley Page Ltd it was for the production of 100 Mk.1 aircraft, to be constructed fully representative of Halifax L7245. This contract was altered before completion to include Mk.2 aircraft with the issue of Contract 73328/40, which is why only 84 Mk.1 aircraft were completed.

Throughout the war Handley Page and its daughter firms were attempting to produce the maximum number of aircraft and develop the full potential of the basic design, yet were continually constrained by military demands and modifications that resulted in at least 27 sub-types and the final production figures as listed below.

Handley Page
Mk.1 Total 84: L9485-9534, L9560-9584, L9600-9608.
Mk.2 Total 116: L9609-9624, R9363-9392, R9418-9457, R9482-9498, R9528-9540.
Total 200: W7650-7679, W7695-7720, W7745-7784, W7801-7826, W7844-7887, W7906-7939.
Total 250: HR654-699, HR711-758, HR773-819, HR832-880, HR905-952, HR977-988.
Total 49: HX147-191, HZ222-225.

Mk.3 Total 101: HX226-247, HX265-296, HX311-357.
Total 225: LV771-799, LV813-842, LV857-883, LV898-923, LV935-973, LV985-999, LW113-143, LW157-179, LW191-195.
Mk.7 Total 15: LW196-210.
Mk.A7 Total 118: NP681-723, NP736-781, NP793-821.
Mk.B6 Total 82: NP822-836, NP849-895, NP908-927.
Total 37: PP165-187, PP203-216.
Mk.C8 Total 27: PP217-243.
Mk.A7 Total 4: PP244-247.
Mk.C8 Total 69: PP259-296, PP308-338.
Mk.A7 Total 40: PP339-350, PP362-389.
Mk.B6 Total 23: TW774-796.
Mk.A7 Total 5: RT753-757.
Mk.A9 Total 145: RT758-799, RT814-856, RT868-908, RT920-938.

English Electric
Mk.2 Total 200: V9976-9994, W1002-1021, W1035-1067, W1141-1190, W1211-1253, W1270-1276.
Total 250: DT481-526, DT539-588, DT612-649, DT665-705, DT720-752, DT767-808.
Total 350: JB781-806, JB834-875, JB892-931, JB956-974, JD105-128, JD143-180, JD198-218, JD244-278, JD296-333, JD361-386, JD405-421, JD453-476.
Total 100: LW223-246, LW259-301, LW313-345.
Mk.3 Total 260: LW346-348, LW361-397, LW412-446, LW459-481, LW495-522, LW537-559, LW572-598, LW613-658, LW671-696, LW713-724.
Total 360: MZ500-544, MZ556-604, MZ617-660, MZ672-717, MZ730-775, MZ787-831, MZ844-883, MZ895-939.
Total 200: NP930-976, NP988-999, NR113-156, NR169-211, NR225-258, NR271-290.
Total 80: RG345-390, RG413-446.
Mk.7 Total 20: RG447-458, RG472-479.
Mk.6 Total 300: RG480-513, RG527-568, RG583-625, RG639-679, RG693-736, RG749-790, RG813-853, RG867-879.
Mk.6 Total 25: ST794-818.
Cancellation of orders at the end of the war: 325 aircraft with ST and SV serial numbers.

Rootes Securities

Mk.2 Total 12: DG219-230.

Mk.5 Total 138: DG231-253, DG270-317, DG338-363, DG384-424.

Total 100: EB127-160, EB178-220, EB239-258, EB274-276

Total 420: LK890-932, LK945-976, LK988-999, LL112-153, LL167-198, LL213-258, LL270-312, LL325-367, LL380-423, LL437-469, LL481-521, LL534-542.

Mk.3 Total 60: LL543-559, LL573-615.

Total 219: MZ954-989, NA102-150, NA162-205, NA218-263, NA275-309.

Mk.A7 Total 121: NA310-320, NA336-380, NA392-431, NA444-468.

Cancellation of orders at the end of the war: 300 aircraft with SV serial numbers.

LAP Group

Mk.2 Total 200: BB189-223, BB236-285, BB300-344, BB357-391, BB412-446.

Total 250: JN882-926, JN941-978, JP107-137, JP159-207, JP220-259, JP275-301, JP319-338.

Mk.3 Total 180: MZ282-321, MZ334-378, MZ390-435, MZ447-495.

Total 80: PN365-406, NP423-460.

Cancelled at the end of the war: 150 aircraft with RV serial numbers.

Fairey Aviation

Mk.5 Total 150: DJ980-999, DK114-151, DK165-207, DK223-271.

Mk.5B Total 96: LK626-667, LK680-711, LK725-746.

Mk.3B Total 104: LK747-766, LK779-812, LK826-850, LK863-887.

Total 180: NA492-531, NA543-587, NA599-644, NA656-704.

Total 42: PN167-208.

Mk.A7/B7 Total 90: PN223-267, PN285-327, PN343-344.

Cancelled at the end of the war: 200 aircraft with RS serial numbers.

Chapter 4
Testing

Testing for the RAF was carried out mainly by the Aeroplane and Armament Experimental Establishment (A&AEE) at Boscombe Down but also, for some investigations, by the Royal Aircraft Establishment (RAE) Farnborough, or the Airborne Forces Experimental Establishment (AFEE) at Beaulieu. These establishments all had a worldwide reputation for unbiased flight testing and analysis. Not only were the prototypes tested but also subsequent aircraft with modifications. Tests were also carried out to improve the performance of aircraft, engines and equipment, and A&AEE tested every 100th Halifax produced by Handley Page, and also every 100th aircraft produced by every daughter firm, to ensure that no performance deterioration had taken place during production.

It would be impossible to deal with all the testing carried out by the various establishments mentioned above — and by the Handley Page flight test personnel — so we will briefly cover some of the various tests involved in developing the Halifax, and how it measured up against the Manchester and Lancaster.

Prior to 1939 Handley Page, as one of the members of what could be called the pre-war professional aircraft industry, had a flight test team headed by Major Cordes, but in July 1941, after guiding the test team and the HP57 through the design and prototype stage and into production, he left to take over as Manager and Chief Test Pilot of No.7 Aircraft Assembly Unit. Major Cordes had been joined by Flt Lt Talbot, who now took over as Chief Pilot with a Flight Team of Fg Off. Marsh. By 1942 there were at Radlett two flight test departments, one covering production with Holland and James as flight test observer/engineers, and the other, on the

Park Street side, doing development and special work, with 'Ginger' Wright, J. Steele, G. Ratcliffe and E. N. Brailsford as flight observers. With the setting up of the York Aircraft Repair Depot (Y.A.R.D) a further flight test team was set up there with flight observers R. Baines, J. Harding and I. Robinson. The test pilots at Radlett carried out monthly tours of duty at York. Their number had by now increased to four — J. Talbot, J. Marsh, T. V. Mitchell and W. G. Sanders.

Flight testing for the pilots and observers was not as glamorous as depicted by the media. Some of it was boring, some involved checking and re-checking theories against fact, but during the war every day was a full day, whether travelling to a Service aerodrome to sort out Halifax problems or flight testing at Radlett. Such a day was Friday 11 July 1941, a straightforward but long day, without heroics and without glamour. For the following account I am indebted to E. N. Brailsford, ex-flight observer for Handley Page.

08.00. A number of flights scheduled for the day. Go to the Army airfield protection guard CO's office to collect colours of the day, needed in the event of an encounter with a Home Defence fighter. Hopefully, firing a Very pistol with the correct colours will avoid being shot down.

First test is on L9485 — due to engine snags the flight is delayed and so time is spent in the wind tunnel with tests at model scale before embarking on the full-size thing. Mr Stafford arrives mid-morning and comes to the tunnel to talk to the Wind Tunnel Superintendent while he waits for the aircraft to be got ready.

'Queen Mary' aircraft transporter. (I. Robinson).

While the aircraft is being cleared for the test Shackley and I collect parachute packs, harness and overalls for ourselves and Stafford. Talbot is the pilot for this flight. We take off at 12.40 and carry out a series of stalls at a variety of flap angles and engine power settings. Shackley is with us to help observations, which concern not only speeds but also controllability, airframe shudder, tail oscillations, etc. Some observations are made from the dorsal turret of both tail and wing. Land at 13.20 and, after reporting engine behaviour and a few snags to Mr Knight, have a late lunch.

Following discussions of this flight, another is called for. This takes place at 18.10 and is fairly brief, but involves operating both upper and lower turrets during the stall to check their effect.

Directly after landing have to prepare for the first flight of L9571. This has Merlin 20 cowlings and a bungee lowering aid on the undercarriage. Pilot is Talbot and we carry two MAP specialists to do some radio tests. They have to wear pilot's harness and seat packs which are very unwieldy and inconvenient.

Have trouble with starboard brakes during braking tests but eventually take-off at 19.05, only to have to curtail some tests due to bad weather. The undercarriage doors are unacceptably slow in closing — the P.O. never shuts completely.

Talbot returns to Radlett with a dive across the airfield at 260 knots. I check that the armoured door latching is O.K. and it does not spring open during the pullout — even when kicked!

Land at 19.30. Mr Cleaver and Mr Knight get the snags, which include a low oil pressure on No.2.

Finish with a mad rush around to get home. Clock out at 19.45.

Early flights with L7244 and L7245 indicated a side-to-side oscillation of the rear fuselage, which became known as 'the shakes'. It appeared to be worse with the flaps down, so Handley Page built on some reflexed extensions to simulate negative flap (immediately dubbed 'clutching hands') but they were not effective and the oscillation was eventually cured by setting the deflectors for the rear turret at 7 degrees out. It was assumed that this rear fuselage oscillation was excitation of a structural resonance by the vortices being shed from the near-cylindrical shape of the rear end of the fuselage. The deflectors would break up the vortices to some extent.

Early flights also proved that the inner engine nacelle fairings were too short and creating unnecessary drag — too sharply tapered a nacelle caused the airflow to separate. The nacelle fairings were eventually extended, after a temporary 'fix' to the trailing edge of the wing, the rearmost portion being fixed to and moving with the flaps. Wind tunnel tests showed that a large drag saving was possible if the inner nacelle fairing was extended to 35 inches aft of the trailing edge, but although this was adopted on three trial aircraft including the Mk.2 Series 2 it never went into production.

During flight testing at Y.A.R.D. at York about 700 take-offs and landings were completed without any major accident. No intercom was available for aircrew in the early days at Y.A.R.D and no 'colours of the day' cartridges were issued until an incident during the summer of 1944 when a Mk.3 which had been reconstructed from parts of Bomber Command and Coastal Command aircraft was presented for flight testing. It had a white/grey front fuselage and outer wings, with the remainder of the aircraft in black/green and roundels missing from the rear fuselage. The route of this particular flight was due east from York. After the test, a Fighter Command Spitfire whose pilot must have been fascinated by the sight of this 'bastard' Halifax formated on it and followed it back to Clifton aerodrome. From that day on 'colours of the day' cartridges were carried.

Much of the flying at Radlett was involved with work carried out in the research section, proving modifications as well as flight testing production aircraft made by Handley Page's and its daughter firms. This could be hard work at times, for in or about January 1941, due to a shortage of hydraulic pumps of the Messier variety, it became necessary to flight test with no hydraulic pump at all. The retraction of the flaps and undercarriage had to be done using a hand-pump; undercarriage retraction took about 5-6 minutes and a lot of sweat by the flight engineer. Fortunately for production and servicing, the Messier pump was replaced by a Lockheed pump and bypass system.

One of the routine items on a production aircraft air test was to feather and unfeather each propeller in turn and, of course, to restart the engine. On the Merlin-powered Halifaxes this always appeared to take a much longer time than on the Hercules-engined aircraft, and one feathering with a difference occurred to a B2 aircraft flown by a Y.A.R.D. crew of W. G. 'Sandy' Sanders and I. Robinson. The starboard outer engine blew up when a conrod broke, pressing the feathering button for that engine appeared to have no effect and the pilot was having a job to control the aircraft — the engine appeared to be ready to shake itself out of its installation. Just as the pilot warned the flight observer to prepare to bale out because the aircraft was becoming unmanageable, the blades feathered and complete control was regained.

Routine test flying was usually done by just a pilot and flight observer, with the latter standing in the second pilot's position — or sitting in this position for take-off. This was a procedure adopted in a number of squadrons where it was felt that the flight engineer was better suited to the job. Other squadrons had the bomb-aimer or navigator in the second pilot's seat for take-off and landing because a number of these personnel had been rejected from pilots' courses and therefore had had some piloting experience.

On 17 July 1941 Flt Lt Talbot, with E. N. Brailsford as flight observer and Shackley as assistant, took off on L9490 to carry out tests of a new fuselage rest bay tank installation. No intercom was used on this type of test, the assistant being the go-between. When the test height was reached a visual OK was given by Talbot to Brailsford, who switched on the rest bay tanks and switched off the port wing tanks, so that Nos 1 and 2 engines would be fed by the rest bay tanks. Apart from a colossal noise, Brailsford's next recollection was of trees and hedges where the clouds should have been; fuel starvation had occurred and the aircraft had made a spiral descent into a field near Hawks Head Lane, North Mimms. With no intercom and the aircraft spiralling down Talbot had been unable to signal to Brailsford to change the tanks back. In spite of this Talbot pulled off a marvellous landing and then helped out

Shackley, who had been stunned by a blow from the armour plated door. In no time at all the local police and Home Guard appeared, and although the crash was in open country numbers of souvenir hunters appeared from nowhere. All the engines were twisted in their mountings, the port wing tip and port fin and rudder were gone and the nose of the fuselage twisted with the under fuselage smashed. As the crew walked away Brailsford called to Shackley to ask if he was now all right; Shackley replied 'Yes' and promptly fell as if pole-axed — he was suffering from concussion from the blow!

The enquiry took place next day at Cricklewood and as a result of this it was decided that intercom must be used for flight tests in future. On 20 August Brailsford went to Dishford. With Fox of the MAP and HP rep Nash and Sqn Ldr Tait as pilot, further tests of these rest bay tanks were carried out; these were successful although Brailsford as an engineer considered the tank set-up a 'ropey' arrangement.

Flight tests at Maintenance Units were not always straightforward either. On 15 October 1944 at No.44 MU, RAF Edzell, a Halifax 3 MZ637 was prepared for a routine air test by Sqn Ldr S. Johnson and flight engineer J. Hampton; the aircraft had been tested previously and had had some snags rectified, so this flight was just a re-test. After taking off and selecting undercarriage up it was noticed that the starboard outer engine cylinder head temperature was falling rapidly, possibly indicating a dead engine, although the airspeed was sufficient to cause the propeller to windmill. Quickly checking for engine failure, which proved positive, J. Hampton then confirmed with the pilot that he should feather. As the feathering button was pressed there was a loud bang and the starboard outer propeller and reduction gear departed. In departing the propeller hit the starboard inner propeller, which split one blade and bent another. This created extreme vibration and the propeller was hard to feather. Flight was continued straight ahead on the two port engines, and as the aircraft was flying well on the two engines it was decided to carry out a

normal landing; however, on the downwind leg, loud bangs began to come from the port outer engine with sheets of flame from the air intake. The pilot told the flight engineer to feather it whilst he carried out the landing — this was made with flaps and undercarriage down and was faultless. Sqn Ldr Johnson received a letter or appreciation from the Senior Maintenance Staff Officer HQ No.41 Group and Sgt Hampton an endorsement to his logbook recording his presence of mind and skill of a high order.

The result of the investigation into the engine failures determined that the starboard outer engine failed because of ignition failure for a short period. The reduction casing had elongated holes and had been unable to cope with the sudden surge of power; the port outer engine failure was due to seized sleeves caused by running at take-off power in excess of the normal time limit.

Test Pilot Flt Lt J. Talbot prepares to carry out another test flight. (IWM).

Aeroplane and Armament Experimental Establishment

With the outbreak of World War 2 both A&AEE and RAE were expanded and their staffs reinforced with more pilots and more scientists. The primary function of the A&AEE was to test new and improved aircraft to ensure that they conformed to the specification and that their flying characteristics and engineering satisfied the RAF requirements, and also to prove that the standard of production aircraft was maintained. The RAE's function was not only basic research and development, but also the investigation of accidents and incidents.

The pilots employed at A&AEE were Service personnel while the flight test observers were A&AEE civilians, their primary function being to carry out tests on new or improved aircraft. Testing the aircraft was not just a case (as the Americans say) of 'strapping an aircraft to your arse'. First a programme of tests was laid down and methodically carried out by the test crews, with readings being taken of all relevant instruments. Testing and re-testing were carried out even when this entailed taking the aircraft into flight conditions which could — and did — prove dangerous. For instance, if during the tests of the aircraft it was found that dangerous buffeting took place during stall tests, then the flight would be continued through the buffeting to determine the point of stall or the extreme of buffeting.

Without being dramatic, it is fair to say that A&AEE and RAE test crews — as well as the manufacturer's test crews — risked their lives time and time again to ensure that the aircraft entering the Service were as proven as possible — a look at the test crews' casualty list will confirm this.

The reports on the Halifax aircraft tested at the A&AEE Boscombe Down are covered by the Report Numbers starting with A&AEE 760 and, naturally, covered the prototype L7245 first.

In a communication from Sqn Ldr Collings on the first A&AEE report the following comments were made:

1. Undercarriage retraction is about 18 seconds and causes slight tail heavy trim. When flaps are raised there is a slight sink and very little change of trim.
2. Elevator reasonably light and effective down to the stall.
3. Rudder heavy but satisfactory up to speeds flown.
4. Ailerons too heavy at all speeds — thought to be due to static friction.
5. One-engine-out flying: on throttling of outboard engine a violent swing occurs which is impossible to hold on the rudder except by throttling down the opposite engine. It is estimated that the climb at all-up weight of 45,000 lb with three engines is satisfactory.
6. Stability: directional is satisfactory at aft C of G; lateral is satisfactory at aft C of G; longitudinal is unstable on climb but stable on glide. Flight in landing configuration; aircraft can be flown away quite easily with full flaps, the loads not being excessive on the stick.
7. Criticism of the cockpit and the entry and exit to seat.

On reading this report Major Cordes agreed with items 1 to 6, but felt that item 7 was exaggerated.

At the end of 1940 L9485 was also at Boscombe Down and with L7245 was the subject of Part 3 of the report dated 21 December 1940, which covered tests made at an all-up weight of 53,000 lb. A summary of the tests showed that on take-off the four throttle levers were opened in unison and that the aircraft had a medium tendency to swing to the left, which could be held by a light touch of the brakes and full rudder until a speed of approximately 40 mph was reached. Otherwise the take-off was normal and straightforward and the aircraft did not need helping into the air. The aircraft's behaviour during stall tests was also satisfactory. The control column had to be pulled back about three-quarters of its travel from the mid position to stall the aircraft. No stall warning was given and little force required but the ailerons became sluggish; the stall was straightforward with no wing-dropping and control was also regained quickly. With two propellers feathered, flight could be maintained at a weight of 45,000 lb under maximum cruise conditions.

Its take-off performance at an all-up weight of 50,000 lb was satisfactory with a take-off distance of 570 yards and a take-off distance to a 50 ft screen of 1000 yards. The ailerons were considered sluggish in response over initial small angles at all speeds, but were effective — although becoming heavy at speeds in excess of 250 mph. Rudders, at speeds below 120 mph, gave little response but were effective at higher speeds, although at speeds below 150 mph there was a tendency for them to overbalance. The elevators were considered light and effective from the stall up to a speed of 250 mph and the aircraft was considered to have sufficient longitudinal stability.

At speeds in excess of 250 mph a certain amount of trim tab was required to overcome the high control column loads and with speeds in excess of 300 mph it needed all the pilot's strength to hold the aircraft in the dive.

Landing was considered straightforward, providing the aircraft's attitude was checked at approximately 25 ft from the ground and the control column brought progressively back to execute a three-point landing. Brakes could be applied at any time during the landing run without any tendency to swing. The retraction jack rod of the tailwheel system was found to be slightly bent on several occasions and was thought to be responsible for any shimmy.

To improve the response of the ailerons at low speed, and over small angles, the ailerons of the first production aircraft were given a slight reflex; in this form the ailerons were considered satisfactory although still a little sluggish.

For these flight tests L9485 had beam guns fitted and firing tests had been carried out in level flights and in a dive to 295 mph IAS. It was found that the guns could only be operated and aimed satisfactorily up to 260 mph IAS. The rear turret was satisfactorily operated up to the maximum airspeed tested,

Halifax Mk.1 L9490 force-landed at North Mimms, Herts., 17 July 1941 during fuel exhaustion trials from Radlett. (E. N. Brailsford).

and the entry and exit were also satisfactory. However, the front turret, although satisfactory from the entry and exit point of view, tended to stick in various beam positions when operated above 260 mph. Also considered unsatisfactory were the fuel jettisoning, rear turret ammunition drum feed, flare fittings, etc.

From this it will be seen that, for a new aircraft, the Halifax had crossed its first hurdle in fair fashion from the handling point of view. The other points were to be cleared up later and the aircraft cleared for higher take-off weights.

Just prior to this report the Manchester had been tested at A&AEE Boscombe Down at an all-up weight of 45,000 lb. All the controls were found to be light, quick and effective and becoming heavier at higher speeds, but longitudinally the aircraft was unpleasantly unstable under all flight conditions though steady in the dive. Take-off at this weight was

Fin and rudders of the two Halifax aircraft HR679 (standard) and HR727 (modified) used in trials to cure rudder locking. (R.A.F.)

660 yards, with the distance to a 50 ft screen being 1175 yards. On take-off the rudders were found to be ineffective until a speed of approximately 50 mph was reached, and a slight backward pull on the control column was needed to assist the aircraft into the air.

Although it was found with the Halifax that rudder overbalance occurred at speeds below 150 mph, with the Manchester the directional stability was initially satisfactory, but when tests were carried out with the central fin removed directional instability resulted. The removal of the central fin was part of the progressive testing, because rotation of the FN7A dorsal turret had been found to cause severe vibration of the fin, causing, in two instances, complete fin disintegration.

The testing of prototype L7245 was interrupted during all-up weight testing to 55,000 lb when, during a final approach, the starboard undercarriage struck a pile of bricks, causing the jack rods to pull out from the jack pistons, as a result of which the radius rods collapsed. Investigation determined that the undercarriage should *not* have withstood the load imposed, and that the way the strut failed and did no further damage was considered satisfactory.

A comparison of the Manchester and the Halifax aircraft tested at similar weights at A&AEE at a slightly later date gave the following results:

	Manchester 1	Halifax 1
Wingspan	90 ft	98 ft 8 in
Wing area	1039 sq ft	1250 sq ft
Tare weight	29,360 lb	33,720 lb
All-up weight at take-off	50,000 lb	50,000 lb
Engines and numbers	Two Vulture 21s	Four Merlin 10s
Total approximate horsepower	3600	4300
Take-off distance	880 yards	570 yards
Take-off distance to 50 ft screen	1250 yards	1000 yards
Service ceiling	17,000 ft	22,000 ft
Time to height	35.8 mins to 16,000 ft	27.4 mins to 20,000 ft
Maximum cruising speed	198 mph at full throttle	218 mph at 13,400 ft
Maximum all-out speed	265 mph at 17,000 ft	270 mph at 18,000 ft
Stalling speed	90 mph IAS	86 mph IAS.

Halifax development was continuing, both at Handley Page's and at A&AEE, but at Avro's the Manchester was being re-schemed into the Lancaster powered by four Merlin engines, with its potential yet to be exploited. On 3 March 1941 a preliminary handling trial was carried out on prototype BT308 at the manufacturer's airfield by A&AEE aircrew. The aircraft was tested at an all-up weight of 38,000 lb and was fitted with the triple-finned tail similar to the Manchester. According to the report, the aircraft started to swing to port immediately it started to move, and in counteracting this it was found that full rudder plus a touch of brakes was ineffective, so it was necessary to resort to throttling the starboard outer engine. So the swing was worse than on the Halifax.

The controls came out better: the elevator was found to be lighter than the Manchester's, and generally superior for handling, the ailerons were light and effective while the rudders were similar to the Manchester's and became heavier as speed increased. Three-engined handling was not completely satisfactory: speed was decreased to 120 mph and the rudder bar was hard over with the trimmer full over to port, but these were not quite powerful enough to counteract the swing. It was suggested that larger fins and rudders should be fitted. This was acted on: the centre fin was removed and the aircraft was powered by Merlin 20 engines by the time

of the second part of the report dated 10 March 1941. Improvement was apparent with the incorporation of the new fins and rudders, but longitudinal stability tests showed that the aircraft was unstable in the climb but stable in level flight — though tending to become unstable as the speed increased. By 16 April it was noticed during the tests that flexing of the wing structure occurred in bumpy flight conditions and there was also distortion of the tailplane. The recommendations here were for stiffening in these areas and an increase in trim tab size.

From this it will be noticed that with the Lancaster Avro's quickly carried out remedial action over the swing at take-off and engine-out conditions, whereas with the Halifax the rudder overbalance was not fully investigated until accidents and incidents increased in 1942. Yet a large amount of time was spent on investigating exhaust flame damping. Who was responsible for authorising the large number of flame damping trials, but not delving deeper into the rudder overbalance, we will probably never know. The only thing in mitigation is that neither steep sideslips nor dynamic engine cuts at low speed were considered part of the testing procedure for heavy bombers in those days; the need for this was only revealed in service when pilots on operations used any manoeuvre to escape from searchlights, flak or fighters, and also when pilots were flying

Halifax Mk.3 prototype R9534 with pre-production D fins and rudders, and standard production E Type rear turret. (RAE).

Meanwhile Avro's and A&AEE had also got on with increasing the all-up weight. Tests had been done at 55,000 lb, with tests on Lancaster 1 DG595 being carried out at 60,000 lb. At an AUW of 55,000 lb and powered with Merlin 20s the Lancaster had a take-off run of 970 yards.

Tests were made on L9485 with large bombs to check the take-off performance. They were done at an all-up weight on take-off of 55,000 lb with a bomb-load of 8000 lb. Three take-off tests were made with two 4000 lb bombs and three take-offs with one 8000 lb bomb. The bomb-doors could not be fully closed with the standard type of bomb-doors fitted, but from these tests it was found that there was no adverse effect on take-off performance.

on three or two engines at too low an airspeed.

By October 1941 L9515 had been selected as a development aircraft and was fitted with Merlin 20 engines, but it had no mid-upper turret, no mid-under turret or beam guns. It was first used for overload tests at Boscombe Down to an all-up weight of 60,000 lbs, still had the jettison pipes installed and the single-exit saxophone-type exhausts were unshrouded.

A comparison of figures for a Halifax and a Lancaster based on A&AEE Reports 760 and 766 in 1942 shows the following:

	Halifax 2 Srs 1	Lancaster 1
Wing section	NACA 23021	NACA 23018
Wingspan	98 ft 8 ins	102 ft
Wing area (gross)	1250 sq ft	1297 sq ft
Chord at root	16 ft	16 ft
Chord at wingtip joint	6 ft 11½ ins	9 ft 2.43 ins
Engine type	Merlin 20	Merlin 20
Rpm and boost at take-off	3000 +12 lb	3000 +12 ins
All-up weight at take-off	60,000 lb	60,000 lb
Service ceiling	21,100 ft	21,500 ft
Time to height (feet)	47 min to 21,000 ft	46.2 min to 21,500 ft
Take-off distance	1010 yards	900 yards
Take-off distance to 50 ft screen	1355 yards	1250 yards
Rate of climb, maximum	800 ft/min	830 ft/min
Maximum speed at height, M gear	263 mph at 12,000 ft	269 mph at 13,000 ft
F gear	264 mph at 18,000 ft	267 mph at 18,500 ft
Maximum cruising speed, M gear	228 mph at 14,000 ft	242 mph at 13,800 ft
F gear	216 mph at 18,000 ft	237 mph at 18,000 ft
Stalling speed, undercarriage and flaps down and power on	80/85 mph IAS	92 mph IAS

During 1942, experience showed that the performance of the Halifax 2 had deteriorated following progressive introduction of external equipment and on increase in all-up weight. This reached the point where the aircraft became incapable of meeting concurrently the twin operational demands of high altitude cruising and high loading. In the early part of 1942 three aircraft were tested with different types of propellers but more than this was required to improve the situation.

In conjunction with these tests an operational aircraft, DG221 of No.78 Squadron with nine operational flights behind it, was investigated at A&AEE. The aircraft was found to carry small extra items of equipment, showed evidence of bad workmanship and poor maintenance and had been treated with a rough special night black finish. Tests indicated that a further loss in performance was apparent — to the point that no attempt was made to flight test it with large bombs fitted, since the take-off performance was already critical. Handling qualities became worse when exhaust shrouds were fitted, with an increase in vibration as well.

It was estimated that with exhaust shrouds fitted and two 4000 lb bombs on board the service ceiling would be approximately 18,500 ft, a climb to 18,000 ft would take approximately 60 minutes and there would be a reduction in top speed of approximately 24 mph.

Meanwhile, Handley Page's were developing a cleaned up Halifax 2 (the Series 1 Special), and this aircraft (W7776) was the subject of tests during August and September 1942. These tests were made at a take-off weight of 60,000 lb and with no shrouds fitted, so Handley Page's, in conjunction with A&AEE, prepared a programme of further cleaning up the aircraft and at the same time installing a more satisfactory mid-upper turret and an efficient flame damping exhaust. The first step was a close-fitting exhaust shroud, the trials of which were carried out on W1008. These proved satisfactory as a glow suppressor but the rear screening of the exhaust flame was still not satisfactory. A four-gun Type A mid-upper turret was due to be tested in the dorsal position in the near future, so it was hoped that this would solve the other operational requirement.

During the various tests at A&AEE the inadequacy of the radiators had been

Halifax Mk.2 Series IA JD212, the only Halifax (trials aircraft) fitted with rocket projectile carriers. (Author).

emphasised. Because the radiator flaps had to be partially or fully open on all operational flights there was a hidden loss of performance, involving a speed loss of 9 mph at 15,000 ft; a redesign and an increase in radiator exit area was being considered by Rolls-Royce — but some operational squadrons were already taking action by cropping the radiator flap and so increasing the effective exit area with shutters fully closed.

The 20th Part of A&AEE Report 760a gave a general review of the Halifax 2 performance that was neither satisfactory nor encouraging. And Handley Page's themselves were not satisfied with the performance of the operational Halifax 1 powered by the Merlin 10. Meanwhile, the Lancaster had gone into production powered by the Merlin 20 — and now the Halifax 2 was loaded down with operational equipment not previously listed and was down on performance. Handley Page's were far from happy and with the approval of the MAP had been further cleaning up the basic airframe of L9515. This had a streamlined metal nose and Merlin 22 engines.

HR679 was then modified to this new standard, but the metal nose had been translated into Perspex and the radiators had the Gallay type replaced by Morris single-block type — the aircraft then became a Series 1A. HR679 was the subject of the 35th Part of the Report and was tested in four different conditions. The results showed that, with or without exhaust shrouds and with or without the type A turret, hardly any difference was made to the level speed or service ceiling, the greatest difference being in the maximum rate of climb and climb to height.

In mid-1940 the Aerodynamics Section had issued a report on a visual check on a one-tenth scale model of the Halifax in the RAE wind tunnel, which had indicated that flow over the nacelles at zero yaw was considerably distorted, with the wake passing inboard of the fins. Also, a vortex was seen to be rolling off the top corner of the fuselage, which was considered to be due to the deep fuselage. By 1942 incidents and accidents had

considerably increased, and the report had some bearing on the rudder overbalancing problem, which was basically a sideslip condition at low speeds, when fin stall occurred and the aerodynamic force had taken the rudder hard over against the stops and locked on. An in-depth investigation was instituted at A&AEE, when in their usual professional manner they carried out a programme of modifications and trials, in conjunction with Handley Page, to eliminate the problem.

On the Halifax the rudder overbalance was basically due to the fins being rather small and the rudders powerful. Thus the rudders could induce a large sideslip angle, enough to stall or almost stall the fins, so the effectiveness of the aerodynamic balance was reduced with the reduction of airflow, and the rudders tended to move and lock hard-over in sideslip. Between 26 February and 5 April 1943 investigations were made with a view to either 'fixing' or curing the problem of overbalance — one of many investigations that entailed both Handley Page as well as A&AEE crews carrying out trials under conditions that had already killed RAF operational crews. Two Halifax Mk.2 series 1A aircraft were involved and the tests included sideslip and comprehensive asymmetric flight handling — the aircraft were not totally identical.

HR679 had a standard rudder with modification 413 incorporated and the inboard nacelles were extended aft of the wing trailing edge. This aircraft's objective was to determine whether a palliative or a cure for rudder locking could be found for retrospective fitting. The second aircraft in the trial was HR727, which had standard nacelles but a new fin and rudder combination designed by Handley Page with the object of reducing overbalance.

When HR727 was tested under general flying conditions the modified rudders were considered to be too light, although at the same time they were considered effective. They were also lighter in asymmetric flight and the footloads were less than on HR679. Unfortunately, sideslip tests proved that rudder locking was taking place at smaller

Halifax Mk.3 LW125, named *Sarie Marais* at Cape Town on goodwill tour 5 December 1944.
(R. T. Mann and HP Association).

angular movements than those found on the other aircraft, although the speeds at which this occurred were lower.

The report concluded that, since no cure or palliative could be found to stop rudders locking over in service, it was recommended that existing rudders be restricted in movement to 17 degrees each way and that a substantial increase in fin area be provided.

Investigations into various rudders and combinations were carried out and Handley Page's finally introduced the large Type D fin referred to earlier, approximately 40 per cent greater in area than the pre-modification fin (the modified fins and rudders were to Drawing 57166FT). This modification solved the overbalance problem, as is shown in the fourth part of Report 760b and the third part of Report 760c. Tests were carried out on R9534 (prototype Mk.3) and DK145 (Mk.5), the conclusions being that the handling qualities were satisfactory with the large Type D rudder/fin combination, that there was sufficient rudder for flight with two engines dead on one side and that turns could be made against the working engines, and that there was no tendency for rudders to overbalance when sideslipping at speeds down to 120 mph IAS.

In June 1943 HR815/G was the subject of a further A&AEE report when a range flight was made by an operational Coastal Command crew with A&AEE flight observers. The flight was made with full fuel load and three 600 lb anti-submarine bombs; the all-up weight at take-off was 61,670 lb

with a crew of seven. All flying was carried out between sea level and 3500 ft, with the major part of the flight at about 1500/1700 ft and with a simulated attack being made at approximately half-way through the flight. The object of the flight was to determine the practical range of the aircraft with two overload tanks fitted in the rear rest-bay positions. The Halifax flew for 14.5 hours and used 2420 gallons of fuel, as measured by flowmeters — although only 2392 gallons were required to refill the tanks. From this it was estimated that the maximum still-air range under test conditions would be approximately 15 hours 46 minutes, or 2320 nautical miles, the practical range being 1870 miles. Handling throughout the flight was normal and satisfactory, but the rest-bay tanks prevented the rest-bay position being used — a point definitely disapproved of by the crew and confirmed as undesirable by the report.

The one and only Mk.2 Series 2, HR756, was the subject of the 37th part of 760a and was tested in April/May 1943. As no Merlin 60 series engines were available when the aircraft was completed at Handley Page's the aircraft arrived at Boscombe Down still powered by Merlin 22 engines and was tested in this condition. The Merlin 22s were installed in lowered nacelles with Rotol XHF 53/W 12 ft 9 in diameter propellers and Beaufighter spinners. The inner nacelles were extended aft of the wing trailing edge, a fixed tail wheel was fitted and the power-plant had six-way ejector exhausts and Morris type radiators and oil coolers.

In December 1943 intensive flying trials were carried out on Halifax Mk.3 HX227, which had completed 3 hours 55 minutes flying before arriving at A&AEE, and Halifax Mk. 3 prototype R9534, which had completed 85 hours before this trial. HX227 completed 54 landings and R9534 45 landings during the trials; both aircraft were subjected to a number of dives up to a limiting speed of 320 mph IAS and sideslipping and evasive manoeuvres were carried out to test the Type D fins. The take-off weights during the tests were either 55,000 lb or 63,000 lb and, although the engines gave no trouble, the airframe had cracks in the wings and fins, and the nacelles appeared to require some strengthening. Also two tailwheels (unstrengthened type) had oleo failures. Nevertheless, under general assessment of maintenance and serviceability the report stated:

> Altogether the aircraft was far better as regards maintenance and reliability than was expected of four-engined aircraft, and the intensive flying was completed in less time than has been taken for any other four-engined aircraft.

Compare this with the Lancaster intensive flying trials, which were completed by March 1942. Three aircraft were involved: L7527, L7529 and L7535. Flying started with L7527, but after 17 hours, when an undercarriage interconnecting bolt fractured, this aircraft was withdrawn because the aircraft was damaged. Flying then started with L7529, but this had to cease as wrinkles developed on the wing upper surface skin after 22 hours. Work resumed on L7535 but after 73 hours' flying it crashed. It was then decided not to complete 150 hours on any one aircraft but to use all the hours on the three aircraft and complete the trial with a further period of flying on L7529, which had by then had the wing skin stiffened. Six engines failures were experienced during the period of the trial.

In late 1944 Halifax Mk.3 LW125 was the subject of an A&AEE report and an interesting route itinerary. This aircraft had a standard airframe with H2S blister and dorsal and tail turrets. It was fitted with extended wing tips to Mod.863 and Hercules 16 engines. After flying to Khartoum for hot weather trials, carried out at all-up weights of 55,000, 63,000 and 65,000 lb, it was decided that it should fly to South Africa so that its behaviour under semi-tropical conditions could be observed. To monitor the trials a comprehensive range of test instruments was installed, covering cylinder and oil temperatures on all four engines and also aircraft performance. A torque dynamometer was fitted to the port inner engine.

The aircraft flew for about 50 hours at Boscombe Down before flying to Khartoum, where a further 50 hours' test flying was carried out. A thorough inspection was then done, and the aircraft departed from Khartoum on November 5th with a crew headed by Sqn Ldr D. Clyde-Smith plus R. Mann (Handley Page rep), R. A. Christmas (Bristol rep) and Sgt Fitter Cheeseman. The route taken was via Nairobi, Ndola, Pretoria and Johannesburg to Capetown, where a *Cape Times* journalist wrote enthusiastically of the Halifax as 'one of the bombers the Germans hate'. An air test for demonstration purposes of 45 minutes' duration took place at Johannesburg and a further one of one hour at Capetown. The return flight was then made via Johannesburg, Bulawayo, Ndola, Nairobi, Khartoum, Cairo, Benghazi and Malta to Boscombe Down. The tour covered approximately 12,000 miles and overall 171 hours 10 minutes' flying was carried out, with a large proportion under tropical conditions. The A&AEE report considered that general serviceability was satisfactory, the maintenance was straightforward, and the aircraft was serviced with the minimum of equipment during overnight stops with main wheel, tailwheel changes and main inspections carried out without difficulty.

By now, Lancaster all-up weights had increased to 68,000 lb and 72,000 lb, although the latter weight could only be used or permitted if Merlin 24 engines were fitted driving paddle blade propellers, with the

Lincoln type undercarriage fitted with modified tyres and adjustments made to tyres and oleo pressures. Results showed that the handling characteristics at 72,000 lb were satisfactory, although in view of the reduced factor in this overload condition and the moderately light elevator it was considered that at this weight the aircraft should only be flown by experienced pilots. The take-off with 20 degrees flap and two divisions nose-heavy trim was considered normal — but how normal was normal when experienced pilots were considered desirable?

Take-off speed	115 mph
Take-off run	1080 yards
Stalling speed, flaps and u/c up	119 mph
flaps and u/c down	98 mph
Max cruising speed,	
FS gear (ICAN)	244 mph at 16,000 ft
Time to service ceiling	50 minutes
Service ceiling	18,600 ft

In comparison with this, a check of a standard production Halifax B6 fitted with H2S and tested in late 1944 gave the following results:

Take-off all-up weight	68,000 lb
Tare weight	39,000 lb
Take-off run to clear	
50 ft barrier	1100 yards
Service ceiling	22,000 ft
Time to service ceiling	31 minutes
Cruising speed	265 mph

Maximum speed in	
MS gear	290 mph at 9000 ft
FS gear	309 mph at 19,500 ft
Stalling speed, u/c and	
flaps down	102 mph
Rate of climb at 2000 ft	1000 ft/min
at 11,900 ft	600 ft/min

The report said that there was no lack of longitudinal stability apparent at any load. Lateral and directional stability appeared good throughout the handling trials, and there was little noticeable change in behaviour of the controls with the change in weight and C of G. The rudder remained very heavy, elevators moderately heavy and ailerons light. In dives with the aircraft trimmed for level flight at 230 mph IAS it was found that as the speed increased the aircraft became increasingly tail heavy until, at 320 mph, the pilot had to exert a very heavy forward stick load to hold the aircraft in the dive.

In other words, the stability of the Halifax was satisfactory in all axes and the diving aspect gave no problems to the crews; for the aircraft was able to fly itself out of dive conditions, as opposed to the Lancaster which tried to go deeper into the dive.

Other establishments

In September 1941 RAE Farnborough issued a theoretical report on the performance of the Hamilcar glider towed by Halifax, Lancaster

Halifax Mk.2 Series 1 (Special) converted to Mk.3 prototype October 1942, with Type F symmetrical fins and rudders. (IWM).

and Stirling tugs. The report was an estimate of the take-off, cruise and climbing performance of the three combinations. It was proposed to use rocket assistance for take-off, 48 rockets being fitted and fired in pairs, each rocket producing a mean thrust of 1800 lbs. The report concluded that, from its estimates, the order of merit for the three tug aircraft in take-off performance for a given cruising range was Stirling, Lancaster and Halifax.

In contrast to these estimates and conclusions, when Lancaster ED842 was used for a trial tug of a Hamilcar glider at AFEE in 1944 to determine and establish performance, cooling and handling characteristics, it was found that, with the Lancaster all-up weight of 49,500 lb and the Hamilcar all-up weight of 36,000 lb, the take-off performance was critical and a special technique had to be employed. With this, the take-off distance to clear a 50 ft barrier was 2600 yards and the tug/glider combination was only at 300 ft when the combination was 4.5 miles from the airfield — hardly a happy situation. The conclusion of this trial report was that, in view of the take-off results, the combination at this load was impracticable from an operational point of view.

In 1943, the year in which RAE Farnborough were experimenting with methods of towing the Hamilcar glider, RAE Report AERO 1857 described the use of twin tugs and the method of towing — and the aircraft to be used was the Halifax. Strange that their third choice was the one used, and was in the end the aircraft determined by AFEE as the aircraft suitable for towing the Hamilcar glider, after trials using all three bomber aircraft used in the RAE report on tug aircraft. It was mentioned in the first part of AERO 1857 that the take-off and climb performance of the Merlin-engined Halifax/Hamilcar combination had proved inadequate for operational use. One wonders if this was based on their 1941 estimates, for the Halifax Mk.2 and Mk.5 were the aircraft cleared by AFEE as the tugs for Hamilcar towing in No.38 Group.

The experiments with twin tugs were carried out from a runway at Hartford Bridge airfield (Blackbushe). A special twin-tow cable was devised that had both a stop on it and a release unit, the latter designed for the disengagement of the assisting tug once operational height had been attained and thus allowing the lead tug to continue to its destination while the assisting tug returned to its base.

Having proved the twin-tug principle (and far more safely than the Germans in their efforts to get the Me321 Gigant glider airborne), the idea was hidden away, for AFEE and No.38 Group were successfully using the Halifax as a tug for the Horsa and twin-towing two Hadrians, and developed it into a single tug for the Hamilcar. This is illustrated in the AFEE report on glider-tug combinations when the Hamilcar was towed by the Halifax, Lancaster and Stirling:

	Halifax 2	Halifax 3	Lanc 1	Lanc 2	Stirling
Tug weight at t/o (lb)	48,500	59,400	49,500	52,800	50,500
Glider weight (lb)	36,000	37,500	36,000	36,000	23,900
Temperature standard	ICAN	ICAN	ICAN	ICAN	ICAN
Ground run (yards)	1200	1470	1400	1260	1190
Climbing speed (mph)	120	135	135	130	145
Initial rate of climb (ft/min)	200	285	285	300	410
Operational height (ft)	5,000	8,000	10,000	5,000	10,000
Cruising speed (mph)	120	130/135	135	135/140	130
Still air range (miles)	620	1270	540	865	380

Non-standard Halifax Mk.3 HX238 at Boscombe Down in 1943, for trial of 0.5 inch D turret and AGLT 'Village Inn' radar. (IWM).

From these tests, further trials were continued which cleared the Halifax as the only aircraft suitable as the tug for the Hamilcar, and the Halifax Mks.3, 7 and 9 as suitable for towing the Hamilcar under ICAN or tropical conditions.

In the middle of 1944 AFEE Beaulieu carried out trials covering the dropping by parachute of a 5 cwt Willys Jeep and six-pounder anti-tank gun. This was duly written up in Report P113, when clearance was given for Halifax Mks.2 and 5 aircraft to carry and drop this armament combination. The AUW of the aircraft was to be a maximum of 60,000 lb and the equipment drop height was to be a minimum of 1000 ft and at an airspeed of 130 mph or less. The load carried was the Jeep and gun, plus six containers of 400 lb each, plus ten paratroops with kitbags. The equipment load was dropped before the paratroops. This type of drop was carried out a number of times by No.38 Group Halifaxes, as practice and in operations, with further demonstrations being made in the Far East by No.298 Squadron in 1945-46.

Another establishment using Halifax aircraft was the Telecommunications Research Establishment (TRE) at Swanage, the aircraft being based at Hurn. Later, TRE moved to Malvern as a precaution against any possible enemy paratroop drop, the aircraft then operating from Defford. Among the developments taking place at TRE were the Klystron and Magnetron valves and H2S. Now H2S was being developed principally as a navigational aid, and when it came to installing the device in an airframe for flight trials the Halifax was chosen because its airframe offered a greater choice of positions for the scanner. The H2S radome was mocked-up at Radlett on W7711, the security at Radlett over drawings being so tight that it drew attention to the project! Work was started on the first installation on V9977 on 4 January 1942 and the aircraft was despatched to Hurn on the 27 March, where TRE personnel installed the 10 cm H2S scanner and associated equipment. This H2S used the Magnetron from an AI Mk.7 and the first flight took place on 16 April. A number of flights took place, and a number of problems appeared as flight heights increased above 8000 ft.

Unfortunately, a major blow to the H2S programme occurred on 7 June. V9977 took off from Defford in the afternoon, flown by Plt Off. D. J. Bearington and carrying five scientists. The aircraft was flying at 2000/3000 ft when the starboard outer engine failed; it was believed that an attempt was made to restart the engine because the generator on it supplied power to the special equipment on board. The engine then caught fire — an inlet valve had fractured — the fire extinguishers failed to operate and the aircraft crashed into the ground near Ross-on-Wye from about 500 ft, killing all on board. Evidence from the investigation suggested that the fire extinguishers were not filled.

Fortunately, W7711 was almost ready and priority was given to its preparation for trials, which resumed later in June, while W7808 and W7823 joined TRE for use on further development. W7808 was the aircraft involved in Service trials with the production H2S.

When the powered Hamilcar (the Mk.10) was developed AFEE carried out trials with it. In 1946 towing trials with a Halifax Mk.3 took place to determine the maximum load of the Halifax tug when towing a Hamilcar 10 under tropical conditions. Consumption tests were also made at 6000 ft and indicated that the limitation on the maximum range of the combination was the fuel capacity of the Hamilcar; it carried a normal fuel load of 390 gallons. The still-air range was 1050 miles under tropical conditions and when the Hamilcar's fuel was exhausted there were still 600 gallons left in the Halifax. From these tests it was established that the maximum tug all-up weight at take-off was 60,000 lb, cruising performance was satisfactory, and the take-off to a 50 ft barrier was 2450 yards with an initial rate of climb of 220 ft/min.

The AFEE cleared the Halifax A9 as a Hamilcar tug in 1947 for temperate and tropical conditions and, later, were concerned with the carriage and dropping of the 25-pounder gun from a Halifax using five 42 ft canopies. The Halifax and its capabilities were by now not in question; what AFEE were interested in was the crating used for the dropping of the gun. The Halifax was by now the accepted Airborne Support aircraft, only to be superseded by the arrival of the Hastings.

Performance comparisons alone are not totally reliable for assessing one aircraft against another, for it must be obvious to the reader that in comparing one aircraft against another the same conditions, engines, equipment and even the crew would need to be the same; so, in quoting figures and making comparisons, the author has taken the average from a number of reports from the various establishments or quoted a specific report.

One point which must be made is that none of the establishments appears to have investigated the emergency escape provisions, so this section closes with three unanswered questions: Why was the Halifax accepted for service if its shortcomings in directional stability were known? Why was the Lancaster accepted for service when it suffered from longitudinal instability at speeds above 200 mph, and, in a high speed dive, was hard to pull out? Why was the Lancaster accepted for service when it had only one escape hatch, which was right up at the front, not sufficiently large for fully kitted-up crew, and through which six crew members had to escape?

Halifax Mk.2 Series 1 (Special) R9534, now fitted with Type A turret, Type E fins and rudders and Hercules Mk.6 engines. (Business Press International Ltd.)

Elevator structure failure on Halifax TW783 during A&AEE testing, February 1945. The elevators were overloaded in an untrimmed dive of 320 mph at a take-off all-up weight of 68,000 lb. (RAF).

Test and trials Halifax aircraft

These are some of the specific Test and Trials aircraft used both by Handley Page and the other test establishments for the development of the Halifax and the extension of its roles.

L7244

First prototype. After flight trials a contract was placed for its conversion into the HP58 Mk.2 day bomber equipped with dorsal and ventral 20 mm cannon turrets with no tail turret. Although a mock-up was made the project was terminated. Used at Handley Page's for production features. Damaged at Boscombe Down. Became 3299M.

L7245

Initially used on armament ground tests at A&AEE, then while landing during trials of aircraft up to an all-up weight of 58,000 lb hit a heap of bricks, which damaged the undercarriage. Loaned to No.35 Squadron to allow crews to obtain handling experience. After completion of tests at A&AEE it was routed to a training establishment as airframe 4204M.

L9485

The first production Mk.1. It was retained as a trials aircraft to prove the capabilities of the Halifax: trials of all-up weight to 53,000 lb, take-off tests with 4000 lb bombs and flame damping. Later used by A&AEE as an armament trials aircraft, having at various times beam guns, Type C and Type A mid-upper turrets and the Boulton & Paul Type K ventral turret armed with two 0.303 in. Brownings. Became training airframe 3362M.

L9515

The 31st production Mk.1 from Cricklewood, nominated as a development aircraft to improve both the range and the performance. An additional fuel tank of 123 gallons capacity was fitted in each outboard position and designated No.6 tank, which increased fuel capacity from 1636 to 1882 gallons. R-R Merlin 20 engines were installed, the engine cowlings revised and the radiator cowling reduced in frontal area. In 1942 the aircraft was further revised with the nose turret replaced with a streamlined metal nose (a metal mock-up of a revised nose) and the Merlin 20s replaced with Merlin 22s — her designation now being a Mk.B2. Upon completion of the trials, authorisation was given for the nose revision in Perspex to mod.452. L9515 was then modified again with inboard engine nacelles which extended aft of the wing trailing edge to overcome the turbulent airflow over the inboard wing section. Also acquired in the process was a mod. 451 Mk.8 Type A mid-upper turret.

L9520

A Mk.1 production aircraft with Merlin 10s which was allocated to Rotol for propeller and de-icing trials. Upon completion of these tests it went to Dowty for installation of the Dowty levered-suspension undercarriage and, with Dowty hydraulic systems, became the prototype Mk. 5. A Dowty tailwheel assembly similar to that on the Lancaster was also fitted to try to eliminate 'shimmying'.

R9387

Equipped with Rotol propellers, as fitted to the Beaufighter, for comparison trials.

R9436

Tested at Boscombe Down and fitted with a Boulton & Paul Type T mid-upper turret in place of the Type C. The T turret mounted two 0.5 in. Brownings with 600 rounds per gun. Tested successfully in October 1942.

R9375

After service with No.76 Squadron this B2 aircraft was allocated to Bristol's for the installation of their B12 low drag mid-upper turret, the first installation being the B12 Mk. 1 with four Browning 0.303 in. guns, then the installation of the B12 Mk.2 with two 0.5 in. guns. Finally the B12 20mm cannon turret was fitted.

R9534

Was a B2 Series 1 (Special) fitted with Type E fins and rudders of symmetrical layout (Mod.624) and was tested at A&AEE; this did not effect a cure for the rudder locking-over and A&AEE recommended a larger fin. It was then fitted with four Hercules Mk.6 engines to become the Mk.3 prototype. Was later fitted with Type D fins and rudders and in March 1943 was routed to A&AEE to prove this installation. The Type C mid-upper turret was replaced with a Type A. Engine cowlings and intake were also changed to the Beaufighter type for tests.

V9977

B2 aircraft used by TRE Malvern for original H2S trials. Crashed.

V9985

B2 aircraft used from Radlett for dropping tests of a dummy 4000 lb bomb in October 1942. Also fitted with bulged bomb-doors.

W1008

B2 aircraft with Merlin 20 engines, selected for cooling tests with different radiators and exit flap areas, then used for propeller tests and flame damping trials. Trials were also carried out to ascertain the effect that the mid-upper turret had on speed. In 1943 handling trials were carried out to ascertain the effect of the mock-up of the AGLT on Type E turret.

W1009

B2 aircraft with Merlin 22 engines. In 1942 carried out performance trials with Rotol propellers.

W7922

B2 aircraft with Merlin 20 engines. Used for trials to determine climb and level speed performance.

DK145

Mk.5 aircraft with Merlin 22 engines. Fitted with type D fins and joined R9534 in the proving of this installation. Fitted with four-blade Rotol XH54 13 ft diameter propellers.

DG281

Mk.5 aircraft used for flame damping trials with various four-way ejector exhausts and others. Trials with FN64 mid-under turret.

HX226

Retained by Handley Page's for test purposes; first production Mk.3. Used for improving air intake efficiency, engine cooling trials in regard to gill positions, spinners, cooling fans and climbing speeds.

HX227

Retained by Handley Page's for test purposes. Used for improving intake efficiency, and in late 1943 was the subject of an intensive flying trial at A&AEE, which it successfully completed as 'far better as regards maintenance and reliability than was expected of a four-engined aircraft'. When delivered to Boscombe Down on 12 September 1943 the H2S blister was not fitted, the tailwheel was non-retractable and the aircraft had modified air intakes. Flight tests to increase all-up weight to 65,000 lb.

HX229

Retained by Handley Page's for test purposes. Used for improving air intake efficiency and flame damping trials of Hercules exhausts.

HX238

Mk. 3 aircraft complete with Type D fins and rudders but without H2S. Used to test Type D rear turret and deflector flaps and the effect they had on handling.

HR679

B2 aircraft with Merlin 22 engines. Used for tests to decrease drag and improve engine cooling as part of the policy to clean-up the Series 1A. After a series of incidents and accidents to the Halifax it was one of a number of aircraft used to investigate the rudder overbalance problem. This aircraft was the prototype Mk.2 Series 1A.

HR727

B2 Series 1A was a further aircraft used for other tests, and alongside HR679 to investigate rudder overbalance. During the tests was fitted with Type C fins.

HR756

This Halifax B2 was selected on the production line for development of the basic design into a high-speed, high-altitude bomber project which would be the prototype of the HP60A (Mk.4). The engine nacelles were lowered to underslung position, similar to the Lancaster, the main wheels were totally enclosed when retracted, the inner nacelles were extended aft of the wing trailing edge, and the aircraft was then designated a Mk.2 Series 2. It had been intended to fit Merlin 65 engines, but when the aircraft was completed these engines were not available and Merlin 22s were fitted. After transfer to Rolls-Royce as a trials aircraft Merlin 65 engines were fitted.

HR845

With the intention of increasing the all-up weight to 65,000 lb the decision was taken to increase the wingspan to 103 ft 8 in, and this aircraft was chosen for this modification. The outer wing attachment area was strengthened and revised wingtips fitted. In January 1944 this aircraft went to A&AEE for trials.

JD304

B2 aircraft with Merlin 20 engines. Used for performance and handling trials with various exhausts.

Close-up view of the failed starboard elevator on TW783. (RAE).

LL615

B3 aircraft modified for towing. Used at AFEE as tug for towing trials of Hamilcar under temperate and tropical conditions.

LV838

With the approval of the MAP, Halifax aircraft were considered for quick conversion to 'Transport A' and the fitment of a 8000 lb pannier to fit into the bomb-bay. The trial installation was on LV838 and was prepared in February 1945. Prior to this, in 1944, the aircraft took part in engine cooling tests. Brief handling trials were also made with a modified rudder balance tab, approval of Hercules 100 power-plant, and trials with various propellers.

LW125

Mk.3 aircraft with Hercules 16 engines. Carried out a series of tests and was then dispatched to Khartoum for hot weather trials. Was a completely standard aircraft fitted with H2S blister and wingtip extensions. With the approval of the MAP, and Handley Page assistance, a goodwill tour was then made to South Africa and back to the UK. This tour was successful from both goodwill and maintenance points of view and just over 171 hours flying was done.

NA644

Mk.3 aircraft used at AFEE on towing duties. Carried out towing of two Hadrians fully loaded under tropical conditions, amongst other trials.

PP225

Mk.C8 aircraft. Was fitted with modified rudder balance tab gear ratio, which had been altered from 0.2 to 0.4 to 1, and handling trials were carried out. Converted from Mk.6 to be prototype C8.

PP285

C8 aircraft acquired by Handley Page as a research vehicle for the testing of a powered control system, and a set of reverse pitch experimental propellers was fitted. Trials of both were carried out and on 9 February 1948, during the landing from one of these tests, the aircraft crashed. The aircraft was severely damaged but the test crew escaped unhurt.

RT758

This airframe was selected for redesign, primarily to develop the airframe for airborne support. The Type E rear turret was replaced with a Type D, the entrance door on the port side was deleted, a large entrance/paratroop door was fitted in the ventral position, and the fuel capacity was altered. The aircraft went to the AFEE in October 1945 and the type was designated as the A9 after trials.

NP715

Mk.6 aircraft. After initial service with RAF it was selected by Handley Page's in September 1946 for flight trials of a new roll control and spoiler system. After use at Handley Page's and at A&AEE the aircraft went to Bristol's for engine fire tests.

TW783

B6 aircraft used for handling trials to clear Mk.6 aircraft to all-up weight of 68,000 lb.

RG815

B6 aircraft modified after VE Day with altered nose and fitted with large selection of radio and radar equipment. Carried out round-the-world demonstration tour of equipment.

HX246

Used by Flight Refuelling Ltd for mainplane thermal de-icing, and at RAE Farnborough for de-icing trials.

W7711

B2 used by TRE Malvern for tests of H2S after crash of V9977.

RG839

Converted by Flight Refuelling Ltd at Staverton as a receiver aircraft for flight refuelling trials for Coastal Command.

Chapter 5
The Halifax Aircraft

The airframe

The Halifax was totally conventional in its shape and construction — an all-metal, stressed-skin, mid-wing monoplane, four-engined bomber. Its fuselage was constructed in four sections: the front, centre, rear fuselage and rear bay. It was of light alloy construction, utilising hoop frames of 'L' and 'U' section, with longitudinal stringers covered with light alloy sheet. Two longeron members ran along either side of the fuselage and carried the loads imposed on the structure by the bomb-load, while at the top side they formed a support for the floor itself. The wing comprised a centre section constructed integrally with the centre fuselage, an intermediate wing and an outer wing; its general construction was of two-spar design with a light alloy stressed skin, each section being joined to the next by means of a special pin joint.

Fuselage

The front fuselage (Fig 6) contained the crew compartment for the pilot and flight engineer and was covered by a glazed roof. The wireless operator's station was below the pilot's position and forward of frame 7, while the navigator and bomb-aimer stations were positioned forward of frame 5. The front fuselage also housed the BP Type C Mk.2 front turret in the marks up to the Mk.2 Series 1 and also Mk.5 Series 1. The flight engineer's position was aft of the pilot's position and an astrodome was provided in the roof at this position. The flight engineer normally acted as the pilot's mate unless a second pilot was carried, as in the case of the RAF C8s or for familiarisation. In the earlier Halifax models the astrodome was mounted on a rectangular tubular frame, which was hinged at two points along its port side to allow exit. In later models the astrodome structure was fixed and the astrodome itself lowered in height.

The flight engineer's bulkhead at frame 11 consisted of 6 mm demagnetised armour plate with a hinged panel to allow access to the F/E's instruments, and a bulkhead door on the starboard side was made from one piece of armour plate — though in some squadrons this door was deleted to save weight. A similar piece of armour plate was fitted over the front end of the bomb compartment. The pilot's roof comprised transparent panels, one of which, directly above the pilot, was detachable for emergency exit use and could be hinged upwards on the ground. An escape hatch in the floor was installed just aft of the navigator's seat. The stressed aluminium alloy skin of the fuselage was stiffened with beaded 'L' stringers and attached to transverse frames; the joint frame at position frame 16 was fabricated from extruded angle and a heavy-gauge plate flange reinforced along its inner edge with a smaller extruded angle. In the marks after the Mk.2 Series 1 and Mk.5 Series 1 (Specials) the nose portion was a streamlined Perspex detachable structure on a frame of drawn light alloy.

The centre fuselage was constructed integrally with the centre section (Fig. 7), the main spars of which passed completely through it. The joint frames were similar to the front fuselage, as was the skinning, the centre fuselage being joined to the front and rear fuselage by bolted flanged frame joints, carrying the bomb-load internally in the centre section and centre-plane. The bombs were covered by bomb-doors, hydraulically operated and of wood/alloy construction (Fig. 8). An emergency escape hatch was provided in the roof at frames 17-18 (though

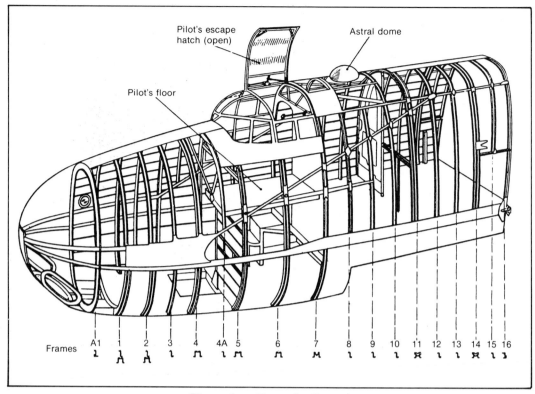

Pilot's escape hatch (open)

Astral dome

Pilot's floor

Frames A1 1 2 3 4 4A 5 6 7 8 9 10 11 12 13 14 15 16

Figure 6 — Front fuselage.

not in the Mk.1), while the centre-plane inter-spar ribs were constructed to take longitudinal rest seats.

The rear fuselage (Fig. 9) was constructed of longitudinal members and transverse frames of box section and 'Z' section, in a similar manner to the front fuselage. In the Mk.1 Series 2 the rear fuselage had openings on port and starboard for beam guns. The openings were constructed of built-up box frames on which the beam gun mountings were fitted. An emergency escape hatch was provided in the roof at frames 23-25, with a well provided in the fuselage floor in the area of frames 29-31, just forward of the rear step, as a paratroop exit or for H2S. The crew entrance door was situated on the lower port side of the fuselage aft of frame 33, while ammunition for the rear turret was accommodated in eight boxes carried in a tubular constructed frame suspended from

the port side of the fuselage roof forward of the main entrance door. The ammunition belts travelled along long chutes to the feed at the lower end of the turret. This ammunition run differed slightly on the Mk.A9, the boxes being mounted further aft to prevent any interference with the paratroop strops and equipment.

The rear bay was similar in construction to the rear fuselage, to which it was bolted and from which it was not normally detached. It housed the BP Type E rear turret and tailwheel unit and carried the tail unit. Six-mm demagnetised armour plate fitted on the port side of the fuselage just forward of the tail turret protected the tail unit controls from rear attack, and a further piece of 9 mm armour plate was mounted vertically at the last fuselage frame under the turret. A heavy-gauge light alloy sheet under the tail turret formed part of the skin covering and served as

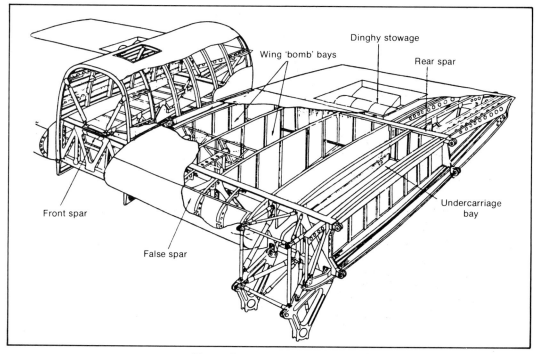

Figure 7 — Centre fuselage.

a bullet deflector plate (Fig. 10).

Production aircraft of the Mk.1 Series 3 onwards — with the exception of the Mk.2 Series 1 (Special) and Mk.5 Series 1 (Special) — had a Type C Mk.2 mid-upper turret mounted in the rear fuselage aft of frame 26. There were, however, many variants of this arrangement over the years.

Mainplane

The mainplane was of two-spar construction with a light alloy stressed skin and comprised a centre section, intermediate port and starboard wing, and a port and starboard outer wing. The centre section was built integrally with the centre fuselage and provided six bomb compartments, and also pick-up points for the inner power-plants, undercarriage and inner nacelles. The front spar consisted of parallel extruded channel booms joined and braced by vertical and diagonal members to form a strong girder construction, while the rear spar used extruded 'T' section booms joined by a sheet

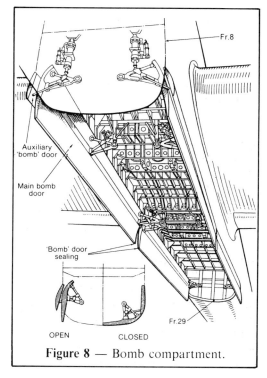

Figure 8 — Bomb compartment.

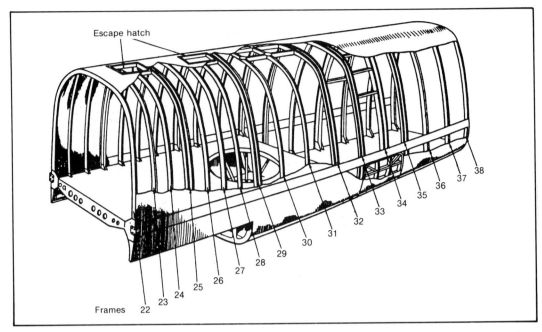

Figure 9 — Rear fuselage.

Figure 10 — Rear bay.

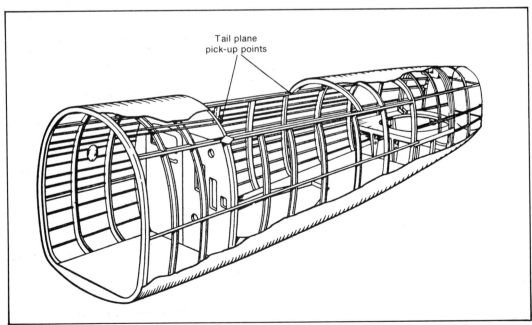

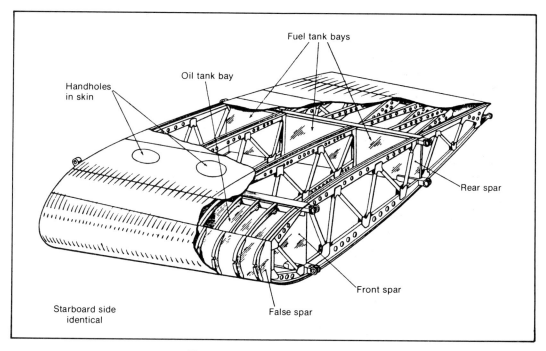

Figure 11 — Intermediate wing.

metal web reinforced by vertical extruded angle section riveted to the front face. The port top surface had a rectangular recess, which provided accommodation for a dinghy.

The intermediate wing (Fig. 11) had spars constructed of extruded booms with sheet webs riveted to them. The front booms were of 'T' section with 'L' section on the rear. The inter-spar ribs were composed of upper and lower booms and diagonal tubular bracing secured by gusset plates. Four fuel tanks were carried in the intermediate wing, with the three inter-spar tanks secured by straps to box-type bearers on the underside. The whole was raised into the wing and the bearers located in brackets on the lower booms of the ribs and bolted into place.

The outer wing (Fig. 12) construction was generally similar, with the front and rear spars having extruded angle section booms with sheet webs. The outer plane provided a superstructure built integrally with the two engine bay ribs and gusseted to the front spar. These engine bay ribs were constructed of upper and lower booms built up with flanged plates and the booms were cross-braced with tubular members. Only on the early aircraft were the outer wings different, in that they had slats fitted which, except on the two prototypes, were locked in. A number of ribs contained aileron hinges and differed from the outer ribs in having booms of flanged channel section. On later Mk.3 aircraft, and on later marks, the outer wings were strengthened at the outboard end and had extended wingtips fitted to make the wingspan 103 ft 8 in to allow an increase in all-up weight to a maximum of 65,000 lb, further increased on the Halton to 68,000 lb.

Trailing edge flaps of fabric-covered metal construction were fitted, one on each side of the centre plane and one extending along each intermediate plane and along the outer plane to the aileron. Each flap was constructed around a spar of aluminium alloy and formed a Type D nose. Frise-type ailerons were attached to the outer wing by five hinges; each was constructed around an aluminium alloy spar, forming a Type D nose. A trim tab was fitted to each aileron, the starboard one a

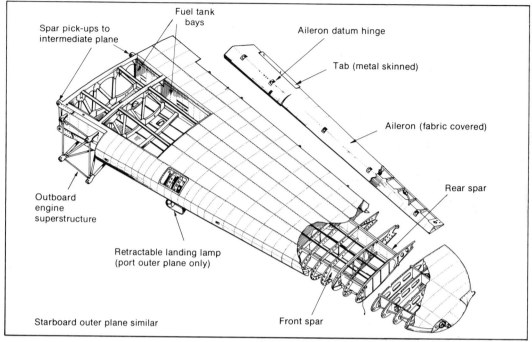

Figure 12 — Outer wing.

pilot-controllable type, the port one adjustable only on the ground. Both were of wooden construction initially, but metal ones were fitted on later models.

At first the fuel was held in eight self-sealing tanks in the wings, but on the Mk.1 Series 3 ten fuel tanks were introduced, followed on the Mk.2, Mk.3 and Mk.5 with 12 fuel tanks, with capacity increased to 1882 gallons. With the introduction of the Mk.6 aircraft the fuel system was arranged in groups and the number of tanks increased to 16 with a total capacity of 2190 gallons, all of which were accommodated in the wings. For long-range use, such as reconnaissance in the Far East or maritime use in Coastal Command, three fuel tanks each having 230 gallons capacity could be installed in the bomb-bay.

The tail unit comprised a straight tailplane with twin endplate fins and was fitted on the top of the fuselage. The tailplane was constructed of two interchangeable sections joined on the centre line by means of bolted spar fittings; the front and rear spars were similar and of extruded angle section joined by a sheet web. A fitting on the rear spar

bottom boom was fitted to provide a pick-up for the tailwheel unit. Six hinge brackets were provided for the elevator. The elevator was constructed in two parts and connected by a flanged coupling on the tubular spar. Each part consisted of a 'D' spar made from aluminium alloy sheet riveted to a sheet web stiffened by diaphragms; aft of the spar the aerofoil section was completed by plate ribs with flanged lightening holes. Built-up box ribs were provided for the hinges. The whole unit was fabric covered.

The elevator trim tabs were similar to the elevator; fabric covered, they were based on a metal tube upon which were assembled a series of plate ribs.

The fin illustrated (Fig. 13) is of the mod.814 type, but the general construction was similar for both modifications. They were constructed as single units with front and rear spars running parallel to the leading edge, which were also at right angles to the tailplane chord line. Each spar was built up from extruded angle booms riveted to a plate web. The tailplane spars extended into the fins and the fin spars were secured to them through

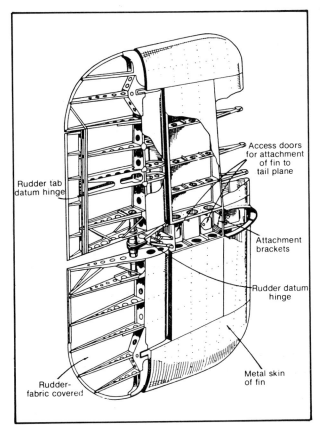

Access doors
for attachment
of fin to
tail plane

Rudder tab
datum hinge

Attachment
brackets

Rudder datum
hinge

Metal skin
of fin

Rudder-
fabric covered

Figure 13 — Fin and rudder.

Figure 14 — Combined tab and main controls.

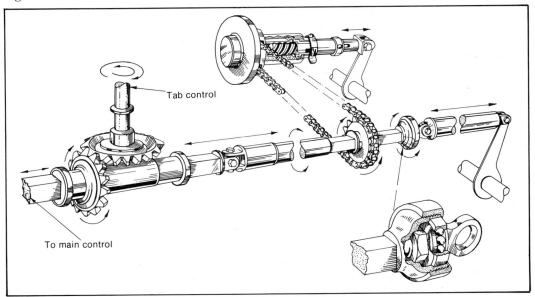

Tab control

To main control

attachment brackets with bolts. The nosing and tips were detachable, the nosing consisting of a light alloy skin stiffened by horizontal lipped angles and vertical stringers. It was held in position by cowling screws in the leading edge engaging with trap nuts carried on tubular structures mounted on the front spar.

The rudders were of similar construction to the elevators and consisted of an upper and lower section, which were joined at the tailplane position by a flanged coupling on the tubular spar; to this the operating lever was attached. The rudder trim tab was similar in construction to the elevator trim tab.

All the main flight controls were operated by tubular push-pull rods, which were also used to supply the basic means of moving the trim controls. The tubes were supported in fibre guides except where there were changes of direction, when universal joints and special ball races were used. The ailerons differed from these systems in that chains were used to transfer movement from the control column spectacles to sprockets, the chains then passing over sprockets to port and starboard to connect with anchorages on the lateral push-pull tubes, mounted aft of the mainplane rear spar. Limit-stops were mounted on the aileron control.

The trimming tab control illustrated in Fig. 14 was based on a gearbox operated by the pilots' handwheel. The gearbox transmitted rotary movement to the main push-pull tubes, totally independent of the tubes' fore-and-aft movement. At the other end of the control tube, a further sprocket transferred this rotary movement to a screwjack which moved the trim tab.

The flap was formed around a spar of aluminium alloy box construction, forming a 'D' nose to which were attached tail ribs similar to those of the ailerons. The aircraft was equipped with four of these flaps, which were fabric covered and operated by means of hydraulic jacks at their inboard ends. The port and starboard flaps were connected by cables which formed a closed circuit and prevented unequal lowering of the flaps. Both

the master lever and the parallel link had jigging holes to allow correct alignment and position when adjusting the flaps and cables.

Engines

Neither of the two types of engine used to power the Halifax was the instant inspiration of the design staffs; rather they were the next steps in general development. The Merlin was still based on the overhead camshaft (OHC) and the 'bang and crash' poppet valve, while the Hercules was based on the silent sleeve valve.

As described in Chapter 2, during the design stage the HP56 with its Vulture engine gave way to the HP57 with four Merlin engines, although within three months of the issue of the contract for the HP56 members of the Air Staff had suggested to Handley Page's that alternative installations should be studied:- the fitting of four Pegasus, Taurus, Napier Dagger or Kestrel engines.

The decisions to upgrade the aircraft size to the HP57 and to fit four Merlin engines were the most sensible, for with the advent of the Merlin engine Britain had an engine in the 1000 hp category and there was no comparable British radial engine in production. The Merlin detail design began in 1932 when the engine was known as the PV12 and was an exactly scaled-up Kestrel. During engine development the cylinder head was altered, but the Merlin engine with this new head — 'the ramphead' — failed to pass the type test and the engine was also down on power. So the ramphead was changed for the scaled-up Kestrel head, and the engine then designated the Merlin 2. The Merlin 10, which was selected to be the power-plant for the Halifax 1, was very similar to the Merlin 2, except for a different reduction gear ratio and Farman type supercharger drive. The ultimate development of the wartime Merlins was of course the 60 Series engines, but unfortunately these were never used on production Halifax aircraft.

The Merlin was a 12-cylinder, poppet-valve, upright 60 degree 'V', pressure liquid-cooled type of engine with overhead

Bore	5.4 ins
Stroke	6.0 ins
Compression ratio	6 to 1
Cubic capacity	1649 cu ins (27.02 litres)
Reduction gear ratio	0.42 to 1
Supercharger — type	Mechanically driven, two-speed, single-stage, centrifugal
— ratios	8.15 and 9.49 to 1
Airscrew shaft	Right-hand tractor
Ignition	Two BTH magnetos
Carburation	SU updraught AVT
Weight of engine dry, nett	1450 - 1455 lb approx
Take-off rpm and boost	3000 +12 (3000 +14 emergency)
Take-off power at 3000 +12	1280 bhp (Mk.20) 1390 bhp (Mk.22)
at 3000 + 14	1470 bhp (Mk.20 and 22)
Maximum climbing rpm and boost	2850 +9
Maximum climbing power	1220 bhp at 9750 ft (MS gear) 1130 bhp at 16,500 ft (FS gear)
Maximum cruising rpm & boost	2650 +7
Maximum cruising power	1080 bhp at 8750 ft (MS gear) 1015 bhp at 15,500 ft (FS gear)

camshafts and a two-speed supercharger. Details for the Merlin 20 and 22 were as follows:

Four overhead valves, two inlet and two exhaust, operated in each cylinder, six of which were formed in each cylinder block casting. Steel liners were spigoted at their top end to form a liquid- and combustion-proof seal. The monoblock assembly was secured by 14 long studs to the crankcase. From the wheelcase drive, inclined shafts drove one overhead camshaft for each head, which operated four rockers per cylinder, one for each valve.

The crankshaft was a six-throw balanced type, carried in seven main bearings. Forward it engaged in the reduction gear and at the rear it drove all the auxiliaries. Forked connecting rods connected the crankshaft to aluminium alloy pistons.

The coolant was a 70/30 ethylene glycol mixture, circulated by a centrifugal pump vertically mounted with two deliveries supplying each cylinder block.

Lubrication was by means of a gear-type pressure pump, with two other gear pumps to drain the dry-sump crankcase, and with hot scavenge oil returning through the carburettor hollow throttle valves and spindle.

The two-speed supercharger was fitted so as to incorporate the efficiency of a moderate gear supercharger (MS) for take-off and low altitude with a higher gear ratio supercharger for higher altitude. The gear drive was transmitted through a friction multi-plate clutch with a driving torque predetermined by centrifugal weights.

A spur reduction gear was fitted at the front end of the engine, arranged at the forward end to drive an airscrew shaft, in which were the oil tubes for the Rotol variable pitch type propeller.

On Merlin 22 engines +9 lb boost was obtained at the gate, +12 lb boost through the gate and, if +14 lb boost was required, the automatic boost control cut-out was pulled — popularly called the 'panic button'. But, on Merlin engines where modification 753 was incorporated, +14 lb boost was obtainable through the gate at ground level without any need to operate the cut-out.

The Merlin engine was in all marks mounted to the engine mounting on four pads. In later marks, all components like header tank and radiators were flexibly mounted, thus eliminating one of the causes of failure of these components.

When Handley Page received their contract for the HP56 the company was worried about the Vulture development programme and suggested the completion of the first prototype powered by the Hercules engines, so as to start development flying as soon as possible. This was rejected, and so, although installation of the Hercules into the HP57 was studied in 1939 and tentatively brought to the attention of the Air Staff in 1941, it never became fact until 1943 with the Halifax Mk.3.

Design work on the Hercules engine began in early 1933 and was completed in December 1935; the first test run was in 1936. The Hercules engine was a 14-cylinder, two-row,

air-cooled radial engine with single-sleeve valve operation. The earlier Hercules engines ran on 87 octane fuel but the Mk.6 was designed from the start to run on 100 octane and was the engine originally chosen for the Halifax Mk.3. The production Mk.3 aircraft went into service with the Hercules 16 engine, which was similar to the Hercules 6 but which had fully automatic Hobson carburettors with single lever control.

The production of a satisfactory sleeve valve was achieved through a successful combination of techniques and an expenditure of approximately £2,000,000. Firth-Vickers produced a high expansion steel centrifugally cast into sleeves which were nitrided. Whitehead at Bristol's found a way to grind the sleeves truly round and High Duty Alloys perfected a special light alloy from which could be forged cylinders with a very low coefficient of expansion; then Bristol's know-how put it all together.

			Max oil temp	Max coolant temp
Mark Comparisons: Merlin 10, 20 and 22				
Mk.10	Bhp at take-off	1075 at SL		
	Rpm and boost at take-off	3000 +9 psi	105°C	135°C
	Max bhp in MS gear	1130 at 5250 ft		
	Max bhp in FS gear	1010 at 17,750 ft		
	Engine weight (nett dry)	1430 lb		
Mk.20	Bhp at take-off	1280 at SL		
	Rmp and boost at take-off	3000 +12 psi	105°C	135°C
	Max bhp in MS gear	1220 at 11,250 ft		
	Max bhp in FS gear	1120 at 19,250 ft		
	Engine weight (nett dry)	1450 lb +2½%		
Mk.22	Bhp at take-off	1390 at SL		
	Rmp and boost at take-off	3000 +14 psi	105°C	135°C
	Max bhp in MS gear	1480 at 6000 ft		
	Max bhp in FS gear	1450 at 12,250 ft		
	Engine weight (nett dry)	1455 lb +2½%		
Maximum for emergency — 15 minutes limit Mks 20 and 22:				
	M gear	3000 +14 psi	105°C	135°C
	S gear	3000 +16 psi		

Hercules 16 details

Bore	5.75 in (146 mm)
Stroke	6.5 in (165 mm)
Cubic capacity	2366 cu ins (38.7 litres)
Compression ratio	7 to 1.
Reduction gear ratio	0.444 to 1.
Engine diameter	52 ins
Supercharger gear ratio	6.68 to 1 (M gear)
	8.35 to 1 (S gear)
Supercharger impeller diameter	13.25 ins
Engine weight (nett dry)	1890 lb
Carburettor	Hobson AIT 132

Power ratings

Maximum power for take-off	2800 rpm $+8\frac{1}{4}$ lb boost
	1580 bhp at SL (M gear)
Maximum power rating	2800 rpm $+8\frac{1}{4}$ lb boost.
	1640 bhp at 4000 ft (M gear)
	1440 bhp at 11,500 ft (S gear)
Maximum cruising power	2400 rpm +6 lb boost
	1355 bhp at 4750 ft (M gear)
	1240 bhp at 12,000 ft (S gear)
Maximum economical cruise	2400 rpm +2 lb boost
	1050 bhp at 10,250 ft (M gear)
	955 bhp at 17,250 ft (S gear)

The crankcase had three sections of forged aluminium alloy; the sleeve drive mechanism was mounted on the front face of the forward portion of the crankcase, enclosed by the front cover. The sleeve drive mechanism consisted of 14 sleeve cranks geared to the crankshaft and attached to the sleeves by universal ball joints. The advantage of the sleeve valve was that the openings gave unrestricted gas flow and allowed the spark plugs to be positioned in the ideal position in the centre top of the combustion chamber. Furthermore, no tappets required setting and thus no alterations to timing could occur.

At the rear of the crankcase was mounted the two-speed supercharger with 'turbine' entry impeller. The gear train to the supercharger impeller consisted of three equally spaced, hydraulically operated clutch units, each containing multiple plate clutches operated by engine pressure oil. To ensure complete cleanliness of the oil it was not only filtered but also passed through two centrifuges, whose job was to filter out any sludge prior to it passing to the supercharger clutches. The centrifuges were driven by the intermediate gear of the lower two-speed clutch.

The crankshaft was in three parts, was of the two-throw type and was manufactured from a special alloy steel. Salomon dampers were fitted between each crankweb and its balance weight to neutralise torsional and flexural vibration.

The front and rear connecting rod assemblies were identical but faced in the opposite direction. Each assembly consisted of a master rod with six articulated rods; the master rod was positioned in Nos 4 and 11 cylinders. The rods at their outer ends connected to the pistons by wristpins. All pistons were identical, although the master rod pistons used different scraper rings.

The reduction gear was of the epicyclic bevel reduction gear type and comprised a propeller shaft with three protruding arms, on which were accommodated the bevel pinions. A driving bevel gear was located on the reduction gear driving wheel on the crankshaft and meshed with the bevel pinions. Another bevel gear was secured by a stationary gear to the reduction gear casing, which was attached by studs to the front cover. The propeller shaft was supported at its forward end by the reduction gear casing and at the rear by a bush in the bore of the crankshaft.

With the development and production of the Hobson-RAE BI/BH5 injector carburettor, Bristol's fitted it to their Hercules engines and developed the engine into the Mk.100 series. This engine mark was the one installed in the Halifax Mk.6 and C8 aircraft.

The power-plant mounting consisted of a tubular structure which picked up at four points on the airframe structure and six points on the engine. Engine cooling was efficiently effected around all the cylinders by cylinder baffles in conjunction with the shoulder-fitting NACA cowling and a controllable gill mechanism. The positioning of this gill

assembly helped to determine the cylinder head temperature and was controlled on the Halifax by the flight engineer.

Before starting a Hercules engine after it had been standing it was advisable to turn it over by hand because, over a period of time, fuel and/or oil could drain into the bottom cylinders, which could cause 'hydraulicing'. This was probably the only precaution that had to be observed with the sleeve valve engine.

The Hercules was the engine that fully developed the Halifax and made her an exceptional aircraft at home and overseas.

Handling – Halifax Mk.2

Take-off
The throttles had to be opened slowly and then up to the gate, controlling the slight swing to port initially with the throttles (or a light touch of brake), and then as the speed increased and the rudders started to bite, by the rudders only. The power for take-off on

Hercules 100 details			
Carburettor	Hobson-RAE BI/BH 5		
Fuel pressure	27 psi with tank pumps on		
Supercharger gear ratio: low	6.679 to 1		
high	8.365 to 1		
Propeller	De Havilland hydromatic 55/18 or 55/19		
Oil cooler	Marston 14 in. AD632		
		Max oil temp	*Cyl hd temp*
Maximum power rating for take-off	2800 rpm +8¼ psi 1675 bhp at SL	100°C	280°C
Maximum power rating M gear S gear	2800 rpm +8¼ psi 1800 bhp at 9000 ft 1625 bhp at 19,500 ft	100°C	280°C
Maximum cruising rating M gear S gear	2400 rpm +6 psi 1520 bhp at 8000 ft 1410 bhp at 16,500 ft		
Maximum economical rating M gear S gear	2400 rpm +2½ psi 1210 bhp at 12,500 ft 1120 bhp at 21,000 ft		

the Merlin 20 was 3000 rpm +12 and on the Merlin 22 3000 rpm +14 psi boost, this being limited to 1000 ft or five minutes.

Initially the elevators felt heavy but became lighter as speed increased and the tail could be raised without difficulty. At an all-up weight of 50,000 lb the aircraft flew itself off, but at 60,000 lb it needed to be pulled off at about 100 mph IAS. The aircraft's safety speed was 145 mph IAS.

Climbing

The climbing power was 2850 rpm +9 psi; the limit was one hour. The initial maximum rate of climb with the aircraft fully loaded was 140 mph IAS. After the undercarriage and flaps were raised the flight engineer closed the flap isolating cocks and engaged the mechanical uplocks of the undercarriage.

Level flight

When the undercarriage was raised, the nose went down slightly and this also occurred with the raising of the flaps.

Power for 'rich continuous cruise' was 2650 rpm +7 psi, and for 'weak continuous cruise' 2650 rpm +4 psi. For maximum range, cruise was in M gear at maximum obtainable boost not exceeding +4 psi (or +7 for Merlin 22). The fully loaded air speed on the outward journey was 160 mph IAS with the homeward journey being made at 150 mph. Higher air speeds than these could be obtained in M gear, but S gear could be engaged if, at 2650 rpm in M gear, the recommended air speed could be maintained — but only if the boost in M gear was less than 2 psi.

The trim tabs on all flying controls on the Halifax were powerful, and especially the elevator tabs. Where the large fins were fitted it was found that the rudders were rather heavy, but where the large 'D' fins were not embodied the rudder was light in comparison with the ailerons and the elevators. Use of the elevator had to be made early and progressively in the turn, rather than letting the nose drop and applying top rudder.

On aircraft where the Type D fins had not been fitted, a large skid or sideslip could stall the fins and cause rudder overbalance, which would cause the aircraft to go into a spiral dive. To rectify this, the nose had to be put down to increase speed to at least 150 mph IAS, the engines throttled back and the rudder centralised. Stalling on the Halifax was gentle and straight with no wing-dropping, but there was no warning on the approach to the stall. Control was easily regained by quickly pushing the control column forward.

Landing

Air intake checked cold, undercarriage down and locked, brake pressure satisfactory, speed reduced to 140 mph, flaps down to 90 degrees, supercharger in M gear, propellers at 2850 rpm. Glide approach recommended speed was 115 mph IAS, while an engine-assisted approach recommended speed was 105 mph IAS. The aircraft was slightly tail heavy with flaps and undercarriage down.

Overshooting

On opening up the throttles for an overshoot procedure the aircraft became nose heavy with normal trim; flaps had to be raised to 40 degree position before selecting the undercarriage up.

Flight limitations

Maximum diving speed	320 mph IAS
Undercarriage down	150 mph IAS
Flaps down	150 mph IAS
Bomb doors opening or closing	320 mph IAS
Maximum take-off weight	60,000 lb
Maximum landing weight	50,000 lb
Bomb clearance angles:	
diving	30°
climbing	20°
bank	10°
bank with 250 lb 'B' bomb	2.5°

Diving

In high-speed dives the aircraft became tail heavy, had to be held in the dive and required trimming into the dive.

Asymmetric Flight (all Marks)

Engine failure on take-off

Provided the aircraft had reached its safety speed of 145 mph IAS, the aircraft could be kept straight on any three engines on take-off; but, in the event of an outer engine failure below this safety speed, the opposite outer engine had immediately to be throttled back partially, while the propeller of the failed engine was feathered and the aircraft retrimmed. The throttled live outer engine could then be opened up and a climb away with three engines at take-off power made with the flaps at take-off position and the undercarriage up, provided the aircraft was lightly loaded.

With heavily loaded aircraft and an outer engine failure on take-off, or immediately after, it was necessary to land straight ahead using the inner engines to control the rate of descent.

Engine failure in flight

If the engine failure occurred on the climb with flaps and undercarriage up, control could be maintained with rudders and ailerons provided that the airspeed was not below 150 mph IAS. If an outer engine failed below this speed it was necessary to throttle back the opposite outer engine, so that the rudder trim could be applied, and the dead engine's prop feathered, when the live engine could be opened up again.

With the failure of one engine at or below 54,000 lb, the aircraft was trimmed to fly at 140 mph; height could normally be maintained to 18,000 ft (Mks 3,7). On Mks 2 and 5 height could be maintained up to 12,000 ft provided the weight was not above 48,000 lb; the best speed to cover distance was 150 mph.

With two engines failed the speed should not be less than 140 mph (Mks 2 and 5) or 135 mph (Mks 3 and 7) and level flight in weak mixture should be possible up to 12,000 ft at a weight below 46,000 lb (Mks 2 and 5); but on Mks 3 and 7 with two engines failed on one side, and at heavy weights, it might be necessary to use 2400 +6 psi boost.

Landing on two or three engines

When landing on three engines, flaps were lowered to 35 degrees and undercarriage selected down on normal circuit. Full flap had not to be selected, nor the rudder trim wound off, until it was ascertained that the airfield could be reached on a straight approach, with the final approach being made at 120/125 mph IAS, using as little power as possible. Care had to be exercised if the aircraft did not have the mod. 814/686 rudder/fins embodied.

When landing on two engines (asymmetric power), the circuit had to be made with the two good engines on the inside of the turn and the speed not allowed to fall below 140 mph IAS. The aim was to have the undercarriage locked down as late as possible, just before the final approach, and the flaps lowered only when the airfield could be reached; the same applied to the rudder trim. Extra height was advisable, with the approach in a glide at a speed of 125-130 mph IAS. Some power might be required during the early stages of the approach.

These handling notes on the Halifax are but brief; if further detailed handling notes are required they may be found in *Pilot's and Flight Engineer's Notes AP1719PN*.

General data on the various marks of the Halifax may be found in the Appendix.

Chapter 6
Armament

When aircraft speeds were around the 100 mph mark it was physically possible for an air gunner or observer to manipulate his guns and their mounting against the airstream, but in the 1930s, as the aircraft speeds increased, it became more and more difficult to do this with any degree of accuracy in marksmanship. The first improvement to come along were windshields, then glazed raisable canopies, followed by glazed-over manually operated gun rings as in the Martin 139W and Avro Anson of the early 1930s. In 1934 Boulton & Paul developed for their Overstrand bomber a pneumatically-powered, glazed nose turret. Movement in azimuth was by compressed air but the elevation was manual, the weight of the gun being level balanced by the weight of the gunner, the field of fire of this turret being two-thirds of a sphere. From then on the power operated gun turret became a must in all new British bombers.

Specification P13/36, to which the Halifax was designed, called for power-operated nose and tail turrets for all round defence, but neither 'HP' nor Volkert were in favour of a tail turret; they preferred a mid-upper turret and a mid-under turret positioned amidships, with the fuselage tapering slimly to the tail. However, the DTD insisted on the fitment of nose and tail turrets. So the provision of turrets for the HP56/57 became a drawn out process of selection and supply. First, in March 1937, Nash and Thompson were asked to supply turrets, but it later appeared that they might not be able to supply a sufficient quantity to satisfy the requirements of both the Avro and Handley Page aircraft, so a further source of supply was sought.

J. D. North, on behalf of Boulton & Paul, had obtained a licence from the Société d'Applications des Machines Motices for a powered turret that had been developed by de Boysson. The turret was self-contained with an electrically-driven hydraulic generator whose independent variable strokes were controlled by a joystick that gave powered motion both in azimuth and elevation. North pursued the development of this turret, adding electric firing, etc, plus the storage of ammunition away from the turret and its feed to the turret by servo-operated power feed.

At the time that Handley Page's were searching for an alternative source of supply of power operated turrets, Boulton & Paul were already involved in development and production of a four-gun, low profile turret for their Defiant fighter. Haynes of Handley Page's paid a visit to Boulton & Paul's factory and on 4 October 1937 in a report to 'HP' was most enthusiastic on his investigation and the operation of the turret. Its only flaw was its weight compared to the Frazer Nash turret — against which was set the fact that the self-contained BP turret was less vulnerable to enemy action.

A mock-up was requested from Boulton & Paul on the order of the Air Ministry while the fitment of the FN4A tail turret went ahead. By 12 July 1938 the Air Ministry confirmed that Boulton & Paul turrets were to be fitted to the HP57 and orders were placed with Boulton & Paul for an 'E' type tail turret and a 'C' type nose turret. The 'E' type had a similar outline to the FN4A that it was to replace and thus created no problems, but the 'C' type was of fuller outline than the fuselage line set for the FN5 and gave further work to the design and production staff in blending it into the fuselage line — hence the pugnacious look of the prototype Halifax nose.

Unfortunately, there were delays with the production of the turrets as Boulton & Paul were preoccupied with the 'A' turret for their

Defiant, and by March 1938 only one four-gun rear turret had been built. Although it had already been decided that the first prototype HP57 would fly initially without turrets installed, turrets would still be required for the second prototype for Service trials, so the Ministry were forced to consider subcontracting the manufacturing of the BP turrets. On 21 April 1939 Disney of the Air Ministry was able to inform Handley Page's that negotiations were well advanced for the transfer of production of Boulton & Paul turrets to Lucas. Thereafter, a few delays occurred due to production difficulties, but generally it was considered that the Lucas production was satisfactory, and Boulton & Paul got on with their own job of development and production.

On 27 October 1938 the Air Ministry confirmed that they required a retractable under-turret on the HP57, although it was agreed that no provision was to be made on the first prototype aircraft. The fitment of an under-gun or under-turret on Halifax aircraft then became something that came and went with the modifications; some squadrons and commands wanted it and some didn't.

'HP' was for the removal of all turrets on night bombers, except the tail turret; he could not see the need for daylight defence armament on night bombers. This point of view was backed by a conference called by N.E. Rowe of DTD in December 1941 when the removal of the mid-upper and nose turrets was discussed, and so was born the Halifax B2 Series 1 (Special). In regard to day bombers 'HP' also felt that more armour and armament was required. In June 1941, when discussing with Air Marshal Freeman the use of the Halifax for day bomber use, he made the point that bomb-load would have to be sacrificed for ammunition and armour, and that, if increased speed was also wanted, it would be possible to reach 340 mph on the Halifax by putting in larger engines in new nacelles. (In fact, A&AEE Boscombe Down had during the war years their own 'Flying Fortress Halifax' in the form of L9485, which was used for armament trials and could be seen flying around with nose and tail turrets,

'C' type mid-upper turret, FN64 under-turret and also side hatch positions — see Plates 13 and 14.)

In an interview with Air Chief Marshal Newall in February 1939 'HP' had been told that a variant of the P13/36 HP57 would be fitted with a 20 mm cannon and for this purpose an underslung gun turret would be tried out. This, like other heavier armament proposals, did not come to fruition due to the advent of war, although in correspondence on 5 September 1939, N.E. Rowe of DTD stated the intention of having four stages of armament development on the Halifax:

First stage
Nose: two x .303 in. gun turret
Under: one set of two hand-held guns
Side: two sets of two hand-held guns
Tail: four x .303 in. gun turret.

Second stage
Nose: two x .303 in. gun turret
Upper: two x .303 in. gun turret
Under: one set of two hand-held guns
Tail: four x .303 in. gun turret.

Third stage
As for second stage, except that the tail turret would have two 0.5 in. guns.

Fourth stage
As for the third stage, but the mid-upper would have two 20 mm cannon.

Although development of the 0.5 in. and 20 mm turrets continued, unarmed Lease-Lend American aircraft were delivered to Great Britain and the most obvious and tried turret for fitment to these aircraft was the Boulton & Paul; the fact that it was self-contained was its greatest advantage. The result was that the production of more heavily armed turrets was delayed, and it was 1943 before the 'D' 0.5 in. turret was flown.

In 1939 a heavily armed day bomber was projected. Under the designation HP58 and termed the Halifax Mk.2, it was intended to have a rear fuselage similiar to a Hampden and to be defended by four 20 mm cannon mounted in pairs in turrets, one above and one below the fuselage, similar to the gun locations on the Hampden. The aircraft selected for conversion was ready, the mock-up inspected, but again the turret development was delayed. 'HP' suggested that 0.5 in. turrets should be installed to avoid delay, but this again was never resolved, so that in August 1940 'HP' suggested the suspension of the Mk.2, and this was agreed to by DTD. The only result of all this work was the installation of the 'C' type turret in the basic Halifax Mk.1 airframe. The fitment of the first 'C' turret was to the second prototype and agreement to this was given by the Chief Designer on 2 September 1940.

As with the Wellington, Stirling and Manchester, no provision had been made in the Halifax requirement for beam defence guns, but by 1940 the interception of Wellingtons and the beam attacks carried out on them by enemy aircraft exposed the fallacy that all fighter attacks would be from the rear, with the result that hurried rethinking brought in the hand-held beam gun installation. Handley Page's had their beam gun mounting drawings issued by July 1940, but the first 50 Halifax Mk.1 aircraft left the factory without side hatches. These were termed the Series 1 and the second batch, which were fitted with side hatches and beam guns, were called the Series 2.

After the conversion of Halifax Mk.2 aircraft to the Series 1 (Special), which was a measure basically brought out to improve the speed and range of aircraft for No.138 Squadron to enable them to fly fast, long-range missions for SOE, modification 452 (the Perspex nose) was introduced and with it the Vickers 'K' 'scare' gun installation. This was followed by modification 421, which was the fitting of a Defiant turret on the standard Hudson turret ring with external fairing. This was because the Air Staff were insisting on the turret having 10 degree depression of the guns. Although No.4 Group aircraft converted to the 'Tempsford nose' and became Series 1s (Special), crew opinion was not favourable to the deletion of the mid-upper 'C' turret, and unfortunately the 'A' (Defiant) turret with the external fairing had as much drag as the 'C' (Hudson) turret. On

24 December 1942 a Halifax 2 Series 1A (HR679) fully modified and with the type 'A' turret fitted in the lowered position (modification 451) was flown at Radlett. It was found to be 10 mph faster than the basic Mk.2 with 'Tempsford nose' and no mid-upper turret. This then became the standard armament, right up to the introduction of the Mk.6 Halifax.

Throughout its service the Halifax was equipped with Boulton & Paul turrets at the main stations, although some aircraft had mid-under positions using a manually moved 0.5 in. Browning gun or the Frazer Nash FN64 under-turret. The FN64 was fitted first on DG281 as a trial installation and was recommended as satisfactory; it had two 0.303 in. Browning guns and sighting was by means of a periscope. In general, aircrew who tried it were far from impressed and its use was mainly confined to Coastal Command. In October 1943 Volkert suggested that further work on its installation be discontinued.

The free 0.5 in. gun in the mid-under position was mainly used by those Canadian squadrons whose aircraft did not have H2S blisters fitted. It was mounted on a Preston Green mounting and manually operated. The covering blister was very shallow and the movement of the gun was quite restricted.

Many Boulton & Paul turrets were manufactured by other contractors, including Lucas, while Boulton & Paul themselves concentrated mainly on design and development. Unfortunately, the Air Ministry was never sufficiently positive in its requirements and ordering policies, so that some designs and developments never became production hardware. The Halifax, and other aircraft, soldiered on to the end of the war with small-bore weapons when heavier armament could have been available to combat the cannon-armed enemy fighters.

The Halifax, up to the Mk.2 Series 1, had a type 'C' nose turret and a type 'E' rear turret, and, with the introduction of the Halifax Mk.1 Series 3, a type 'C' mid-upper turret was installed. On the introduction of the Mk.2 Series 1A, the type 'C' turret was replaced with the type 'A' Mk.8 mid-upper turret.

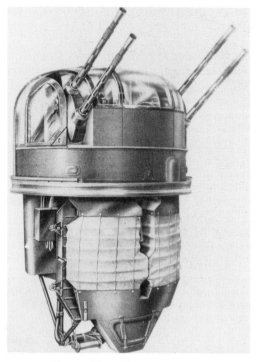

Figure 15 — Turret structure.

All these turrets were based roughly on the same layout, the guns being held on recoil mountings attached to the gun plates. The main structural parts of the turrets (Fig 15) were the mounting ring, support table, gun plate assembly and gun recoil mountings. This assembly was mounted on the airframe structure by means of a ball-bearing mounting ring, which was attached to the airframe by 12 retaining bolts. A manual mechanism was provided for rotating the turret in case of an emergency or when no power was available.

The electric power to the Boulton & Paul turrets entered the turret through a slip-ring feed, operated an electric motor of the constant speed type, and drove a duplex hydraulic generator, which provided power for the rotation of the turret as well as the elevation/depression of the guns. The operational speeds of the turret were controlled only by the amount of displacement of the gunner's control column, which governed the volumetric output of the pumps. The pressure generated in the hydraulic system varied with the external resistance against its operation. Provision was made for the turret to operate at approximately double normal speed for short duration, for which a high-speed switch was incorporated.

The closed hydraulic system was wholly self-contained in the turret, with the turret being rotated by a reversible hydraulic motor through a reduction gear (Fig 16). The guns were elevated by the double-acting hydraulic ram. This ram operated on the gun plate which carried the guns — in the case of the type 'E' turret, two pairs of guns.

On the rear turret — the type 'E' — the ammunition supply of 2500 rounds per gun was carried in boxes located in the fuselage forward of the turret. Due to the weight of the ammunition belts from the boxes to the guns, a feed assister was employed in the turret; this was driven by the turret electric motor to draw the ammunition belts through the feed ducts to the guns. The guns were fired by means of electrical solenoids and sighted by means of the Mk.3A reflector sight or the GGS Mk.2C. To facilitate sighting, the air gunner's seat was raised and lowered by a hydraulic ram connected in series with the gun elevation ram.

Being self-contained the turret was not so vulnerable to enemy fire. Its serviceability was

Figure 16 — Turret details.

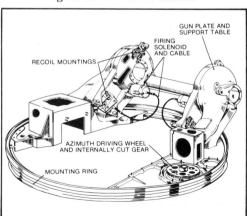

Boulton & Paul D type turret with 'Village Inn' AGLT radar fitted for tests on Halifax B3 HX238 at Boscombe Down. (RAE).

Figure 17 — Type 'D', Mk. 1 turret, showing location of components.

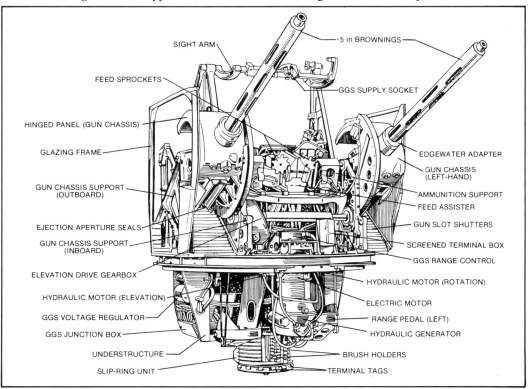

SIGHT ARM

·5 in BROWNINGS

FEED SPROCKETS

GGS SUPPLY SOCKET

HINGED PANEL (GUN CHASSIS)

GLAZING FRAME

EDGEWATER ADAPTER

GUN CHASSIS (LEFT-HAND)

GUN CHASSIS SUPPORT (OUTBOARD)

AMMUNITION SUPPORT

FEED ASSISTER

EJECTION APERTURE SEALS

GUN SLOT SHUTTERS

GUN CHASSIS SUPPORT (INBOARD)

SCREENED TERMINAL BOX

GGS RANGE CONTROL

ELEVATION DRIVE GEARBOX

HYDRAULIC MOTOR (ROTATION)

HYDRAULIC MOTOR (ELEVATION)

ELECTRIC MOTOR

GGS VOLTAGE REGULATOR

RANGE PEDAL (LEFT)

GGS JUNCTION BOX

HYDRAULIC GENERATOR

UNDERSTRUCTURE

BRUSH HOLDERS

SLIP-RING UNIT

TERMINAL TAGS

exceptional, judging by the correspondence received by the author — ample evidence of fine Boulton & Paul technology.

With the *Schrage Musik* installation on the German night fighters the British night bombers without undergun protection became easy victims. Unfortunately, it took quite a time for officialdom to accept that a new type of gun installation and new forms of attack were being used by the German night fighters, with the result that the FN64 and BP type 'K' mid-under turrets were not pursued with vigour. In the end, it was nearly August 1943 before the installation of a Browning 0.5 in. under-gun was considered, and August before an aircraft mock-up of the mounting and position was inspected at Handley Page's (Stirling and Lancaster installation inspection was about the same time).

Authority for the 0.5 in. under-gun defence mounting on the Halifax and the Lancaster was given on 6 October 1943, and at about the same time it was pointed out that new 0.5 in. Brownings must be used, as old ones tended to jam more easily. Further problems occurred in the installation of these under-guns, mainly in the manner of firing them, so that it was January 1944 before 4 Group HQ were able to authorise the first ten mountings for No. 77 Squadron for trials.

Experience with this gun installation seemed to vary with different people; some crews found that the guns overheated and vibrated badly — was this a case of using old guns? — while some never used them. Trials indicated that the 0.5 in. mounting and blister had little or no effect on performance up to 20,000 ft, but above that height the aircraft lagged behind the ones without mounting blisters.

Figure 17 shows the type 'D', Mk.1 turret. Full data on each type of turret is given in the Appendix.

Chapter 7
Undercarriage and Hydraulics

The use of the Messier hydraulic system and undercarriage in the Halifax started with the determination of one man to have his own business and to produce precision hydraulic equipment; that man was Louis Armandias, who acquired from Messier of France a licence to produce Messier equipment in the United Kingdom. This included the rights acquired by Messier to produce the hydraulic system and pump that was designed by A. de Boysson of S.A.M.M.

In 1936 Armandias arrived in the UK with the intention of finding a customer and a factory and producing the Messier equipment. He could not have picked a better time, for Specification P13/36 had been issued and hydraulically operated undercarriages, flaps and gun turrets were the fashion. After meeting him, Volkert of Handley Page's was sufficiently impressed to arrange a meeting with 'HP' in person. Volkert expressed a desire to use the Messier system because the hydraulic pressure was higher than normal and the system utilised stored-up energy for the lowering operations. The de Boysson-designed Messier pump had a built-in clutch unit having the desirable quality of only clutching in when hydraulic power was required; i.e., when the undercarriage or flaps were raised. The interview with 'HP' was quite satisfactory and he gave Volkert his blessing for the use of the system.

But this only solved one problem for Armandias, for he had no production capability and 'HP' indicated clearly that he was not prepared to put up capital to start another company for the production of hydraulic equipment. After discussion with Baron L. D'Erlanger and Alan Goode of Petters, Louis Armandias formed his own company with its head office and drawing office at Grosvenor Gardens, London, and a search for production facilities began.

In Handley Page's tender to the P13/36 specification the Messier system was entered and in March 1938 the Drawing Office was proceeding on the assumption that the Messier undercarriage and hydraulic system would be installed, only for Volkert to find in November 1939 that the Messier undercarriage system did not fulfil the standard test requirements of AP 970 — although at the same time he noted that the requirements included two tests which conflicted badly with each other. Further tests were made and modifications carried out and eventually the requirements were satisfied.

Meanwhile Armandias and Company had been joined by Owen of Rubery Owen and a new company was launched, called Rubery Owen Messier. A factory was found at Warrington, subcontractors organised and new machinery ordered for the factory. As at this time there was no production and Handley Page's would be requiring components for the prototype, it was decided to order the main undercarriage arch — a huge magnesium alloy casting of Messier design — from the French Messier Co, as well as the prototype hydraulic system, while production planning started in the UK.

When the parts did begin to roll out from the Warrington factory there was already a hold-up at Handley Page's which had resulted in the MAP requesting Handley Page's to consider an off-the-peg undercarriage from Dowty. Dowty were instructed that the main undercarriage arch design must fit in the bearing forgings exactly as the Messier arch, that the levered suspension system must use a simple shock absorber based on the Manchester one, and that the stroke was not to be less than 12 inches.

Although unable to supply off-the-shelf, an alternative undercarriage was eventually produced by Dowty, but when it was introduced in the Halifax a Dowty hydraulic system was also introduced. The Halifax so fitted was designated the Mk.5; but in the production of the undercarriage a certain number of parts was produced from castings instead of forgings as on the Manchester. 'HP', in a letter to the MAP, urged that the decision to produce these should not be put into effect until a complete check on the stressing and strength was made as they might be required to meet higher take-off and landing requirements. Nevertheless the undercarriage was fitted, and in a short period of time stress cracking occurred with the result that the maximum all-up landing weight was reduced.

Returning to Messier, the original undercarriage using a magnesium casting was very strong and very few instances of failure occurred, but in 1939 no-one realised the significance of take-off drag of the undercarriage. In regard to the design for the Halifax main undercarriage arch this drag was very bad. At a meeting at Handley Page's on 5 January 1941 Messier were asked to go ahead with an alternative design of built-up strut-type arch so that the drag of the Halifax could be reduced; this never came about on the Halifax and the eventual open tube design with lower drag was incorporated on the Hastings.

The Messier tailwheel assembly was the weakest part of the Halifax design, and in early 1941 Volkert asked Rubery Owen Messier to investigate this assembly thoroughly and come up with a redesign of the retractable tailwheel. The main fault of the tailwheel assembly was that while retracting it did not always centralise — with disastrous results. Messier therefore introduced the 'solid strut' — a non-retracting type of oleo strut — which was quickly produced and installed; the retractable tailwheel assembly was re-introduced on the Halifax Mk.3. The solid strut was a completely new design, non-retractable, and was in no way similar to the retractable type.

In getting the Messier system into production as quickly as possible no attempt was made to change over from metric to British threads, although AGS pipe fittings were used. The Messier hydraulic system used Messier fluid (DTD 391), as opposed to the DTD 44 mineral oil used in the Dowty system, which created an added item to the stores inventory. Requests were made later for the Messier hydraulic system to utilise DTD 44 fluid. This never came about, and airframe fitters were for years to talk of 'mess-ee-er' fluid. Similarly, the MAP would have liked to have had interchangeable Dowty and Messier jacks, but the Dowty equipment was built to British Imperial standards and the Messier to metric.

Although the beauty, simplicity and heart of the Messier hydraulic system was the engine-driven pump with its built-in clutch unit, in practice the Messier pump proved unreliable. This was due initially to a manufacturing fault with a case-hardened washer, but later to incorrect setting-up of the flexible drive and pump. This was probably due to lack of information being passed to the personnel concerned.

In 1942 it was decided to change over from the Messier pump to the Lockheed pump, which had been running satisfactorily in other installations. With the introduction of this type of pump it was necessary to introduce an automatic cut-out so as to provide an idling circuit when no service was selected, as the Lockheed pump was pumping continuously. The system using the Lockheed pump superseded the Messier system and continued in use throughout the rest of the life of the Halifax.

The magnesium alloy main undercarriage arch was produced in three places — at High Duty Alloys, Slough, at Birmal, and at Magnesium Castings & Products of High Wycombe — and the castings were then machined by Messier's at Warrington and Trafford Park. Numbers of other components were cast and forged by subcontractors but machined by the company. The Lockheed pump was the exception to this, for it was produced outside the company and was an embodiment loan item on the Halifax.

G. Orloff was the Chief Designer of Rubery Owen Messier, and was to continue in that position when it became British Messier after the war. At the request of Volkert of Handley Page's he commenced the design of a strutted undercarriage to replace the large magnesium alloy arch. Also considered by Volkert in November 1941 was a single-leg type with twin wheels, but it appears that Messier never became involved in any design work on this project, although a design of this type appears on the Halifax Stage 1 replacement, the HP65.

In spite of the initial problems with the Messier hydraulic system and undercarriage it would be fair to say, based on Handley Page documents, that Volkert himself was pleased with the potential of the Messier system, for more than once he spoke of the efficiency of the system, and this was borne out in later years when it was used by many manufacturers of aircraft. Once the initial problems were overcome and the air and ground crews educated in its use, the Messier products were fully accepted and appreciated; but, before that, it was production that most bothered Handley Page's.

Handley Page's were by now having the Halifax production held up by shortage of main undercarriages because Messier were only producing 16 sets per month. As Rotol were withdrawing from the Rubery Owen Messier organisation, 'HP' proposed to the MAP that a Mr. Coverley be placed in complete control of the part of the company manufacturing the undercarriage and hydraulic equipment. Further to this, 'HP' was prepared to guarantee the MAP up to £50,000 against any claims against the Ministry — but firmly stated that he did not want any interest or profit in or connection with the Rubery Owen Messier organisation. All this resulted in a two-month trial period for the company to increase production; although by now production was already on the increase and, as explained earlier, Dowty were being called in to produce an alternative undercarriage.

By October 1941 the Dowty alternative undercarriage was a reality and a test was arranged between L9515 fitted with a Messier undercarriage and L9520 fitted with a Dowty undercarriage. The result indicated that there was no practical difference in unstick distance between the two, but to clear a 50 ft barrier the aircraft with Dowty undercarriage took 90 yards less, with both aircraft at all-up weight, of 60,000 lb.

The heart of the Messier system, the Messier clutched pump, was by now in such short supply that at Radlett production Halifaxes were being tested without the hydraulic pump — much to the disgust and physical overloading of the flight test observers who were developing over-size arm muscles in the pumping up of undercarriage and flaps. The pump was also giving problems at the squadrons, as explained earlier, and, to try to solve this, in November 1941 Halifax L9505 was tested at Radlett with the Messier pump replaced by the Lockheed pump. This

Figure 18 — Messier power circuit using Lockheed pressure pump.

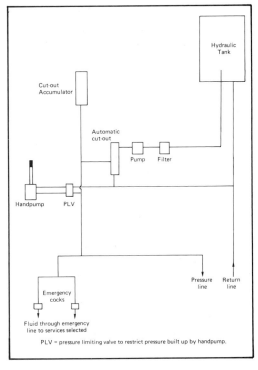

drew from a large Vokes filter and incorporated in the Messier system was an automatic cutout (Figure 18). From this test the conclusion was reached that the system functioned satisfactorily, for operating times for nearly all services were less than those recorded for the original Messier system, so the decision was taken to make this system the basis for production.

But by early 1942 doubts were being expressed about the Dowty undercarriage and hydraulic system, for it was found that, apart from the use of castings instead of forgings, there was a substantial increase in weight of the aircraft compared with the Messier equipped one. On 28 March a meeting was called by the Ministry of Aircraft Production to discuss this, and it was agreed to hasten production of forgings to replace the cast suspension levers, etc and to hasten the approval of a common Dowty design for Halifax and Lancaster. In the end, of course, the Halifax Mk.5 with its Dowty undercarriage had so many undercarriage failures that the production of that mark was shortened.

The Messier hydraulic system was used for the retraction and lowering of the undercarriage and operation of the landing flaps, as well as wing and fuselage bomb-doors, landing lamp and other auxiliary services. An emergency system was also incorporated, which allowed the undercarriage to be lowered in the event of flak or cannon fire damage to the accumulator. This allowed the use of either the engine-driven pump or the hand-pump to lower the undercarriage and meant that the aircrew (namely the flight engineer and pilot) had four methods of lowering the undercarriage: (a) normal method by accumulator; (b) emergency method by engine-driven pump; (c) emergency method by hand-pump; and (d) bungee-assisted lowering aid.

The undercarriage itself consisted of the main undercarriage and tailwheel assembly. The main undercarriage itself had three main components: (a) the undercarriage arch, axle and wheel with brake units; (b) the radius rods; (c) two retracting jacks to each radius rod.

The layout of the undercarriage is shown in Figure 19. The lowered position was maintained by: (a) the geometric lock of the radius rods; (b) the hydraulic lock on each hydraulic jack; (c) the accumulator pressure, (d) the internal mechanical lock in the jacks.

From this it will be seen how effective and safe was the lowering of the undercarriage and its positiveness in the locked-down condition. Furthermore, the Halifax with Messier undercarriage and hydraulic system was 650 lb lighter than the Dowty-equipped Halifax.

The Dowty-equipped Halifax — the Mk.5 — utilised two Lockheed pumps, fitted on the inboard engines, which drew DTD 44 hydraulic fluid from the reservoir and pumped out through the automatic cut-out. The delivery operated the jacks either way and the automtic cut-out by-passed the fluid back to the reservoir when the pressure was full and no service being operated. An accumulator in the system damped out fluctuations and prevented 'machine gunning' of the automatic cut-out valve.

In the Dowty system, if a complete failure of the hydraulic system occurred there was an emergency air system to blow down the flaps and open the bomb-doors. The use of emergency air of course entailed the complete bleeding and refilling of the hydraulic system.

As the Halifax Mk.5 became 'worn in' in service it was found that when the undercarriage lever was placed in the neutral position, leakage across the selector rotary valve occurred, which in a number of cases resulted in the back pressure building up on the down line of the undercarriage jacks, which sheared the uplocks, and down came the undercarriage — most embarrassing when stretching the range on a flight to and from Norway. The answer to this problem was to select 'undercarriage up' and leave the lever in this position, which meant that the pumps were pressure pumping continuously.

Although a Halifax (L9520) was allocated to Dowty for development of their system for the Halifax Mk.5, no aircraft was allocated to

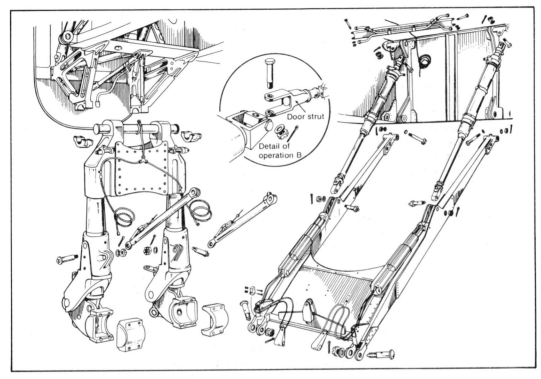

Figure 19 — Undercarriage layout.

Messier for the development and improvement of their system, which meant that no individual company testing was possible, or climatic testing carried out, except by A&AEE.

In late August 1943 the Air Ministry ruled that provision was to be made for tropicalisation of Halifax Mk.3s (Specification P13/36 called for operation at home and overseas and the Halifax already had operated at home and overseas). This meant that further alterations would need to be made to the hydraulic system to operate the aircraft continuously in tropical summer conditions. For instance, an aircraft parked outside in the tropical sun would have its hydraulic fluid expand, as well as the oleo seals drying out in contact with the hot walls of the oleos. So not only better seals but also thermal relief valves were required for the hydraulic system. These were designed and the Halifax Mk.7 had them incorporated as standard.

Finally, while on the subject of oleos, it must be recorded that the Dowty type on the Halifax Mk.5 used to collapse with very little warning — typically and embarrassingly about ten minutes before take-off! Fortunately, the shock absorber struts were fairly easy to replace, though of course the aircraft had to be jacked up to carry this out. Most Bomber Command squadrons who operated this mark of Halifax soon prepared themselves for this eventuality and had a van ready with a supply of shock absorber struts and lifting jacks.

G. E. Curtis (ex-Sgt Fitter of No. 428 Squadron) says of those days: 'The Dowty levered shock absorber struts were easy to change, but of course the aircraft had to be jacked up to do it, and the collapse inevitably happened in the middle of the line up for take-off.' Having had experience of Mks 2, 3 and 5 Halifaxes, and therefore of both Messier and Dowty systems, he, like many others, felt that the Messier was the better.

Chapter 8
Operations

From the Heyford of 1933 with its fixed undercarriage, maximum bomb load of 3500 lb, open cockpits and gun rings, an all-up weight of 16,750 lb and a top speed of 138 mph, to the Halifax of 1939 with an all-up weight of 50,000 lb, a period of only six years had elapsed. Now the maximum bomb-load was 8000 lb, as per Specification P13/36, soon to be further increased, and new tasks for the new bomber were to be thought out. Although the maximum power from the engines was increased throughout the life of the Halifax the cruising speed remained almost the same at around the 220-230 mph mark rather than the 275 mph required by the specification; for with an ever-increasing power output came an ever-increasing load. This figure of 275 mph was to prove unattainable at normal loaded weight in the cruise by any of the designs or derivatives orginating from Specification P13/36.

The Halifax Mk.1 went into operation in early 1941 with a power operated twin-gun nose turret and a power operated four-gun rear turret, which was at that time considered sufficient; then for daylight operations beam hatches fitted with twin Vickers 'K' guns were installed. This was followed by the Hudson type mid-upper turret and then a mid-under position — and so the service load increased as the all-up weight increased from 55,000 lb to 68,000 lb.

Radio, radio aids and radar were added as the demands for better communications and bombing and navigational equipment increased. These were *Gee*, H2S, *Boozer*, *Monica*, *Tinsel*, and, in No.100 Group aircraft, *Airborne Cigar* and *Mandrel*. The demand for the equipment originated when long-distance propaganda raids (code-named *Nickels*) proved that peacetime dead-reckoning navigation and astro shots did not work under wartime conditions.

The Battle of Britain was without any doubt both a military and a psychological victory for RAF Fighter Command, for this was the first time that the Luftwaffe had failed to achieve their objective, but in no way was the Luftwaffe beaten, and in no way could Britain win the war in the skies over Britain; the only way was by the use of bombers. But at that time neither the Stirling nor the Halifax was even in squadron service, there were no radio aids, no radar aids — in fact we even started the war without bullet-proof tanks. Yet from this situation eventually emerged a force fully equipped with every radio/radar aid, nearly always a jump ahead of the enemy — and with Halifax aircraft not only fitted with bullet-proof tanks but with nitrogen protection for the tanks as well.

RAF Bomber Command in the early years of the war was not keen to adopt Operational Research — complacency over our bombing efficiency was prevalent — and in spite of the Luftwaffe's success the idea of a Pathfinder Force was anathema to Air Marshal Harris. Fortunately he was overruled on this and then Churchill gave priority to Bomber Command as the major striking force against Germany. Pathfinder Force was formed in 1942 under Group Captain D. C. T. Bennett (later Air Vice-Marshal), who was an experienced civil and military pilot with exceptional navigating ability. From then on, with more radio and radar aids, Pathfinder Force led the way in, and from November 1943 they were joined by No.100 Group who disrupted and misled the German night-fighter controllers.

The first and only Halifax squadron in Pathfinder Force was also the first to receive the Halifax — No.35 Squadron. It was then operating Halifax Mk.2 Series 1As with an all-up weight of 60,000 lb. These were later

A Halifax BII being serviced by Groundcrew.

fitted with H2S and, with Stirlings of No. 7 Squadron, were to mark Hamburg on 30 January 1943 for the main force. In December 1943 the squadron converted to Halifax Mk.3s and completed its last Halifax operation on 1 March 1944.

Unfortunately for the RAF, Bomber Command was not the only front-line Command to be engaged with the German military machine, for Coastal Command were struggling not only to combat the U-boats and German coastal traffic but to expand as well. In 1942 two squadrons of Halifax bombers — Nos. 158 and 405 Squadrons — received orders to place detachments under the operational control of Coastal Command. Inside a year more Halifax squadrons were formed, or joined, Coastal Command.

Although the Short Stirling was often considered the Cinderella of Bomber Command, in fact the Handley Page Halifax was never given due credit for its achievements or its versatility. For of all the designs or derivatives developed from Specification P13/36 only the Halifax during the war years fulfilled the Air Staff's requirement for a bomber, general reconnaissance and general purpose aircraft for home and overseas. Furthermore, in its role of airborne support it was only superseded when the Handley Page Hastings entered service in 1949. This was also the same type that superseded the Halifax in Meteorological Flight duties — the last flight by a Halifax on Met. Flight was a No.224 Squadron aircraft from Gibraltar, on 17 March 1952.

From its basic design to P13/36 with a continuous application of technology the Halifax was developed into a number of successful roles and was the only four-engined British-built bomber during World War 2 to be based and operated from the Middle East and Far East as well as in Europe.

It was the first four-engined British-built bomber to bomb the German heartland; the first four-engined British bomber to carry the 4000 and 8000 lb bombs; the first to use FIDO operationally; the first to be fitted with H2S; the first along with Stirlings to use H2S operationally; and the first four-engined British-built landplane to operate in Coastal Command.

It was operated: as a bomber in Europe, the Middle East and Far East; on photographic mapping duties in the Far East; on long-range radar reconnaissance in the Far East; on electronic counter-measure duties with No. 100 Group in Europe; as a maritime reconnaissance aircraft with Coastal Command; as a transport aircraft in Europe, the Middle East and Far East; as an airborne support aircraft in Europe, the Middle East and Far East; on long-range Met. Flight

105

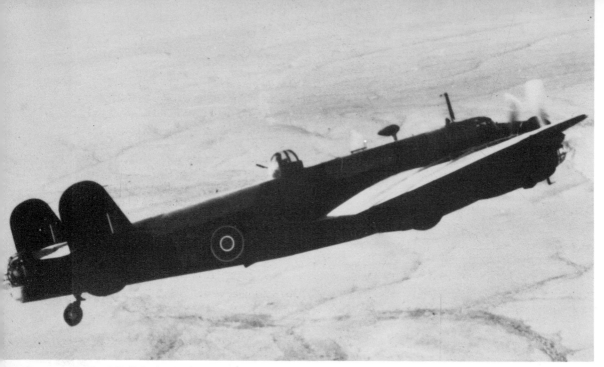

Halifax Mk.2 Series 1 of No.10 Squadron detachment, Middle East 1942. (W. McCree).

duties in Europe and Middle East; and on SOE duties in Europe and Middle East.

It was the only British-built bomber to fly the 'Hump' to China; the only bomber variant capable of towing a loaded Hamilcar glider in tropical or temperate climates; and the only bomber variant cleared by the AFEE to carry and drop by parachute the Paras' gun and jeep combination.

And from an analysis of ditching reports by Bomber Command it was found that the Halifax had a better ditching record than the Lancaster; its survivability record was far superior to most other aircraft and a testimony to its structural integrity.

When Bomber Command recommended daylight operations over enemy territory in 1944 the Halifax aircraft of No. 4 Group established a record in Bomber Command by the destruction in air combat of 33 enemy fighters. In fact, on daylight operations throughout the war Halifax aircraft failing to return represented 0.56 per cent of those despatched, while the Lancaster loss rate was 0.77 per cent. In August 1944 the Halifaxes of 4 Group flew 3629 sorties and by the end of the same year had flown 25,464 sorties for the loss of 402 aircraft. This was further improved

in March 1945 when the Group dropped its largest weight of bombs and had the lowest rate of lost aircraft in Bomber Command.

These are the basic records of the Halifax in service, proving the strength of its structure, its versatility and its right to recognition as one of the great aircraft. We now follow it into operations, when its first operational sortie against the enemy was on 11 March 1941.

Into battle

The Group chosen for re-equipping with the Halifax was No.4 Group, which had its bases in the Vale of York and its headquarters at Heslington Hall, which is one mile South East of York (and now provides the core of York University).

By the end of 1942 No.6 (RCAF) Bomber Group had moved into the northern part of the Vale of York, and was equipped with Halifax aircraft. No.6 Group had its headquarters at Allerton Park, east of Knaresborough, a market town north-west of York. Allerton Park was an old Victorian mansion house and was known to the

106

Canadians as 'Castle Dismal'; they controlled seven operational stations, all north of Harrogate. No.4 Group had the distinction of being the world's first night bomber Group and numbered among its commanders some of the most experienced pilots there were, such as Wg Cdr D. C. T. Bennett, Wg Cdr Cheshire and Sqn Ldr Tait — all to be promoted as the Group expanded.

By the spring of 1944 the squadrons of No. 4 Group had introduced distinctive fin and rudder markings on some of their aircraft; at least nine squadrons did this, while a number of the aircraft also had their vertical fuselage surfaces and wing/fuselage under surface finished in a glossy black. No.6 Group Halifaxes sported unofficial artwork on their noses that must have equalled any found on the USAAF's B17s; a number of No. 4 Group Halifaxes followed suit.

The Halifax was the second British-built four-engined bomber to enter RAF service in the 1939-45 war, being preceded by three months by the Short Stirling. The first squadron, No.35, had been reformed at RAF Leeming in November 1940 after a number of its crews had had a short spell of duty at A&AEE Boscombe Down to obtain handling experience with Halifax aircraft under test there. The squadron moved to its operational station at RAF Linton-on-Ouse in December 1940, and during this period flew the prototype L7244, which had been loaned to the squadron to gain experience on type. Shortly afterwards, the first operational Halifaxes started to arrive, one of these being the second production aircraft L9486. All these early aircraft were completely fitted with dual controls, which of course made the conversion of pilots that much easier, though it did restrict the movement of occupants in the nose section if they needed to use the Elsan in the aft fuselage.

On the night of 10/11 March 1941 the squadron carried out the first Halifax raid, seven aircraft being detailed. Due to a hydraulic failure on one, only six Halifaxes took off: L9486, L9488, L9489, L9490, L9493 and L9496. The primary target was Le Havre with Boulogne as the secondary. Due to cloud cover over Le Havre only four aircraft were able to attack the primary target, and that from a height of 10,000-13,000 ft. L9493, piloted by Fg Off. Warren, was hit by heavy flak and the navigator injured, but he commendably carried on with his duties. The starboard inner engine's radiator was punctured, causing the engine to overheat, and hydraulic failure caused the undercarriage to fall down, but the aircraft returned safely to base on three engines. L9489 was piloted by Sqn Ldr Gilchrist, and after a successful attack was returning to the UK, only to be mistaken for an enemy aircraft

Halifax Mk.1 Series 2 of No.35 Squadron over the city of York in the winter of 1940. (Air Cdre P. A. Gilchrist)

by a British night-fighter and shot down in flames, crashing near Normandy in Surrey at 22.40 hours with only the pilot and the flight engineer escaping by parachute. To quote Sqn Ldr Gilchrist:

'Shot down by night fighter (RAF), Aldershot-Guildford, Sgt Aedy wounded — crew killed. A rather sad beginning'.

The second raid by No. 35 Squadron was an attack on the Blohm & Voss Works (shipyards) at Hamburg on the night of the 12/13 March. This was considered a successful attack; flak was not too strong, and in those days was usually accurate around the 8000-10,000 ft mark.

In April 1941 C Flight of No. 35 Squadron was hived off to become the nucleus of No. 76 Squadron, which then moved to Middleton St. George, to become operational in June under Wg Cdr Jarman.

On 13 June 1941 in an interview with Air Marshal Freeman, 'HP' was told that they were considering the use of the Halifax for daylight operations, in which case they would have to sacrifice some bomb-load for more ammunition and armour. It would thus appear that the Air Staff had visions of using the Halifax as then equipped as a day bomber, in spite of past experience in 1939-40 with day bombers defended with small-bore weapons.

This became fact on 30 June 1941 when six Halifax aircraft of No.35 Squadron were despatched on a daylight raid on Kiel without escort. A successful raid was made from 17,000-18,000 ft with all bombs being seen to burst on target. Three Me109s made an attack on L9499, which was shot down, but not before one Me109 was also shot down. L9501 was also attacked but got safely home, as did the other four.

The next main target was the *Scharnhorst*, on 24 July. While the main force was attacking Brest in daylight, nine Halifaxes of No.35 Squadron and six from No.76 Squadron attacked the *Scharnhorst* at La Pallice. Fourteen aircraft reached the target and were met by between 12 and 18 Me109s and heavy flak. Every aircraft was hit by either flak or fighters, with the result that five Halifax aircraft failed to return. L9527 was

shot down on the approach and four more around the target area; five more that reached base were severely damaged. To expect small-bore weaponed bombers to defend themselves effectively against cannon-armed fighters in daylight again indicated the naive approach of some of our operational planners. The damage to *Scharnhorst* was minimal — five direct hits and 3000 tons of water inside — and the same evening she sailed for Brest.

On that evening, news of the daylight raid and of the existence of the Halifax bomber was officially disclosed to the British public, but it was not until the September that the HP57 was officially named 'Halifax' by Lord Halifax at a ceremony at Radlett. In his address Lord Halifax quoted from an old Yorkshire prayer: 'From Hull, Hell and Halifax Good Lord deliver us,' remarking that in the months and years ahead the Germans might well make the same plea.

'Veracity 1' was an attack on the *Scharnhorst* and *Gneisenau* at Brest by a mixed force of Halifaxes, Manchesters and Stirlings. The Halifaxes were from No.10 Squadron (five aircraft), No.35 Squadron (six aircraft) and No.76 Squadron (six aircraft). This time a fighter escort was to be provided to cover the attack and withdrawal. The attack was opened by the Stirlings, which were heavily bracketed by flak. The Halifaxes went in, having had one aircraft withdraw with engine trouble, and the attack was pressed home. R9367 was damaged and was forced to ditch before reaching England; V9978 was damaged by flak and had two engines out but landed safely at Boscombe Down.

On 30 December a repeat performance was carried out, code-named 'Veracity 2'. This time only three Halifax squadrons were despatched, but they had an escort of Polish Spitfires. Sixteen Halifaxes went into the attack on the *Scharnhorst* and *Gneisenau* this time. Both the flak and enemy fighters were more concentrated, and V9979 crashed after being hit in the port wing. Then L9615 and R9374 were damaged but, escorted by Spitfires during the withdrawal, they escaped and ditched safely.

By the end of 1941 the German flak and fighter opposition had increased to the point where daylight attacks by unescorted heavy bombers were yielding such poor results for the losses in aircraft and crews that the Halifaxes, along with other heavy bombers, were withdrawn from daylight operations.

The Halifax became the main heavy weapon of Bomber Command's offensive during the winter of 1941-42 and by the spring of 1942 twelve heavy bomber squadrons of No. 4 Group in Yorkshire were fully equipped with the aircraft; these included No. 10 Squadron at Leeming, No. 77 Squadron also at Leeming, and No. 158 Squadron, which had been reformed from the base unit of No. 104 Squadron and was based at East Moor.

To help the Royal Navy in its protection of North Sea convoys to Russia — in spite of the Senior Service's habit of shooting at RAF aircraft — several attacks were carried out on the German battleship *Tirpitz* which was sheltering in Aassfjord near Trondheim in Norway. The first was on the 30/31 January 1942 when nine aircraft of No. 76 Squadron made the journey, but the attack was aborted because of bad weather over the target. A further attack was made as a protective measure for convoy PQ13 on the 30/31 March, but this time the German early warning system was as effective as the weather had previously been; a smoke screen had quickly been laid over the target and the raid was foiled.

On the 27/28 April 1942 twenty-six Halifax aircraft of No. 4 Group were called up to make a further attack on the *Tirpitz*, this time using 250 lb, 500 lb and 4000 lb bombs and modified Mk.19N Royal Navy mines. The use of the mines was the Admiralty's idea; they reasoned that, with the *Tirpitz* close in-shore, the mines could be dropped on the hillsides and so roll down and under the ship, where the depth fuses would operate and so explode the mines under the ship. The problem was to get the mines onto the hillsides, which entailed the Halifaxes detailed for this part of the operation descending from 2000 to 200 ft at the dropping point, while the remaining aircraft carried out a high-level attack.

Four aircraft failed to return from this operation, one of which was W1041 flown by Wg Cdr D. C. T. Bennett (CO of No. 10 Squadron). During the attack the smoke

Halifax Mk.2 Series 1 ZA-T of No.10 Squadron detachment at No.5 MU in the Middle East, 1942.
(N. West).

screen started to develop and W1041 was hit in the starboard wing on the approach and set on fire; more unfortunate was that the bomb-aimer could not see the ship and so Bennett had to make a second run. By now the starboard wing was badly on fire, the starboard undercarriage had fallen down and the starboard flap was trailing down. Turning the aircraft towards Sweden, Bennett found the aircraft unable in its damaged condition to rise above the mountains, so he was forced to give the order to abandon the aircraft. He held the aircraft steady with the port outer engine throttled back and with full port rudder while the crew baled out. The flight engineer's last action was to clip the pilot's chute onto Bennett, who baled out just as the starboard wing folded up. Bennett later met up with the wireless operator and together they escaped to Sweden, from where he was repatriated to the UK and back to No.10 Squadron (later to command Pathfinder Force).

Another of the casualties was Halifax Mk.2 Series 1, W1048, TL-S of No. 35 Squadron, flown by Fg Off D. McIntyre. This aircraft had been despatched from the English Electric factory only 12 days previously and was on its first operation. W1048 was the eighth aircraft to attack and, almost as soon as the mines were released, suffered a direct

Halifax being overhauled in the open at No.5 MERU, Egypt 1942 (N. West)

hit. Smoke filled the cockpit and carrying out the fire-fighting drill for the starboard outer engine had no effect, so, with Plt Off P. Hewitt guiding him through the mountains, the pilot decided to put the burning aircraft down to save the crew — in fact there was no alternative but to crashland. Missing the first landing spot on another lake the pilot landed gently on Lake Hoklingen, which was frozen over. All the crew escaped safely, but the flight engineer (Vic Stevens) was injured, so two of the crew volunteered to stay with him while the pilot, bomb-aimer and wireless operator escaped to Norway. The ice melted and W1048 sank into 90 ft of water; but 31 years later, on 19 June 1973, Norwegian volunteers and the RAF Sub-Aqua Club team raised her to the surface again.

The next major operation that involved the Halifax was the first 1000 bomber raid, target Cologne. On the 30/31 May 1942 1046 aircraft were despatched, led by Wellingtons and Stirlings equipped with *Gee*. The last wave was composed totally of Halifaxes and Lancasters, of which 118 were Halifaxes — from which four failed to return. Initially there was low cloud on the route which raised doubts about the operation but nearer the target the visibility was perfect. When the Halifax squadrons arrived the raid had been on for an hour and the blazing inferno that was Cologne could be seen 60 miles away. Some crews couldn't believe what they saw — it appeared like a huge forest fire, but the Rhine bridges and the twin towers of the cathedral confirmed their target as Cologne. The fires were so intense that the flames were reflected on the aircraft.

A total of 898 aircraft claimed to have attacked the target, with the AOC of No.3 Group (AVM Baldwin) flying as second pilot on one of the first Stirlings, but 40 aircraft failed to return. It was estimated that 1445 tons of bombs were placed on the target, resulting in total destruction of 2,904,000 square yards, which included more than 250 factories or workshops either destroyed or badly damaged; 12,000 fires were started, some of which were still burning for days afterwards.

Halifax Mk.2 Series 1 (Special) of No.10 Squadron steep-banking into photographic aircraft. (T. Thackray)

'HP' sent a telegram of congratulation to A. T. Harris, AOC-in-C of Bomber Command, on the night's work, to which the AOC-in-C replied on the 2 June:

'My Dear Handley Page
We all very much appreciate your telegram of congratulation on Saturday night's work, the success of which was very largely due to your support in giving us such a powerful weapon to wield. Between us we will make a job of it.'

From this it would appear that Harris was satisfied with the Halifax. But, as time passed and the 'powerful weapon' was further

Result of mid-air collision of Halifax MZ465 of No.51 Squadron over Saarbrucken 13/14 January 1945, flown by Plt Off A. L. Wilson. Considered to be the most heavily damaged four-engined bomber ever to return and land in the UK. (IWM).

improved, the AOC-in-C Bomber Command changed his attitude to Handley Page, for the Lancaster became his chosen instrument.

On the 1/2 June 1942 the second 1000 bomber raid took place; the target was Essen in the Ruhr, which was the industrial heartland of Germany and which was notorious not only for its industrial haze but also for its formidable defences of radar controlled searchlights and flak. So the target was neither an easy one to find nor one easy to hit. Altogether 956 aircraft were despatched, including 130 Halifaxes from No. 4 Group. Due to the weather conditions only 767 aircraft claimed to have attacked. Of these, 20 Wellingtons were briefed to act as Pathfinders with flares for illumination of a pinpoint target in the Krupps works, the aiming point for seven No. 76 Squadron aircraft prior to the main attack. Crews found on arrival that there was 10/10ths cloud as well as flak, and the attack was far from successful; 31 aircraft (3.24 per cent) failed to return, of which eight were Halifaxes (6.15 per cent). A further 99 aircraft were damaged in various degrees and five were destroyed on landing.

In June 1942 a detachment of No. 10 Squadron was despatched to Aqir in Palestine to carry out operations in North Africa; these were:

W1170 W1171 W1172 W1174 W1176
W1178 W1151 W7659 W7679 W7695
W7697 W7756 W7757 W7758 W7716
W7717

Of these only 14 aircraft arrived; W1178 crashed at Gibraltar and W7695 ditched off Alexandria. Then a detachment of No. 76 Squadron was despatched to join the No. 10 squadron detachment; these were:

W1144 W1148 W1149 W1156 W1161
W1169 W1177 W1183 W7671 W7672
W7655 W7614 W7702 W7754 W7755
W7762

The two detachments supplied aircraft for the night bombing of targets in North Africa, which by now included enemy-occupied Tobruk, and they used Fayid in Egypt as an advanced base. On the night of 13/14 July 1942, W1171 became the first casualty when it received extensive flak damage and was forced to crash-land in the desert. Altogether 154 sorties were carried out by the two

Halifax Mk.3 PN369 operating in SEAC on long range radar reconnaissance, 1945. (IWM).

detachments until September, when the decision was made to amalgamate the detachments and designate them No. 462 Squadron RAAF.

The squadron's aircraft suffered from engine overheating — denoted by a plume of steam issuing from the header tank — and engine failures after overhaul naturally impaired the squadron efficiency: engine as well as airframe overhauls were carried out in the open. No replacement aircraft, old engines and sand did nothing to improve things — and spares would have helped a lot! One improvement in this respect did take place when a 'sand devil' swirled across the aircraft, missing the Wellingtons but wreaking havoc among the Halifaxes awaiting repair and overhaul. In a very short space of time a number of Halifax aircraft had been blown into each other — and their cannibalised remains helped the spares situation considerably.

The conversion of crews for the Halifax squadrons was originally carried out by No.28 Halifax Conversion Unit, which was formed in late 1941 with aircraft supplied by Nos 35 and 76 Squadrons — usually the most tired or the unwanted ones. This HCU was the forerunner of a number of Heavy Conversion Units that was brought into being to convert twin-engined aircraft crews to the Halifax. For instance, No. 1652 HCU was formed at Marston Moor for No. 4 Group, but some squadrons formed their own conversion flights to achieve a quicker rate of conversion. This was possible because a number of Halifaxes had been delivered initially with dual controls.

The HCU was the point in the crew training programme where the flight engineer joined the crew. The flight engineers' training was at first a little chaotic. All were ex-ground crew and thus trained as fitters, but some further training was given at Speke, they learned gunnery at Dishforth, and sometimes had a spell at Rolls-Royce; but no training was given on fuel or flight management, which was only brought into the curriculum when complete flight engineers' courses were started at St. Athan. So the first flight

Halifax Mk.3s over the French coast at Calais, summer 1944. (L. Buckell).

engineers had a heavy burden placed on them, not only to fit into their crew but to obtain all the technical data and so complete their own training.

During the month of August 1942 the Halifax squadrons carried out further raids on enemy territory, but by the end of the month it was found that Halifax losses were 10 per cent, which attracted the attention of both Lord Cherwell and the Prime Minister, who demanded an explanation. After much analysis it was confirmed that the Halifax had suffered greater casualties than either of the

Halifax Mk.2. Series 1A JP228 fitted with Merlin 20s, D Type fin and H2S blister, February 1944. (IWM).

other two heavy bomber types, but when examined in detail it was found that at that particular time the Halifax was carrying at least 2000 lb more than the Lancaster, had attacked more heavily defended targets and had also not been used on mining operations as had the other two — mining operations usually resulting in lower losses. Nevertheless, the casualties were higher than was satisfactory, and it was felt that one of the contributory factors was that, at the all-up weight at which the Halifax was operating, the performance in regard to rate of climb and operating height was inferior, partly due to the shrouded exhausts with which this aircraft was equipped.

Some members of Bomber Command HQ felt that the losses were due to the operating height being too low — though not as low as the Stirling — while others suspected that the rudder overbalance during evasive manoeuvres at too low an altitude was causing the Halifax to spin into the ground. It was also found that where the pilot of an aircraft had flown a number of sorties as a second pilot he had a better chance of survival — but this extra training was not always possible in squadrons that were suffering high casualties.

What was very obvious to all who had tried to analyse the results was that the Halifax performance had deteriorated with the increase in load; that it was falling victim to the German night fighters possible partly due to lack of performance and partly because its exhaust was giving it away. At about this date, Linton-on-Ouse had stated officially that the

Halifax at an all-up weight of 60,000 lb was sluggish in the climb up to approximately 3000 feet.

Set against this was the fact that the Lancaster commenced its career powered by the Merlin 20 while the Halifax had started operations powered by the Merlin 10. It is apparent that at this date many Halifaxes were still powered with the Merlin 10 and yet its all-up weight had increased from 50,000 lb to 60,000 lb. A number of aerodynamic as well as operational factors did contribute to the inferior performance of the Halifax, as explained in previous chapters, and this only changed with the increase in span, the cleaning up the airframe and the fitting of the Hercules engines.

Pathfinder Force was formed on 11 August 1942 under the command of Air Cdre D. C. T. Bennett and initially comprised No.7 Squadron with Stirlings, No.35 Squadron with Halifaxes, No.83 Squadron with Lancasters, No.156 Squadron with Wellingtons, and No.109 Squadron with Wellingtons and Mosquitoes (ex-Wireless Development Unit).

The first two raids in which PFF took part were quite unsuccessful, if not calamitous, but on 27/28 August 1942 a raid was made on Kassel, which turned out better; fires were started all over the town, including the Henschel works, but three PFF aircraft were missing. An improvement in efficiency — and safety for the crews — was essential, and with Bennett in charge everything was geared to this objective.

On 4/5 September 1942 an attack was made

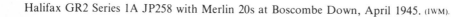

Halifax GR2 Series 1A JP258 with Merlin 20s at Boscombe Down, April 1945. (IWM).

Halifax Mk. Met 6 RG778 of No.224 Squadron over the Rock of Gibraltar 1945. (RAF Museum).

on Bremen, with PFF operating in three groups. The first were Illuminators with white flares, the second were Primary Visual Markers with coloured markers, and the third group were the Backers-up, who dropped their incendiary bombs on the markers. The main force then followed, with the result that several shipyards, factories and railway sheds were gutted.

By the end of 1942 Pathfinder Force had flown 1091 sorties with a loss rate of 2.5 per cent for the Halifaxes, 3.7 per cent for the Lancasters, 5.4 per cent for the Stirlings, and 6.0 per cent for the Wellingtons.

To improve the effectiveness of Pathfinder Force and to utilise efficiently the small number of H2S sets that were then available it was decided to equip two squadrons in PFF with this navigational aid. Those chosen were No. 7 Squadron and No. 35 Squadron. Their first use operationally came on the night of 30/31 January 1943 in a raid on Hamburg.

Halifax Mk.5 Series 1 (Special) on a North African airfield preparing to tow off a Horsa glider prior to invasion of Sicily, July 1943. (IWM).

115

A Halifax GR11 believed to be from either No.58 or No.502 Squadron at St. Davids, Pembrokeshire circa 1944.

Red flares were dropped as route markers, the H2S aircraft marked the target with red target indicators, Backers-up then dropped their markers, and then in came the main force.

It was the turn of Wuppertal-Barmen on the night of 29/30 May 1943 to feel the growing weight of Bomber Command. This was a successful attack, with 719 aircraft despatched and 611 claiming to have attacked the target. The force was led in by PFF *Oboe* Mosquitoes, who accurately placed red TIs, followed up by the Backers-up keeping the aiming point marked, so Main Force was able to hit hard and devastated 90 per cent of the target. Thirty-seven aircraft failed to return, some of these being the victims of Me110s, who pursued the bombers across the North Sea and caught the crews as they relaxed their vigilance. The Halifax squadrons taking part were Nos 10, 35, 102, 158 and 419, who reported the raid as well concentrated, with one pilot reporting smoke up to 16,000 ft. Conditions were a slight ground haze and good visibility, while the defences were reported as saturated. Nevertheless, ten Halifaxes failed to return, which included four from No. 35 Squadron and six from Nos 4 and 6 Groups (HR717 and HR840 from No. 158 Squadron).

By now the C-in-C of Bomber Command had made the Lancaster his chosen weapon, even referring to it as his 'Yardstick' for performance, and goading 'HP' with assertions that Lancasters were being sent in first on attacks to take the brunt. This can be proved to be inaccurate, for in some cases it was not the first wave of aircraft that was attacked but the last waves. From this it is obvious that Harris disliked the Halifax, a point made in AVM Bennett's book *Pathfinder*.

When this dislike of the Halifax started is not known, for with the entry of the Halifax into service Harris appeared to be most enthusiastic. But at a meeting on 21 December 1943, which was attended by Air Chief Marshal Portal and Air Chief Marshal Freeman, as well as by Harris and four others, Harris was most condemning of the Halifax, with the result that consideration was given to switching production from the Halifax to the Lancaster. Further to this, he was apparently

116

not prepared to accept that the Halifax B3 and B6 would be comparable to the Lancaster in regard to speed or ceiling.

Whether Harris's dislike of the Halifax was due to its loss rate or the clash with 'HP', or whether it was because the Lancaster carried the larger bombs — which it has been reported he favoured over incendiaries — is not known. In fact, although the Halifax loss rate by the end of 1943 was in excess of that of the Lancaster, the Halifax B3 and B6 were then entering service with Bomber Command, and both these marks had an improved performance. Initially their entrance into service did not bring down the loss rate in a dramatic fashion, which was partially due to the fact that a number of older marks were still in use, but by the end of 1944 the Halifax loss rate had dropped to 2.5 per cent.

The decision was made in 1943 to re-equip the Main Bomber Force with Merlin-powered Lancasters and Hercules-powered Halifaxes, with the result that some Halifax squadrons were re-equipped with Lancasters while some

Lancaster 2 squadrons got Halifaxes. Nos 427, 428, 429, 433 and 434 were re-equipped with Halifaxes in mid-1943; and others in 1944. The Lancaster 2s, Stirlings and Halifax 2s and 5s were routed to the HCUs to increase the training of Bomber Command crews for the bitter battles ahead.

After an attack on Peenemunde on 17/18 August 1943 (vividly and accurately described by M. Middlebrook in his book *The Peenemunde Raid),* on the evening of 23 August the target was the 'Big City'. Now the trip to Berlin represented a flight of approximately 500 miles across enemy territory to a target which was one of the most heavily defended areas in Germany, a target which some people in authority felt was too large to destroy by air attacks from Britain at that period of the war. For this particular raid 727 Bomber Command aircraft took off, the German radio operators detected the operation, the German fighter controllers managed to read the signs and by 23.04 hours the night-fighters were ordered to Berlin. Survivors reported 80 fighter interceptions

A Halifax Mk.III in trouble. The photograph speaks for itself.

and 31 actual attacks before Berlin, and when the night fighters shot down some of the PFF aircraft they knew they had the rest of the bomber stream to attack. The weather was good with very little cloud.

From this raid on the 'Big City' 56 aircraft failed to return; No. 158 Squadron, for instance, despatched 28 aircraft and lost five.

During the first few months of operation with H2S its serviceability was not very good. In fact, by the time the H2S aircraft had reached the target area not much more than half the sets were serviceable. These early sets also suffered from 'clutter' and the interpretation of the plot could only be made by a well-trained operator, though large targets like Hamburg and Cologne could be easily identified by the difference of land and water or river shape. H2S, even with all its faults, interested the Americans enough for them to produce their own version of it, called H2X.

On 3 November 1943 Air Chief Marshal Harris told Churchill that with the help of the USAAF a combined operation could completely wreck Berlin at the cost of 400-500

aircraft, but the USAAF were not to be drawn in at this stage, so Harris decided to go it alone. Between the middle of November 1943 and the third week of March 1944 the RAF carried out 16 heavy bombing attacks on Berlin and in this period 500 aircraft and their crews were lost. With shorter nights and the preparation for the invasion of Europe intervening, this was the end of the 'Battle of Berlin'.

No 6 (RCAF) Group

Canadian squadrons of No 6 Group were often adopted by various cities or organisations and were also given names. For instance: No. 408 Squadron (Goose), No. 429 Squadron (Bison), No. 419 Squadron (Moose), No. 431 Squadron (Iroquois), No. 427 Squadron (Lion), No. 433 Squadron (Porcupine), No. 428 Squadron (Ghost) and No. 434 Squadron (Bluenose).

Nos 408 and 419 Squadrons supplied 20 Halifaxes for the 1000-bomber raid on 5 March 1943 on Essen, from which DT646 failed to return. The same two squadrons

Halifaxes in action during World War Two.

No.76 Squadron Halifax BII LK 911 at Linton-on-Ouse. Failed to return from a raid on Frankfurt 21 December 1943. Crashed near Hungen, Germany.

supplied 42 Halifaxes for the Peenemunde raid from which five failed to return: DK243, EB211, JD158, JD163 and JD458.

In 1944 other Canadian squadrons converted to the Halifax and were likewise named: No. 415 Squadron (Swordfish), No. 425 Squadron (Alouette), No. 420 Squadron (Snowy Owl), No. 426 Squadron (Thunderbird), No. 424 Squadron (Tiger) and No. 432 Squadron (Leaside).

No. 427 Squadron was adopted by Metro-Goldwyn-Mayer in May 1943 and a number of their Halifaxes were named after MGM stars; for instance, DK186 was named *Lana Turner* and EB246 *Robert Donat*.

No.6 Group in 1943 carried out over 6200 successful sorties and dropped more than 13,600 tons of bombs and mines, while their

air gunners claimed 19 German night-fighters; but the price paid was 340 bombers lost.

The Advent of the Halifax Mk.3

In November 1943 Halifaxes of No. 78 Squadron took part in a raid on Frankfurt, and the remarks of one crew member (Plt Off Harrington) emphasised how the performance of the Halifax had dropped with the increase in all-up weight and equipment: 'To Frankfurt, bombed from 20,000 feet on a Mk.2 Series 1A . . . considered that this must have been ideal flying for it to have bombed at this height.'

Encapsulated in this brief statement is the reason for withdrawal of the Mks 2 and 5 aircraft: the handling and performance had

Halifaxes in formation over the sea heading towards the enemy coast.

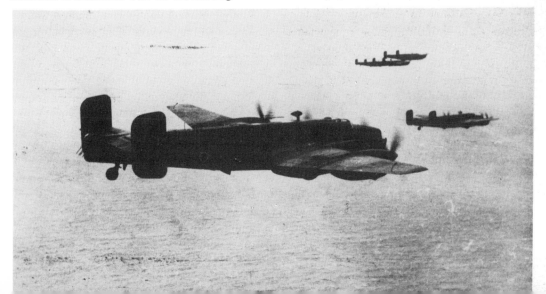

Halifax LK640 of No.431 Squadron, RCAF Tholthorpe (failed to return from Ludwigshafen, 19 November 1943). (Yorkshire Air Museum)

were sometimes still routed at operating heights below the Lancasters, when they were quite capable of being flown at or above the Lancasters.

In January 1944 Halifax losses in No. 4 Group were rising until they reached a peak of 5.1 per cent for 644 sorties against all targets. It was therefore decided to withdraw all Mks 2 and 5 aircraft from operations over Germany, but this only affected Nos 10, 77, 102 and 519 Squadrons as the remainder were equipped or were re-equipping with the Mk. 3 aircraft.

Of these other squadrons, C Flight of No.158 became the nucleus of No. 640 Squadron and so left No. 158 Squadron as a two-Flight squadron. No.640 Squadron carried out their first two ops from No. 158 Squadron's base at Lissett before moving to Leconfield, from where it operated until the end of the war, dropping in that time 8484 tons of bombs and winning No. 4 Group's monthly Bombing Cup five times.

deteriorated as the weight was increased with extra fuel, extra equipment and shrouded exhausts. The Halifax, when introduced on operations, was found to be pleasant to fly — confirmed by pilots who flew it then — but by the end of 1943 it was underpowered, and the Halifax Groups were flying below the Lancasters over the targets — so receiving damage and incurring losses from the aircraft above as well as receiving more attention from the enemy below. In fact, with the introduction of the Halifax Mk. 3, squadrons

In 1943 it had been decided by the Air Ministry that two Halifax Mk.5s and two Lancaster aircraft should be despatched to the Far East to determine their performance under tropical conditions, so Halifaxes DK254 and DK263 and two Lancasters, all operated by Service personnel, were sent to India. The two Halifaxes were accompanied by R. T. Mann (the Handley Page

Halifax Mk.III, *Z-Zombie* of No.158 Squadron, Lissett. Flt Lt Watson and crew. Photograph taken just after returning from a raid on Cologne.

representative), who arrived at Salboni in India on 9 October 1943, where all the aircraft came under the control of 1577 Flight of No. 221 Group. According to the report from Mann to the Handley Page Service Department the Officer Commanding the Unit expressed the opinion that he didn't require civilian representatives around. What was obvious was that he was biased in favour of the Lancasters, having accumulated his heavy bomber time in No. 5 Group and, where interchangeability of spares was concerned, the Lancasters were given priority.

After the Halifaxes had been in use for some time with little trouble the whole atmosphere improved. Mann also reported that the general performance of both Halifaxes compared favourably with figures compiled under English climatic conditions.

The Lancasters were withdrawn later in the year and were replaced by two Halifax Mk. 3s (NA642 and NA644), which were used on various trials and other duties until, in 1946, they were sent to Chaklala (India) for Airborne Support work. The trials of these two aircraft resulted in the operational use of the Halifax in the Far East.

The first two squadrons in Britain to receive the Halifax B3 were No. 433 RCAF (Porcupine) Squadron and No. 466 RAAF Squadron. The latter used their new aircraft for the first time on a mine-laying mission on 1 December 1943, having received their first Halifax Mk. 3 on 3 November. Between that date and March 1944 the squadron blasted away at enemy coast defences, early warning radar sites and targets like Frankfurt and Berlin.

In the Middle East in early March 1944, No. 614 (County of Glamorgan) Squadron was reformed and took over No. 462 (RAAF) Squadron's Halifaxes — B2 aircraft that had seen many owners. Its debut was an attack on Genoa on 11 March with seven aircraft, which deposited 24 1000 lb bombs and 54 500 lb bombs on the target without loss. It was tragically different on the night of 14/15 March when, in an attack on the Sofia marshalling yards, four aircraft and three crews were lost due to severe weather. The squadron also took part in raids on the Ploesti oil fields and other targets, and acted as the target marking force for No. 205 Group, dropping 4000 lb bombs. The squadron's last operation with the Halifax was against Porto Marhamo on 3 March 1945, after which they converted to Liberators.

Hercules Halifax superiority

So in 1944 began the superiority of the Mk.3 Halifax with its Hercules engines. Pilot Officer (later Sqn Ldr) A. L. Wilson, who flew with Nos. 51, 77 and 102 Squadrons on various aircraft including the Halifax Mks 2, 3, 6, 7 and 9 says of the aircraft, 'apart from being slightly heavy on the ailerons, a

Halifax B2 Series 1A JP246 of No.148 (SD) Squadron at Brindisi, Italy 1943-44. Flown by Sqn Ldr R. G. N. Pryor. (RAF Museum).

beautiful aircraft to fly, excellent visibility'.

A further point is made by Ken Chapman (ex-pilot of Nos. 640 and 171 Squadrons): 'The best feature of the Halifax was the excellent rate of climb over the Lanc, although this did fall off at altitude. I also flew Lancasters after the war finished, I preferred the Halifax by far, much more power on take-off'.

By the middle of 1944 the twin-engined night-fighters of the Luftwaffe represented its most efficient arm and comprised 15 per cent of the Luftwaffe's first line strength — a token of the respect that Germany placed on Bomber Command's attacks and the damage these were doing. By the end of 1943 the German night-fighters were equipped with SN-2 radar, which could pick up emissions from *Monica* and home on them, while another set (FuG350 *Naxos*) homed on H2S transmissions.

On 30/31 March 1944 came the raid on Nuremberg that almost broke Bomber Command's back after its unsuccessful attempts to obliterate Berlin. The main force was composed of 701 heavies and was led in by 119 aircraft of PFF.

The route as planned was opposed by AVM Bennett as being too direct and too close to fighter beacons, but this opposition was overridden by Harris. It did not help that the weather as forecast bore little relationship to the actual.

German ground control again read the signs correctly and fed 246 night-fighters into the bomber stream, while Luftwaffe bombers flew over the bomber stream to illuminate them from above with parachute flares. The first night-fighters intercepted the bomber stream south of Bonn, and near Frankfurt-am-Main fighters of Nos. 1 and 7 Divisions joined in the decimation of the bombers, with the result that some bomber crews donned their 'chutes as they saw their friends (or decoys) going down. PFF marked the target at 01.05 hours and the main force commenced their attack at 01.10 hours. It was estimated from crew reports that in the space of 90 minutes from midnight 80 bombers were shot down, some of the nightfighter 'aces' claiming four and five bombers each.

From this operation 94 bombers failed to return, 17 more received minor flak damage, four were damaged beyond repair, three damaged beyond unit repair with 15 others damaged by other than enemy action.

One of the Halifaxes damaged over Nuremberg was LK797, flown by Plt Off C. J. Barton of No. 578 Squadron. About 70 miles from the target the aircraft was attacked by a Ju88c and then by a Me110. The first attack damaged the intercom, then further attacks damaged an engine and caused other serious damage; amid the confusion and misunderstood signals the wireless operators, navigator and bomb-aimer baled out. In spite of this Barton pressed on to the target and released his bomb-load by his pilot's bomb release, then the propeller of his damaged engine flew off. With the aid of his remaining crew but without intercom or maps the pilot set course for home. Eventually the aircraft crossed the English coast 90 miles north of his base and low on fuel. Searching for base, with fuel now almost exhausted, Plt Off Barton made the decision to force-land, ordered the remaining crew to their crash positions and attempted to land by Ryhope Colliery, near Sunderland. The three crew members survived the crash but Plt Off Barton died shortly afterwards, and was awarded the only Victoria Cross ever given to a Halifax crew member.

Many crews felt that there had been treachery and that the Germans knew of the target beforehand, but there has been no proof of this whatsoever. There, is however positive proof that many aircraft ran low on fuel, and some crews felt that this was another cause of the high losses.

Against the loss of 94 bombers could only be set five enemy fighters shot down. By now RAF Intelligence was aware that some German night-fighters were fitted with obliquely mounted guns, and in 1943 the design and installation of 0.5 inch Browning machine-guns in under-gun positions had started. In October 1943 such an installation was on trial on Halifax JD380 at Park Street. Trials at HDU found that up to 20,000 feet the

LAC Barton, training in USA, 20 February 1942. (IWM)

installation made no difference to performance, but above that altitude performance fell off quickly compared to the standard machine. Near the end of 1944 the under-gun installation was approved and was being installed, No.6 Group Squadrons being some of the first users.

Mention has been made of *Monica* and its detection by SN-2 equipped night-fighters. *Monica* was fitted on the bombers as a rearward-looking search radar, which detected aircraft approaching within a 45 degree wide cone. When an aircraft was detected it gave a series of bleeps in the crew headphones, but unfortunately it did not distinguish between friend and foe, which was a little nerve-wracking in a bomber stream. As the battle changed in favour of the night-fighter again, technicians developed a device called *Perfectos*, which when fitted to Mosquito intruders placed the night-fighters

in an unenviable position, for it not only triggered off their IFF (identification sets) but also gave an accurate range and bearing to home on. Though this did not directly affect the RAF bombers it certainly affected the night-fighter force morale, for in August 1944 the night-fighters shot down 164 aircraft but lost 38 aircraft of their own.

By April 1944 the air raids on Germany were easing off as the Allied Air Forces concentrated more on targets in France, so the Luftwaffe reinforced their night-fighter force there with three squadrons, and another carried out intruder operations over Britain. Targets in France were not always a soft touch; one such, on the night of 2/3 June 1944, was Trappes marshalling yards. For this target 123 Halifaxes of No. 4 Group went into the attack; visibility was perfect with a nearly full moon — just right for fighter interception — and that night the German night-fighter force concentrated on Trappes, with the result that 16 aircraft failed to return.

One of the aircraft on that raid was Halifax LV792, and the damage this aircraft received that night was enough for it to qualify at that time for the title of 'most heavily damaged bomber to return to base'. This was a Mk.3 aircraft flown by Plt Off D. Bancroft (RAAF) of No. 158 Squadron. The bombing run was made at the specified height of 7500 feet, the bombs were dropped on the green marker, and the aircraft turned for home. Just over Evreux a Ju88 came in under the starboard tailplane and caught the aircraft with a burst of cannon fire, raking the fuselage. Fierce fires broke out in the shattered bomb-bay and

Plt Off C. J. Barton, with crew, before the incident for which he was awarded the VC. (IWM)

Wreckage of Plt Off C. J. Barton VC's aircraft Halifax LK797, LK-E of No.578 Squadron.
(IWM)

forward of the rear bulkhead, a large hole was all that was left of the H2S scanner and the DR compass was destroyed. Another large hole was in the port side of the fuselage by the wireless operator and the hydraulic system was hit, which allowed the bomb-doors to fall open and the wings flaps to droop; the undercarriage would have fallen down as well but was held up by the uplocks. With the starboard wing tanks damaged and the port inner engine on fire, the pilot quickly feathered the propeller and carried out the fire drill — and Doug Bancroft clearly saw the Ju88 break away on the starboard bow, obviously convinced that he had finished off the Halifax.

The aircraft was by now in a bad way, for the ammunition in the racks and tracks to the rear turret was being fired off by the heat, the mid-upper and rear turrets were out of operation, all intercom was gone, and then the starboard inner engine stopped due to the tanks being holed, though changing over tanks rectified this and the engine came back to life. Meanwhile, due to misunderstood signals, some of the crew had baled out, but those left continued to fight the fires.

The pilot had allowed the Halifax to

continue in a diving turn to port and eventually levelled out at 3000 ft. With all compasses out, a north-westerly course was set by the North Star and the slow drag home continued. Staggering over Le Havre at about 2000 ft, and gradually losing height, the crew expected to have to ditch but continued with their efforts to get home. LV792 eased across the Channel and the pilot headed for Hurn airfield firing red Very signals. On receiving the green to land, the pilot ordered the uplocks pulled and the undercarriage fell down and locked; a straight-in landing was made and satisfactorily carried out, in spite of both mainwheel and tailwheel tyres being burnt off.

Three days later LV792 was struck off charge and the instrument panel was claimed by Plt Off Bancroft; this panel now rests in the Australian War Museum, a fitting tribute to a fantastic flight, for aircrew and aircraft. No. 158 Squadron was unlucky that night for, besides LV792 being written off, LK841, LK875, LK877 and LV921 failed to return.

Radio/radar counter-measures were introduced early in the war, but it was not until November 1943 that No.100 Group was formed under the command of Wg Cdr E. Addison to give back-up support to Bomber Command by carrying out an electronic listening watch, radio/radar counter-measures and 'Window'/bombing spoof raids. The electronic listening watch was so effective that there was no German radio or radar equipment unknown to the RAF at the end of the war.

No. 100 Group's first success was in support of the D-Day landings in Normandy, when three Halifax aircraft (LW613, LW621 and LW624) patrolled throughout the night along a route between Tonbridge and Yeovil maintaining a *Mandrel* screen to cover the activities of the Airborne Forces. These Halifaxes were from No.192 Squadron, which had been formed in the previous January and was classed as a 'special duty' unit until incorporated into No. 100 Group.

The major RAF measure against German interception radar was 'Window', which was backed up by a number of airborne and

Air Ministry Bulletin No.14238 10 June 1944 — 'BEES IN A BOMBER: Q FOR QUEENIE. A swarm of bees searching for a home decided to take up their quarters in the port rudder of 'Q' for Queenie, a Halifax bomber at an airfield in the North of England*. Queenie was on operations that night, and while her crew were quite ready for the Germans, they were not prepared to take off with a flight of intruders already inside the bomber. The flight sergeant in charge of the ground staff was called and after a discussion on how to get rid of the swarm, someone remembered that there was a man in the next village who kept bees. So he was called in to do the job, and 'Q' for Queenie took off that night to sting the Germans — but minus the bees!
*No.578 Squadron, RAF Burn.

Bees swarming in tail unit of Halifax Mk.3 LW473 (LK-Q) of No.578 Squadron, RAF Burn, June 1944. Sgt Hugh Sloan and Sgt. Jack Clague, 'Q' for Queenie's air gunners. (IWM)

Ground and aircrews watch while the apiarist dislodges the bees. (IWM)

ground-based transmissions that formed a screen behind which the bomber stream was able to operate, a screen that only the most experienced German radar operators had any success against and which rendered the FuG227 and FuG350 homing radars ineffective. The most serious interference to the German night-fighter force was the jamming of the R/T and W/T links between the ground stations and the fighter force. This was carried out by *Airborne Cigar* and *Jostle 4*, carried by the Halifax and B17 respectively. Unfortunately the electronic jamming equipment suffered from low serviceability.

On 8 September 1944 the second bomber support squadron was formed and was equipped in October with Halifax B3s. Eight of these were ferried to St. Athan on 24 October for the fitting of *Mandrel* equipment. This squadron was No.171, formed from C Flight of No.199 Squadron, and was initially equipped with Stirlings and Halifaxes. The third squadron to join No. 100 Group was No.199, which began its operations on 1 January 1945 and also had its *Airborne Cigar* installation fitted in that month.

Adolf Galland, the most respected of German fighter pilots, must have paid No. 100 Group their highest compliment when he stated that the decrease in night-fighter successes from the middle of 1944 onwards was due to fuel shortage, interference and the activities of No. 100 Group. In his words, this specialist unit did its job so well that it was hardly ever absent from any British night operation and could claim to have set really difficult problems for the German night fighter force.

An attack was made on Bergen on 4 October 1944 by 15 of No. 420 Squadron's Halifaxes. They took off from Tholthorpe just after 05.00 hours and flew to Bergen, with seven aircraft hitting the primary target and the remaining eight attacking the alternative target; ships in the harbour put up a flak barrage. According to the squadron records, bombing of the U-boats was thought to be scattered, but one stick of bombs straddled ships in the water adjoining the U-boat pens. A terrific explosion was heard which resulted

in a big fire, and smoke could be seen for 75 miles on the way back to base. All the aircraft returned safely although four had to land away from base due to fuel shortage.

Fishpond night-fighter search radar had been incorporated into No.4 Group Halifaxes by September 1944 and *Visual Monica* had been withdrawn. The new search radar was not only proving to be more effective but also had better serviceability. It was of the passive type with its CRT in the wireless operator's position; he operated the set and upon the approach of enemy fighters gave the gunners the bearing and distance reading of their target. H2S was also improving in its serviceability, having only 80 failures in 3000 sorties.

By the middle of 1944 the Luftwaffe night-fighter force had increased to 685 aircraft, and by October 1944 to 830 aircraft; this allowed reconnaissance flights to be flown over the North Sea to pick up early warning of British Bomber Command raids, and made possible the feeding-in of night-fighters to the bomber stream much earlier.

The synthetic oil plants, oil refineries, and oil stocks had now become the main targets for both the USAAF and the RAF, so in May the defence of the oil plants in central Germany became the responsibility of the 14th Flak Division. The main synthetic oil plants were at Leuna, Blackhammer, Gelsenkirchen, Ludwigshafen and Wesseling, and, with the major attacks commencing, their defences were further increased, with as many as 300-400 guns around each plant, some guns with calibres up to 12.8 cm. Post-war analysis indicates that the flak defences took a greater toll of the USAAF daylight raiders, while the night-fighters took a greater toll of the RAF night bombers.

RAF Bomber Command joined the USAAF in attacks on the German oil plants in June 1944 after a directive was issued to make them a primary target. One of these attacks was on Gelsenkirchen on the night of 6/7 November 1944 when 738 Bomber Command aircraft took part. Cumulus tops were at 10,000 feet and visibility was good. Halifax loads varied from incendiaries through 500 lb MCs — some with time delays — to 2000 lb HCs. The target was fired up and covered in bomb bursts in a short space of time so the Master Bomber told the crews to bomb on the markers, but as some squadrons could see the Green TIs they bombed these. Flak was intense before the target but only moderate afterwards and no fighters were seen.

Proof of the Halifax's structural strength was given on 13 January 1945, when B3 MZ465 of No. 51 Squadron, piloted by Plt Off (later Sqn Ldr) A. L. Wilson, took part in an attack on Saarbrucken. This account is Sqn Ldr Wilson's own:

. . . Shortly afterwards as I scanned right I saw the other Halifax on collision course from my right. I heaved back on the stick, too late, and as his port wing went underneath me, his port fin knocked the front ten feet off my nose just forward of the rudder bar. My navigator and bomb-aimer were killed and fell to earth with the aircraft's nose section, and the signaller was thrown from his position past the engineer. The four props were all damaged, the dinghy shot out of the wing, damaging the port fin, and the electrics failed. All the flight instruments and engine gauges failed. Whilst we sorted ourselves out we lost some 14,000 feet before stabilising at about 7000 feet. Navigating on the stars, we eventually carried out the distress pattern when we thought we were over England. Descending through 8/8ths cloud we eventually landed at Ford, having had to carry out one overshoot as on the first approach the aircraft was difficult to land.

This was considered to be the most heavily damaged four-engined bomber to return to and land safely in the United Kingdom — and for this magnificent effort the pilot did not receive any flying recognition.

Luftwaffe night-fighters were becoming adept at infiltrating homeward-bound streams of bombers. The No. 4 Group Operational Report dated 1 April 1945 stated that a total of 16 Halifaxes had reported 21 attacks by enemy fighters which resulted in the shooting down of eight aircraft. One of these Halifaxes was NR179 'C' of No. 466 Squadron, which had been called down to 1400 feet after arrival at its base airfield (Driffield). Later given 'Prepare to land', the pilot prepared to approach, but when no permission to land was given he carried out an

Allied troops load containers for No.148 (SD) Squadron Halifax for SOE drop to Partisans in the Balkans. Brindisi, Italy, 1943-44. (RAF Museum).

Halifax Mk.5 Series 1A of No.644 Squadron getting ready to tow off a Hamilcar. Tarrant Rushton, May 1944. (IWM).

overshoot. Then, on his second approach, the airfield lighting was switched off, so the pilot carried out a further overshoot and climbed eventually to 4000 feet because the flight engineer had reported only 15 minutes' fuel left; this was in preparation for baling out. The aircraft was then attacked by a German night-fighter. Both engines and the fuselage on the forward port side were set on fire and there were strikes on the nose; only three of the crew escaped as the aircraft went into a dive — the altitude was too low.

Harry King (ex-flight engineer with No. 466 Squadron) was in the circuit on that night, and says:

The trip itself was normal; our endurance was 6 hours 35 minutes. Only when we called up base did we really discover that there were intruders around, but our rear gunner had stayed in his turret because he had sensed something was wrong. We were instructed to land, on entering the funnels we were told to land, I remember 'C' Charlie calling up and being told to overshoot, as he did this the fighter got in a burst at him and we landed with all our fingers out; when we arrived at the crew room another fighter flew across with all guns going.

The Bomber Command Night Raid Report on the raid on Kamen that night was a typical piece of Lancaster bias. Its summary listed 234 Lancasters and Mosquitoes despatched to raid Kamen; in fact the figures of aircraft taking part were: 201 Halifaxes, 21 Lancasters and 12 Mosquitoes (Night Raid Report 854).

The Halifax squadrons of No. 4 Group had in 1944 carried out 25,464 operational sorties and lost 402 aircraft, which was a great improvement over 1943, when 11,607 operational sorties were carried out for the loss of 485 aircraft. Further to this the Group aircraft had also ferried 432,840 gallons of fuel to Brussels for the British 2nd Army in its push to Arnhem, and the Halifax air gunners shot down 73 enemy aircraft — a record for Bomber Command. No. 4 Group over March 1945 were to drop the largest weight of bombs as well as to have the lowest percentage rate of lost aircraft in Bomber Command.

By the completion of hostilities the Halifaxes of Bomber Command had carried out 82,773 operational sorties in bombing, mining, RCM and other operations; their total casualties were 2236 aircraft missing or wrecked, and they had dropped 224,207 tons of bombs.

At least four Halifaxes are known to have completed 100 operations, the best known being Halifax B3 LV907 of No. 158 Squadron at Lissett. Named *Friday the Thirteenth* and embellished with all manner of bad luck items, it completed its hundreth op on 22/23 January 1945 with a raid on Gelsenkirchen and went on to complete 128 operational sorties by VE-Day. The pride of No. 158 Squadron and its crews, LV907 never failed an operation.

With VE-Day over, eyes turned to the Far East but, while 'Tiger Force' and its Lancasters were being prepared, 1341 SD Flight had already been formed and sent to

India. The Flight came into being at West Kirby on 21 December 1944 with Halifax B3s, and arrived in the Far East on 14 February 1945. It was then amalgamated with No. 159 Squadron and pinpointed radar installations of the Japanese for the attention of Liberator bombers. The Halifaxes had long-range bomb-bay tanks and were fitted with RCM equipment. Some of the aircraft serial numbers were PN369, PN370, PN371, PN381 and PN382. After numerous long flights the final operation was on 1 September with a flight to Port Blair.

At the end of this section on Bomber Command operations the conclusion must be drawn that Avro's ignored the P13/36 specification requirement and produced a specialist aircraft for the carriage of large bombs, while Handley Page's, heeding the specification, produced the Halifax, which successfully accomplished a range of tasks, from bombing to transport, and in its final marks was an aircraft of superb performance. So in the end the RAF reaped the benefit, for

they had two aircraft types to cover all tasks, with the Halifax available to do everything bar carry the extra-large bombs.

One final thing needs saying. It must be remembered that behind each crew and every operation were scores of other ranks, the 'Erks', the Service ground-crews whose unglamorous role was vital in getting the crews and aircraft airborne. The aircraft ground-crews in particular worked out on the windswept dispersals in all weathers, servicing their aircraft without benefit of special warm clothing; struggling with pipe unions or removing spark plugs, struggling to load bombs slimy with rain and mud, while the wind and frost froze their fingers or rain dribbled down their necks. The ground crews saw the aircraft off and were still there in the early hours of the morning, waiting on the safe return of their crew and aircraft.

No special medal was struck for Bomber Command crews, but neither was any medal or recognition ever given to the ground-crews in recognition of the long cold days and nights

Halifax Mk.5s of No.298 Squadron with Horsas and Hamilcars at Woodbridge, 24 March 1945. (IWM).

making the bomber offensive a success. Yet most Halifax ground crew members that I have met or corresponded with never groused about this; they have a warm affection for the old 'Halibag', found that servicing it was in general easier than with other aircraft types, and most felt that the 'Halibag' was 'short-changed' in regard to recognition of its contribution to the war effort.

Anti-submarine operations

The Halifax entered the Coastal Command scene on 24 October 1942, when detachments of five Halifax aircraft from No. 158 Squadron and five more from No. 405 Squadron were placed under control of Coastal Command HQ for anti-submarine duties.

Prior to this decision, and early in 1942, the Luftwaffe had been able to carry out offensive operations against merchant shipping in the North Atlantic, and submarines were operating across the Bay of Biscay into the Atlantic. But from May 1942 the Flag Officer U-boats in the Bay of Biscay was requesting the help of the Fliegerführer Atlantic for defensive protection over the Bay against Coastal Command anti-submarine aircraft, which were attacking the U-boats in their passage to and from their bases at Bordeaux, La Pallice, Lorient and St. Nazaire. This resulted in June in the formation of a Luftwaffe unit of nine Ju88 fighters for anti-Coastal Command duties, the strength of the unit eventually being increased to 34 aircraft.

So by the end of the year the Halifax was on anti-submarine operations in the form of the detachments from No. 158 and No. 405 Squadrons, and although the No. 158 Squadron aircraft returned to Bomber Command in December, those of No. 405 Squadron continued until March 1943, when they also were withdrawn.

By that date two Coastal Command squadrons were operational with the Halifax: Nos. 58 and 502. A group of Coastal Command officers had in late 1942 approached Handley Page's to discuss the conversion of Halifax aircraft for anti-submarine employment. This resulted in the equipment of No. 58 Squadron in December 1942 with Mk.2 Series 1A aircraft, followed by the equipping of No. 502 Squadron with the same aircraft in January 1943. These aircraft were powered by Merlin 20 or 22 engines and had an all-up weight of 60,000 lbs; their armament was modified by the replacement of the nose Vickers 'K' VGO with a Browning 0.5 inch and the fitment of a FN64 mid-under turret — although a few of the early aircraft did join the squadrons fitted with the 0.303 inch Vickers 'K' gun up front. It appears that No. 58 Squadron were the first to mount a 0.5 inch Browning in the nose, as it was felt that a heavier calibre weapon was required to keep the U-boat crews from their AA guns.

In February 1943 servicing crews moved into the two Coastal Command squadrons and began fitting ASV Mk.3 and *Boozer* equipment. Later on, Halifax aircraft destined for Coastal Command were picked up by ATA crews from the parent factory and delivered to Marwell Hall (the dispersal site for Eastleigh) for conversion to Coastal Command requirements by Cunliffe-Owen; approximately two weeks later they were collected and flown to St. Athan for the fitting of ASV equipment.

Coastal Command were more silent than the supposed Silent Service, spending month after month surveying countless miles of ocean, scanning the ASV for a possible indication of a U-boat, scanning the sea's surface for a periscope's trace; countless hours of noise, boredom and discomfort, coupled with the possibility of ditching in near-freezing seas. Yet for some crews there was the satisfaction of a successful attack: after 13 previous unsuccessful attacks by No.58 Squadron Halifaxes, on the 7 May 1943 Wg Cdr W. Oulton (CO) in 'S' of No.58 Squadron stalked and sank U-663. This appears to have broken the run of bad luck, for on 15 May Wg Cdr Oulton and crew, after a long, arduous patrol over heavy seas and after many false sightings, caught U-463 on the surface. The depth charges landed close to

No.298 Squadron Halifax A5 towing a Horsa Mk.2 glider from Tarrant Rushton airfield. (David Wells).

the port side of the U-boat and in a few seconds its bow had risen vertically, then slowly subsided into and under the waves with just debris coming to the surface — success after a long flight.

As the year 1943 progressed and the attacks on both U-boats and enemy coastal shipping became even more successful, Ju88 fighter packs began roaming the Bay of Biscay, with the result that three of No.58 Squadron's Halifaxes became the victims instead of the hunters; U-boats were gradually fitted with more anti-aircraft guns and of larger calibre, remained on the surface when attacked and began to fight back. This was countered by the aircraft being fitted with heavier armament too, such as 20 mm cannon or rockets.

Coastal Command Beaufighters now joined the hunt for U-boats, enemy shipping and for Ju88s, so with the Beaus roaming the seas from the Arctic to the Bay of Biscay the enemy seaborne traffic was forced to travel at night. This resulted in the Halifax and other Coastal Command heavy aircraft concentrating their searching by night, flying at 1000 ft scanning their ASV for a trace and dropping flares once a contact had been made. To help improve the situation a new low-level bombsight was tested in February 1943 and Mk.5 Series 1 aircraft were also

passed over to Coastal Command.

In April the Air Ministry advised the Halifax squadrons that the all-up weight for take-off was restricted to 60,000 lb, which resulted in No.502 Squadron dispensing with their armour plating because they wished to carry their maximum depth charge load and as much fuel as possible.

With their night sorties Coastal Command was denying the seas to German shipping, which resulted in the Luftwaffe introducing anti-Coastal Command Ju88 night-fighter patrols to counter the Halifax and other aircraft's night attacks; this in turn was countered by the Halifaxes flying even lower, so as both to evade the attentions of the Ju88s and to get below the radar cover. This unfortunately also placed the Halifax in an unenviable position when attacking an enemy vessel, for any and every weapon could then be brought to bear on it — and flying at night over sea at low level was a most dangerous pastime in any case.

After long-endurance flights Coastal Command aircraft often arrived back at base low on fuel and with their airfields 'clagged in', and the diversion from the coast in such circumstances often spelled disaster. This happened to HR688 of No.502 Squadron on 29 March 1943, when it was diverted due to bad weather and crashed at Maundown Hill,

Somerset. It happened to other aircraft as well, although some just disappeared over the Atlantic 'cause unknown', such as LL123 of No.518 Squadron which vanished over the Atlantic while on Met. Flight duties on 21 January 1945.

When it was decided to extend the meteorological services, which was one part of Coastal Command's responsibilities, Halifaxes were modified and took over these duties in early 1944. They were thus able not only to extend the operating range of search further into the Atlantic, but also to check the pressures, temperatures and winds from sea level to heights that had not been possible before. On the basis of meteorological gatherings carried out by two Halifaxes (one from No.517 Squadron and one from No.518 Squadron) and an American Met. aircraft just prior to D-Day the decision was taken for the invasion of Europe to begin.

The Halifaxes selected for conversion to Met. duties were Mk.5s and were delivered from the factory to Cunliffe-Owen where conversion was carried out. This entailed the fitting of special Met. equipment and a Met. observer's station with what has been termed 'a reasonable amount of comfort'! One Met. pilot, when asked his opinion of these flights, remarked, 'Bloody boring and too much water'.

By the end of the war Coastal Command Halifaxes had been responsible for the sinking of eight U-boats, possibly nine — how many more were damaged by attacks is not known. The Met. role was continued until the end of the war and after, commencing with Halifax Met. 5s of No.517 Squadron, until in 1945-46 there were five squadrons flying Halifaxes, though by then the aircraft were Met. 3s or 6s.

The potential of the Halifax for Coastal Command was almost seen in the original requirements of P13/36 and Handley Page's interpretation of them: the use of wing bomb-bay position for flotation bags, carriage of two torpedoes and the production of the Halifax with ample room inside for crew, equipment and rest-bay, with plenty of room for fully equipped aircrew to scramble over the main spar. Even Fairey Aviation during the production of the Halifax recognised the potential in the Halifax for conversion into a tricycle undercarriage freighter, so there was room indeed. It is just sad to relate that, like Bomber Command, upon the cessation of hostilities Coastal Command's establishment was reviewed, so that by the start of 1947, the number of Halifaxes in that command began to decrease.

Special/Airborne Support Operations

The Halifax with its commodious fuselage and lifting capability was an ideal aircraft for many roles, not least of which was the Special Duty, Special Operations Executive (SOE) and Airborne Support roles. Unfortunately, most of the aircraft supplied to the squadrons carrying out these operations were initially of the 'time expired' variety from other Commands and thus short of breath (power) and low on serviceability. In point of fact Air Chief Marshal Harris was strongly against any attempt to use bomber aircraft for anything other than bombing Germany, and ignored the necessity, and in some cases the soundness, of diverting aircraft for use in SOE or Airborne Support operations. This was partly because, over a period of time, he had already lost squadrons to Coastal Command or the Middle East theatre of operations, so was obviously wary of any other diversion of aircraft and crews. Nevertheless, at a time when more aircraft were required to sink U-boats and win the Battle of the Atlantic, and so ensure supplies to the UK — including fuel for Bomber Command aircraft — bombers were being used to carry out attacks against bomb-proof submarine pens in Occupied Europe.

This in no way questions the stature of Sir Arthur Harris as one of the great Commanders, for in many cases he was acting on orders from above, but for all that he never appreciated the need for aircraft for SOE and Airborne Support squadrons. A few SOE operations with supplies dropped to the resistance movements in Europe could do far more damage, more cheaply, to some of the smaller targets than could the bombers — and with fewer casualties to the people of Occupied Europe.

Two instances of this will illustrate the point. In July 1943 four SOE agents not only killed 12 of the Gestapo but also brought the canal system connected the Ruhr to the Mediterranean to a complete halt at a critical period in the war. The damage took four months to repair, no aircraft or crews were lost and no civilians were killed or injured; the cost was the price of the explosives and the use of the aircraft to transport the agents. The second instance occurred in June 1944, when an SOE agent met the foreman of the Ratier propeller factory, which was then turning out 300 propellers a week for the Luftwaffe. By the judicious use of small explosive charges half a dozen irreplaceable machine tools were ruined and production stopped until the area was liberated.

The aircraft side of SOE began in late 1940 with the formation of No.419 Flight, which was later renumbered 1419 Flight to prevent confusion with No.419 Squadron; but the Halifax did not come on the SOE scene until late 1941 when the Flight, under orders from Portal, was given squadron status and establishment and renumbered 138 Squadron.

The first operation with the Halifax aircraft of No.138 Squadron did not take place until the 7/8 November 1941, as initially the aircraft was not considered to have sufficient range for the SOE flights to Poland. This first operation was by one aircraft and the drop in Poland was at the extreme end of the aircraft's range. Unfortunately, as on so many aircraft operations during the war, actual weather and weather forecasts didn't tally and aircraft were lost; in this case, on the return journey stronger headwinds were encountered than had been forecast and fuel began to run low, so the Polish pilot decided to divert to Sweden, where he crash-landed the aircraft.

The No.1 route was across Denmark and entailed a journey of 960 miles to Warsaw and a flight time of 10-14 hours to central Poland, but when the German night-fighter force became effective and casualties started to rise the No.2 route was opened, which ran across Sweden but reduced the distance that the Halifax could penetrate into Poland. Drops continued, mostly of arms, explosives, etc, but also including Polish resistance fighters — termed 'Joes' by the aircrew, as no names were known or exchanged.

On 18 December 1941 came a move for No.138 Squadron to Stradishall, when the squadron had on its strength three Halifaxes — hardly enough to bankrupt Bomber Command, and far from sufficient in numbers to have any effect on the demand for the transport of supplies to the various resistance groups in Occupied Europe. Special Duty squadrons on SOE drops operated around the 500 ft mark and their navigators had to be spot on, for unlike Bomber Command they had no H2S, no flares or target indicators to drop on, and the dropping zone (DZ) was minute in size. If the DZ was not 'live' on arrival, the aircraft circled for a while before being map-read by the bomb-aimer to the next (alternative) dropping zone.

On 14 March 1942 the squadron moved again, this time to Tempsford, which had been specially built and equipped for the SOE squadrons. It was at Tempsford that the squadron joined the newly formed No.161 Squadron, and it was at Tempsford that the Halifax 2 Series 1 (Special) originated, as explained earlier.

Halifax A9 RT764: one of the first manufacturing batch. (David Wells.)

SOE flights to Poland entailed flights of approximately 2000 miles carrying a payload of 2400 lb, so range and speed were required as well as sufficient accommodation and a good exit. To suit all these SOE requirements the Halifax was suitably modified, including the provision of a dropping hatch in place of a mid-under turret. It will be remembered that one of the requirements of P13/36 was the provision of a dropping hatch.

In No.138 Squadron was a Polish Flight, designated 301 Polish Flight and equipped with three Halifax and three Liberator aircraft. This flight was later withdrawn from No.138 Squadron and transferred to Tunis, where it was attached to No.148 Squadron, re-designated 1586 SD Flight and came under the control of No.334 Wing. No.148 Squadron had been reformed as a SD squadron and re-equipped with Halifaxes as from 18 February 1943; its eventual establishment was ten Halifaxes and four Liberators and it supplied the various resistance movements in the Mediterranean area.

SOE operations were not the sole prerogative of the SD squadrons, for Airborne Support squadrons of No.38 Wing (later Group) were also called on to carry them out — the same squadrons being used for bombing operations when not involved in air support exercises or operations. The Halifax was suited to all these roles and its versatility and strength were appreciated by the crews who flew her.

No.38 Wing was formed in Army Co-operation Command in June 1942 for the purpose of providing transport for the British Airborne Forces, which had been set up at the Central Landing Establishment at Ringway in September 1940. This was followed by the establishment of the Airborne Forces Development Unit in October of the same year, but the Halifax did not join the AFDU until 12 months later, when R9435 was the first to arrive. It was engaged on various trials at Ringway, being joined by other Halifaxes on the trials with the Horsa and Hamilcar gliders.

The Halifaxes in No.38 Group were suitably modified and used for glider towing, paratrooping, SOE drops and bombing. These were originally Mk.2s and Mk.5s, which first entered service with No.295 Squadron. The strengths of No.38 Wing squadrons were in low-flying and pinpoint navigation; no radar aids were used until later years when airborne *Rebecca* was used in conjunction with *Eureka* at the DZ, for the location of the dropping zone.

On 9 November 1942 two Halifax-Horsa combinations took off from Scotland; their destination was the German heavy water plant at Ryukan in Norway. Each glider carried 15 sappers, with the whole ground party under the command of Lt Methven, while Sqn Ldr Wilkinson (flying one of the Halifaxes) was in command of the detachment. The heavy water plant was located in a deep forested valley with 3000 foot sides, and the dropping zone was manned by Norwegian underground personnel. One combination opted to fly low to Norway but, partly due to an inaccurate weather forecast, landfall was not where planned, with the result that the tug aircraft flew into the hills and its glider crash-landed, with its occupants severely injured or dead. The other tug could not locate the landing zone, so after a search and with fuel running low the combination was forced to turn for the UK. Unfortunately, due to turbulence over the Norwegian coast the tow parted and the second glider crash-landed. The survivors from both gliders were tortured and eventually killed by the Gestapo. The tug, flown by Sqn Ldr Wilkinson, managed to make landfall safely in the UK, though low on fuel,

When it was decided to have a 'heavy lift' on the Sicilian invasion it was imperative that Horsa gliders be taken to North Africa. With this in view, a number of long flights by Halifax-Horsa combinations around the UK were undertaken by Gp Capt Cooper and Sqn Ldr Wilkinson to determine the feasibility of towing the Horsas to North Africa. The results of these tests showed the practicality of using the Halifax for such a task — the Halifaxes being fitted with bomb-bay fuel tanks. As no night flight towing had been

A No.298 Squadron Halifax A7 carrying a Jeep, Far East 1946. (Author)

carried out up to that date the flights across the Bay of Biscay to Gibraltar were made in daylight. Each Horsa carried three glider pilots because the glider had no autopilot and because the long flight placed an exceptionally heavy physical and mental strain on the glider pilot, who had to maintain the glider in the right tow position to try to prevent any possibility of the tow-rope parting.

The RAF Halifax-Horsa combinations took off from RAF Portreath in Cornwall with orders to deliver 30 Horsas to Salle, near Casablanca; waiting air and ground crews watched the first combination lift off, then disappear below their line of sight, to appear again a little later climbing away, with the familiar smoke trail belching from the Merlin engine exhausts. The first glider was flown by Major Cooper and Sgts Hall and Antonopoulos, but their luck was out and the flight ended with the tow-rope parting and the Horsa ditching, the glider pilots being safely picked up later. The first combination to arrive safely in North Africa was the second one to take off, the tug being flown by Flt Lt 'Buster' Briggs and the glider by Col. G. Chatterton, P. Attwood and H. Flynn.

During these delivery flights, which were

given the code name of *Turkey-Buzzard*, one combination disappeared completely while another was attacked by German aircraft over the Bay, approximately 140 miles west of Cap Finisterre. The glider pilot gallantly wanted to cast off, but the tug pilot insisted that he stay on tow while the rear gunner of the Halifax tried to fight off the enemy aircraft. This one-sided fight finished with the Halifax being shot down and the glider ditching. Two of the glider pilots had been in the first glider that had ditched, so their remarks were unprintable.

It may be of interest to point out that it was an unwritten law among glider-towing crews that no matter how bad a situation they were in — engine on fire or engine failure after take-off — they must not cast the tow-rope off first, but order the glider to cast off before releasing the tow-rope; in other words the well-being of the glider and crew had to take precedence over their own safety. With both glider and tug crews living on the same airfield, messing and flying together, a bond of friendship and comradeship built up.

The Halifax-Horsa combinations were used on both airborne assaults on Sicily along with Dakota para-transports and Albemarle tugs; neither of these operations could be classed as classics in airborne assaults, although the extreme gallantry and fortitude on the part of the airborne troops and paratroops ensured that the objectives were taken. During the attacks one of the casualties was Sqn Ldr Wilkinson's Halifax, which was lost on the attack on Ponte Grande.

With the development of the Airborne Forces the Halifaxes modified for No.38 Wing were mainly the Mk.5 Series 1 (Special), though some Mk.2s were used. These were later replaced with Mk.5 Series 1A aircraft — and again, some of these had seen better days in other Commands. Alterations to the aircraft were the removal of the mid-upper turret, moving the rear turret ammunition tracks and boxes to new positions nearer the turret, the fitting of a No. 6A towing and release unit on an outrigger under the tail, with a release handle fitted on the right-hand side of the throttle box, and the installation of a paratroop exit in the position where the H2S or under-turret was normally fitted. A requirement of glider-towing aircraft of the Halifax series was that they must be fitted with either 12 ft 9 in or 13 ft diameter propellers; sometimes a combination of three or four-blade propellers was fitted.

Halifax glider tugs took part in all glider operations involving British Airborne Forces in Europe, from and including the Sicilian landings. On D-Day their involvement was not only the towing of gliders but also the dropping of troops, and dummies to simulate paratroop attacks.

From September 1944, and after the Arnhem operation, three Albemarle squadrons of No.38 Group converted to the Halifax 5 aircraft: Nos 295, 296 and 297 Squadrons. No.644 had been formed from C Flight of No.298 Squadron on 16 March 1944 and this also re-equipped with the Halifax in the August of the same year. Both Nos 298 and 644 Squadrons operated alongside each other from Tarrant Rushton in Dorset, which was an ideal airfield for learning the glider towing business.

A mass take-off of Halifax-Horsa (or Hamilcar) combinations was an exercise in good discipline. The gliders were stationed along the runway while the Halifaxes were positioned each side of the runway and connected by their tow-ropes to their individual gliders. Upon clearance being given, the Halifax moved onto the runway and took up the slack in the tow-rope, then checked with the glider pilot that he was ready for take-off.

When the answer was 'yes' and the green given for take-off the Halifax tug commenced to roll, with the glider lifting off and moving into the high tow position and the next combination by now moving into the take-off position and starting to roll, and so on. An average time for each take-off was 45 seconds. The dangerous part of glider towing — apart from enemy action — came on the mass release of the gliders, with tugs left, right and centre getting out of the landing zone area with tow-ropes flailing around behind them; each tow-rope was 350 ft long with a diameter of $3\frac{7}{8}$ ins for the Horsa and $4\frac{1}{4}$ ins for the Hamilcar.

For the RAF D-Day operation, No.38 and No.46 Groups had available a total of 362 aircraft plus 61 in reserve and 1120 gliders, of which 70 were Hamilcars and thus only towable by Halifax aircraft. For this task there were only two Halifax-equipped squadrons (Nos 298 and 644). One of No.298 Squadron's pilots was Geoff Cunliffe, who remembers D-Day as follows:

D-Day operation, Horsa tow; we were told at briefing that there would be turbulence. What we were not told at briefing was that besides turbulence there would be cloud over the French coast at precisely the height we were flying, and amongst all this we were attracting the attention of light flak at the same time. The aircraft was being pulled all over the place with me trying to keep some form of control by instruments. On coming out of cloud and spotting the drop zone I found that all I was towing was a broken tow-rope. Fortunately, I learned later that the glider had been able to land within a reasonable distance of his landing zone.

A Halifax GTV towing a Horsa glider.

Prior to the Arnhem operation No.38 Group had carried out night glider-towing exercises, as well as a number of daytime mass exercises and demonstrations, but on 17 September 1944 the landing of the 1st Airborne Division began in daylight; still only Nos 298 and 644 Squadrons were equipped with the Halifax, 40 of which were available. There were three lifts and the first day sorties were flown without incident, but by the third day the enemy opposition was organised and flak lined each side of the flight corridor. The story of Arnhem has been told and retold so little more needs to be said, except that more information on the pre-planning would be of interest to some of us, and secondly, that the Halifax again played its part, towing both Horsas and Hamilcars.

While all these operations were happening in Northern Europe the Halifaxes in the Middle East were stirring things up in their area, with both special duties and bombing operations. No.148 Squadron had been equipped with Halifax and Liberator aircraft in March 1943 and in January 1944 moved to Brindisi as part of No.334 Wing. The squadron crews became the modern gun-runners of 1943-45, for more than 5000 tons of arms, ammunition and equipment as well as resistance personnel were dropped to patriotic groups in the Balkans. The Halifaxes went in at about 200 feet, looking for a light at the DZ. When it was given a reply identification was sent down and the drop commenced. Time spent at the DZ was minimal, mainly for the sake of the resistance group, for obviously the longer the Halifax spent around the DZ the longer the Germans had to hunt for and locate the area.

Before a pilot new to the squadron could carry out a job he had to do at least one successful drop with an experienced crew, which was understandable as the drop was made in open fields miles from towns, with the only identification being an open fire or a torch; so it was essential to have a good navigator and a good map-reading bomb-aimer.

The squadron also took part in trying to supply Warsaw during the Polish rising

against the Germans there, which meant flights of the order of $9\frac{1}{2}$ to 10 hours duration, made over dangerous mountains in extremely bad weather. As the Halifaxes and Liberators approached the burning city, it appeared as if it was one complete sheet of flame with smoke billowing into the sky. Flying as low as possible and with the flaps down to get the airspeed down to about 120/130 mph the aircraft were the target for any and every calibre of weapon. Soon the smoke even found its way into the aircraft, while on the ground it obliterated the landmarks and made it almost impossible to identify any of the DZs. From these RAF operations to supply Warsaw 245 Polish, British and South African airmen failed to return and of the 192 drops made to the Poles very few reached the hands of the resistance.

Typical of an SOE drop in Northern Europe would be a briefing in mid afternoon, covering the weather, routes into and out of the area concerned, flak areas, time for the drop, the DZ, the code letter for the resistance group, and also any other air activities in that area. Aircraft would take off at individual times, climb on course to approximately 7000 feet — though flights to Holland usually kept as low as possible to creep under the radar — then dive across the coast and level off at about 200-250 feet until reaching the DZ.

Prior to the Arnhem operation the Halifax had added another transport duty to its repertoire: a heavy duty beam was slung in the bomb-bay and from this a Jeep and six-pounder gun could be slung, transported and dropped by parachutes; this was used in conjunction with SAS troops and with supply containers in the wings. The gun and Jeep were dropped first, followed by the containers and then the troops jumped from the fuselage dropping hatch.

These Jeep and gun combinations with SAS troops were dropped just before and just after D-Day by Halifaxes of No.38 Group, and the task for these troops and combinations was to join up with resistance groups and so add a mobile and heavy 'thump' to the small arms of the resistance, thus forcing the Germans to use more troops

A No.298 Squadron Halifax A7 without its bomb doors, Far East 1946. (Author)

on security duties.

The final major airborne support operation of the war in Europe took place on 24 March 1945 with the transport of the Allied Airborne Army across the Rhine. The time between the Arnhem drop and the Rhine operation was taken up with conversion to Halifax aircraft, re-equipment with Halifax A3s and exercises with mass formations. One pilot of No.297 Squadron, who converted onto the Halifax during this period, was Flt Lt K. Garnett, who says of the Halifax: 'Very strongly constructed, good pilot's visibility, crew area spacious, excellent handling. With four radial engines it had good performance even on three engines'.

For the Rhine crossing the operation was codenamed *Varsity* and USAAF General Brereton was placed in charge of the air operations. He had already decided that another Arnhem must not occur and insisted on one massive airlift; 1795 troop carriers were available and 1305 tugs. For the British contingent there were 440 Horsas and Hamilcars, and six squadrons of tugs in the heavy category.

The planning and preparation for this operation were excellent, although, like all airborne support operations, the results were 'By guess and by God'. Over 21,000 airborne

troops and paratroops were transported in; Halifaxes towed in fully loaded Hamilcars with No.298 and No.644 Squadrons operating from Woodbridge and Nos 296 and 297 Squadrons from Earls Colne. Of this operation Geoff Cunliffe remarks:

The Rhine crossing was a fairly straightforward operation with not a lot of opposition. Two things remain strongly in my memory. The first was the escorting fighters literally forming a queue to knock out any flak position

Gun and Jeep load on Halifax A9 of No.47 Squadron, Fairford 1947 (Author)

which dared to fire. The other was of the Hamilcar directly ahead of me suddenly bursting open at the nose and the tank and tank crew coming through and falling to the ground.

The operation was a total success and opened the way for the 21st Army to strike deep into Germany and roll up the North German armies to the Elbe. An interesting innovation was the use of three Halifaxes fitted with special radios to act as Master Supply aircraft and direct the aircraft to the six dropping points. From this operation 41 aircraft were lost, including five Halifaxes shot down by flak.

In May 1945 No.38 Group took part in the transfer of the 1st Airborne Division's troops and equipment to Copenhagen to take over from the Germans, and this was followed by Operation *Doomsday*, which was the airborne transfer of 7000 troops and 2000 tons of supplies to Norway. The landing of British troops in Norway was to forestall any German idea of fighting on or any possible incidents after the German surrender. No.38 Group aircraft flew the troops to Oslo, Stavanger and Kristiansand on 11 to 14 May,

a little later than anticipated due to bad weather, which also caused the diversion of some Halifaxes to airfields different from the intended ones. The Halifaxes later returned to their home airfields with souvenirs of their flights — not flak or fighter damage, but German flags and paraphernalia; though rumours spread that the odd one or two military Volkswagens found their way back via a Halifax bomb-bay!

After the war in Europe the next area for liberation was the Far East, which would mean airborne landings at vital spots, so the Halifax A3 would be required for the heavy tow. No.298 squadron was one of those chosen to move eastwards with their Halifaxes: new crews were posted in, new A7 aircraft were delivered, and lectures given on flying in the Far East, with stress laid on the predilection of the Japanese for suicidal attacks. Starting in June 1945 the squadron began to fly eastwards in groups. Then came the atom bomb and VJ-Day, so out of the 38 Group squadrons to move to the east only No.298 Squadron actually got there. Afterwards, Nos 620 and 644 Squadrons left for the Middle East and a base in Palestine.

Chapter 9
The Transport Halifax

The aircraft and its operators

The potential of the Halifax for conversion into a transport aircraft was considered over a long period. In Specification P13/36 one of the original requirements called for the provision in the design for the accommodation of personnel inside the fuselage, and even while the P13/36 was still a project Air Commodore Verney in June 1937 was asking Handley Page's whether it could be converted to carrying passengers. The aerodynamics section at Handley Page's investigated this but considered that the HP56's high structural weight and the Vulture engines would not make it an outstanding civil aircraft and notified 'HP' to this effect.

From 1942 Handley Page's were considering the possibility of a Halifax being converted to a freighter for carrying Halifax spare parts. On 22 May 1942 'HP' in a letter to Volkert referred to future policy and development in design work on the Halifax, with the first proposal being basically a large diameter fuselage of at least 9 ft for the transport of Halifax components. The third proposal was a large diameter fuselage similar to the first proposal but adaptable as an ordinary civil freight or mail carrier; the fourth proposal was similiar to the third but adaptable as a high-speed passenger carrier or trooper.

In January 1943 Handley Page's submitted proposals to the MAP for a civil transport — a look to the future at a time when Britain and its Allies were still fighting their way back. No encouragement was forthcoming from the MAP, but this did not dissuade Handley Page's from beginning preliminary design work under the type designation of HP64, which progressed to the point where an approach was made to H. Roxbee Cox and

Walter Tye to discuss civil airworthiness of the project. By August the Second Brabazon Committee had before them Paper No.44, which was a note from BOAC giving a comparison between York and Halifax transport conversions. Meanwhile, in mid-1943 the Air Staff had carried out an exercise to produce a cheap and quickly adaptable interim military transport named 'Transport A' and an unarmed production version of the 'A' named 'Transport B'. In November, in a conference with DTD and DOR, Volkert discussed the HP64 and HP66 — the HP64 being considered both for civil use and as a military transport carrying 20 paratroops and a total of 12 containers. DTD referred to his 'Transport A' and 'B' and said that the 'A' must be a conversion of maximum simplicity, and that the H2S might be retained as a navigation aid, so no priority was given to the HP64 ('Transport C'), which faded from the immediate scene but reappeared against Specification 15/43, finally to emerge, much modified, as the HP67 Hastings.

At Handley Page's the 'Transport A' was finally envisaged as a stripped Halifax Mk.3 or Mk.7 with the minimum of conversion. The first such conversion was a Mk.3 (LV838) with a trial installation of a bomb-bay pannier (mod. 1377) that had been developed by RAF Transport Command Development Unit. 'Transport B' was an unarmed version of the Halifax, with a tail cone replacing the rear turret, and was fitted with a mod.1377 pannier. This version was the HP70 Halifax C8 — the prototype being a converted Mk.6 PP225 — and fulfilled the need for a high-capacity, high-speed freighter, so an order was placed for 100 aircraft for the RAF and given top priority; all were to be produced at Handley Page's at Cricklewood. The C8 model had mod.1192 features (freight or 11

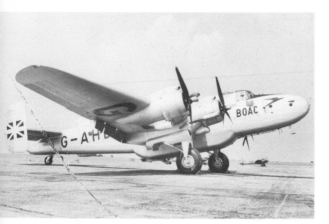

BOAC Halton Aircraft G-AHDU (*Falkirk*)
(British Airways).

passengers or 10 stretchers), mod 1377 pannier (8000 lb) and the fuselage had extra windows in the fuselage forward of the crew entrance. The crew for the RAF Halifax C8 was two pilots, wireless operator, navigator and flight engineer.

The first Halifax production C8 was PP217 and was delivered for trials to the Air Transport Development Unit. But prior to this a number of Halifax aircraft to 'Transport A' specification had been delivered to various units for trials and also route proving; one of these units was No.187 Squadron. In November 1945 No.301 (Polish) Squadron was nominated for re-equipment with Halifax C8s — typical serial numbers were PP221, PP223, PP225, PP233, PP236, PP328, PP334 — and after a period of training began to carry out freight/passenger flights to the Middle East. Then No.304 (Polish) Squadron also converted to Halifax C8s but before they began to operate an order was issued cancelling all flying by both squadrons due to repatriation of personnel. Some of No.304 Squadron's aircraft were PP232, PP236, PP270, PP275, PP283 and PP319. Only these two squadrons were equipped with the C8, although a few aircraft were used by other units and experimental establishments.

After the war and upon its release from RAF service the C8 was the main version to fulfil the needs of the civil market as a fast freighter in the post-war years, both in Great Britain and Europe. The first civil Halifax C8 was PP336, which was purchased through Thomas Cook & Son Ltd on 25 February 1946 for HRH the Maharajah Gaekwar of Baroda, who required a fast transport to get him from his home in Baroda to his horse-breeding and racing stables at Newmarket. The aircraft was flown to Radlett for conversion, Rumbolds doing the cabin soundproofing and furnishing, while Handley Page's fitted heavy duty tyres and wheels and more powerful brakes. It received its C of A on 20 March 1946, was registerd G-AGZP and was operated on behalf of HRH by British American Air Services, who supplied the operating crew and were responsible for the servicing.

The best-known civil conversion of the Halifax was of course Captain G. N. Wikner's *Waltzing Matilda*, which was originally a Mk.3 NR169, HD-T, of No.466 (RAAF) Squadron and which had carried out 51 raids. Upon its purchase from the Ministry of Aircraft Production by Captain Wikner it was sent to Handley Page's at Radlett in the February of 1946 for conversion to a civil transport for the carriage of 15 passengers and baggage, being given the registration G-AGXA. Apart from getting his family and passengers back to Australia, Captain Wikner wished to use the aircraft for exhibitions and fund raising. Upon its reappearance after conversion it appeared very much as it had in wartime; although all its armour and armament had been removed the gun turret cupolas were still in place, and basic seating had been fitted.

Taking-off on 26 May 1946 with all seats filled with returning servicemen, crew and the Wikner family, Captain Wikner headed for Australia, estimating that G-AGXA had a still-air range of 2000 miles and was good for 11 hours in the air. G-AGXA touched down at Sydney on 15 June with a flying time from England of 71 hours. It was then registered as VH-BDT ready for exhibition flying, but unfortunately no financial support for this could be obtained and the aircraft was sold to a group of pilots and engineers for air trading in the Far East. They in their turn went into

1500 gallon bulk fuel lorry tank installed in Halifax bomb-bay by Airtech Ltd for use on Berlin Airlift. (Airtech Ltd).

liquidation and *Waltzing Matilda* was sold at an auction to a scrap dealer. The full story of the flight was told by Captain Wikner in *Aeroplane Monthly* in September 1979, which he concluded with: 'A sad ending for such a wonderful aeroplane'.

In the previous year, in September 1945, BOAC had requested and obtained the loan of three Halifax C8 aircraft for a three-month period, these aircraft to be run extensively with inspections and overhauls being done at night at the terminal point. The three guinea-pig aircraft — PP325, PP326, and PP327 — operated on the West African routes from London, 4500 miles of varying conditions and temperatures, from October to December, one flying the equivalent of 3061 hours per year while another had a utilisation almost as high. The average flying time was 45 hrs 27

min and servicing was 3.43 man-hours per flying hour. Comments and criticisms from BOAC covered weatherproofing and draughts, hydraulic system minor changes, fuel contents gauges unreliable, sharp projections in the fuselage, rough edges on controls, and numerous small items. These must be seen against the fact that the C8s were basically bomber airframes, but the criticisms were not ignored by Handley Page.

In April 1946, Handley Page issued a brochure on their HP 70 Halton interim civil transport, which was a passenger conversion of the Halifax C8 carried out by Short & Harland of Belfast. The main features of the Halton were the replacement of the glazed nose by a skinned 'solid' nose in which mail, etc could be carried, and a large entrance door on the starboard side which replaced the crew entrance door on the port side. The portholes were replaced with 15 by 12 inch windows and a fully equipped galley was provided forward of the main cabin. A pannier (Figure 20) capable of taking loads up to 8000 lb was fitted below the fuselage in what used to be the bomb-bay — similar to the C3 and other conversions. The all-up weight of the aircraft at take-off was 68,000 lb. General data supplied by Handley Page's for the Halton were:

Wingspan	103 ft 8 ins	(31.6 m)
Length	73 ft 7 ins	(22.4 m)
Height — tail down, static	20 ft 8 ins	(6.3 m)
Undercarriage track	24 ft 8 ins	(7.54 m)
Wing area	1275 sq ft	(118.3 sq m)
Tare weight	37,750 lb	(17,100 kg)
Basic equipped weight — passenger	41,000 lb	(18,600 kg)
Maximum all-up weight	68,000 lb	(30,800 kg)
Fuel capacity, normal	2190 I gal	(9950 litres)
Oil capacity	128 I gal	(581 litres)
Maximum level speed	320 mph	(515 kph)
Max weak mixture cruising speed	270 mph	(434 Kph)
Economical cruising speed at 15,000 ft	210 mph	(338 Kph)
Max load	12,100 lb	(5490 kg)
Range with max load	1810 miles	(2910 km)
Range with 10,000 lb load	2150 miles	(3460 km)
Maximum range with normal fuel load	2530 miles	(4060 km)

After completion of their development flights PP325, PP326 and PP327 joined a number of other Halifax aircraft operated by BOAC in the training role, ready for the introduction of the Halton. They and the Halton aircraft were operated by No.1 Line Halton Fleet based at Bovingdon but carried out training sessions from Aldermaston. It was at Aldermaston that PP325 was damaged and, along with PP326 and PP327, was sold. Both PP326 and PP327 were given civil registrations but PP325 was sold as scrap/spares.

Although the Halifax and the Halton were the same basic airframe and had been designed as bombers, crews in general found them neither different nor more difficult than other aircraft of that period, though obviously the DC3 Dakota was more sophisticated. Weatherproofing was typical of unpressurised aircraft of that period, no better and no worse, and general flight handling was satisfactory although crosswind landings were a bit of a problem, as on all tailwheel aircraft. But what was appreciated was the strength of the undercarriage on some of the unmade runways of West Africa, and the general strength of the airframe to withstand the heavy turbulence, cumulo nimbus and lightning experienced on the routes — some of those around India and West Africa have to be experienced to be believed. No *Gee* or

Halton G-AHDV (ex-PP314) of Westminster Airways on the Berlin Air Lift 1949 as a tanker.
(G. F. Mahony).

Loran was fitted and navigation depended on QDMs by D/F loop and by taking star shots. The biggest problems were the possibility of someone putting the wrong hydraulic fluid in the tank — and the spilling of fluids on the radio operator! — plus water seepage through the windshield.

BOAC ordered a fleet of 12 Haltons and the first one delivered was G-AHDU (ex-PP310), which was named *Falkirk* at Radlett on 18 July 1946. The fleet operated on the West African route carrying six crew and ten passengers, the route sometimes being LHR to Lisbon, Rabat, Port Etienne, Bathurst, Freetown, Takoradi to Accra, while at other times it was via Casablanca, Bathurst and Accra to Lagos. The Halton was also introduced on the Indian routes and then the route to Ceylon. Its low cost of maintenance in service was 3.94 man-hours per flying hour, extremely good for a converted military aircraft — a point made in a letter from BOAC to Handley Page Ltd. BOAC's Haltons operated six services a week to Lagos and it was from this route that the last Haltons were withdrawn on 2 May 1948 upon the introduction of aircraft carrying more passengers and designed initially for the carriage of passengers.

The Haltons were then sold and joined over 100 Halifax aircraft already operating with foreign and British charter companies. Eleven Haltons were sold to Aviation Traders who leased or sold them to other operators like Bond Air Services or Westminster Airways, and so joined the British charter companies on the Berlin Airlift under the operation of British European Airways. One Halton (G-AHDR) was sold to E. M. Sutton who sold it in June 1948 to the Breguet Co as F-BECK. A list of civil aircraft with their operators is included at the end of this chapter.

Other operators of Halifax/Halton aircraft were British American Air Services, who besides operating G-AGZP for the Gaekwar of Baroda also operated their own Halifaxes, which were overhauled by the other part of the company, Airtech Ltd. BAAS were mainly engaged in the carriage of soft fruit and drilling equipment, etc. They were also

Halifax C8 LN-OAS at Radlett awaiting delivery, 18 August 1947. (I. M. Burns).

responsible for two flights of Hercules engines slung in the bomb-bay for delivery to Paris, and the carriage of a boxed Humber car to Spain — the boxed car slung in the bomb-bay; this again was a Halifax first.

Eagle Aviation was one of the most successful Halifax companies and was formed on 14 April 1948 by H. Bamberg with a fleet of two Halifaxes, G-ALEP and G-AIAP. It operated on the Liverpool-Belfast 'Milk Run' before joining the Berlin Airlift. After the Berlin Airlift the company set up a base at Aldermaston and retired their Halifaxes in January 1950, replacing them with Avro Yorks.

Another large operator of Halifax aircraft was London Aero & Motor Services (LAMS), which was formed by Dr. G. Humby and Dr. M. Humby; their first Halifax, G-AHZN, received its C of A on 14 December 1946. The company took over the running of Stansted airport and moved there with three Halifaxes.

LAMS Halifax G-AIWT, named *Port of Sydney*, made a charter flight round the world early in 1947, and flew from Stansted to Iceland and the USA, on to New Zealand and Australia and back to England, arriving back with seven tons of dripping. LAMS then set up LAMS (Australia) and LAMS (South Africa), all services to be operated with Halifax C8s. The end of the company came with the serious illness of Dr. G. Humby, and it closed in the second week of July 1948.

The Lancashire Aircraft Corporation was also another successful operator of Halifax aircraft, the company purchasing a large number of these aircraft in September 1946, the first one being G-AIHV. The first passenger charter was on 12 September with a flight to New York with 20 seamen. Cargo flights were made worldwide, carrying anything from ship prop-shafts to fruit. Two Halifax aircraft were operated on the Liverpool-Belfast 'Milk Run', and when the

Halifax C8 PP285 accident at Radlett, 13 February 1948. (I. M. Burns).

Berlin Airlift started LAC moved their aircraft to that. The Halifax aircraft were withdrawn from operations when the company acquired Avro Yorks in June 1952.

During those days of charter operations, the air and ground crews were the poor relations of aviation. With most companies operating on a shoe-string their personnel supplied their own overalls or uniforms; in fact, most charter aircrew and ground-crew could be recognised by their ex-RAF battledress or demob suits! If the aircraft suffered any defects en route it was up to the flight engineer to rectify them and use his initiative to get the aircraft back; hours worked did not come into it. Fortunately, the Halifax and its Hercules engines were reliable for that period, and providing the aircraft was worked hard the main points of trouble were oil cooler leaks and magneto failures.

Another company involved with the Halifax was Airtech Ltd, formed in February 1947 as a subsidiary of Chartair Ltd. Airtech's first year was taken up with recruiting people to handle the repair and maintenance of aircraft, including the Halifax. One of these aircraft was acquired by British American Air Services, which was also an associate of Chartair. Airtech obtained ARB approval in January 1949 and was responsible for the conversion of Halifax aircraft, the fitment of 1500 gallon lorry tanks in the Halifax bomb-bay, and the installation of radio equipment;

altogether, 50 or more Halifax aircraft were acquired from the MoS and converted, maintained and sold to various operators.

Foreign operators also used the Halifax: Air Globe of Switzerland had Halifaxes HB-AIF, HB-AIK and HN-AIL; and in France there were three operators of Halifax aircraft as well as the French Air Force. These were Aerocargo, S.A.N.A. and SOCOTRA, who between them operated nine aircraft. Norway also had two Halifax C8s registered, LN-OAS and LN-OAT, which survived until 1953. In fact, Eagle Aviation's *Red Eagle* G-ALEF (PP337) was originally registered to Vingtor Airways as LN-OAT, but was never operated by them.

In August 1948 the Russians created a situation in Germany that resulted in the Western Allies supplying West Berlin by air. British European Airways were authorised by the British Government to organise the civil component of the Berlin Airlift, and the charter operators were offered contracts to carry supplies and so supplement those carried by the RAF.

When the demand for aircraft to carry liquid fuel to Berlin increased it was decided to modify Halifax/Halton aircraft. For this, Airtech Ltd purchased from various surplus dumps a number of 1500 gallon lorry bulk-fuel tanks, refurbished them and fitted them to the Halifaxes in the bomb-bay. The tanks were hoisted into place by the standard hoists and were retained in position by means of three heavy-gauge, light alloy straps, which were secured to the heavy duty bomb racks. To satisfy ARB the tanks were joined to the aircraft's venting system, and to improve the unloading of the fuel special drainage valves were fitted. To complete the installation, light fairings were fitted fore and aft of the tank to streamline it into the fuselage line.

Neither the tank nor the pannier had any effect on the handling of the Halifax, though there did appear a 'hump' in cruise flight, in which a small increase in engine power gave a disproportionate increase in speed. Most charter pilots, as well as BOAC, found the Halifax/Halton satisfactory to fly, the only snag being the tendency on training to bounce

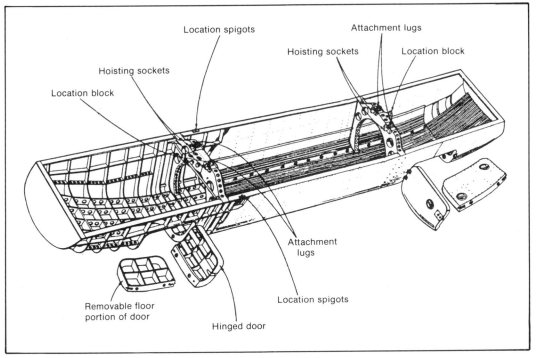

Figure 20 — Freight pannier.

on landing, which could result in a 'golf ball' effect and a go-around, but wheeling the aircraft in with the tail below the horizontal usually resulted in good landings, and the aircraft could be braked quite quickly after touchdown without any ill effects or swinging.

In February 1949 the ARB decided that no C of A would be issued to the Halifax/Halton for it to carry petrol in the 1500 gallon tank, because of the fire hazard if a belly-landing and subsequent disintegration of the tank occurred, so it was restricted to the carriage of Derv.

When the civil Halifax/Halton was first introduced on the market the AUW was given as 65,000 lb with a payload of 12,100 lb, and the maximum landing weight as 55,000 lb. The maximum all-up weight was later revised to 68,000 lb, and the maximum landing weight increased to 56,000 lb. During the Berlin Airlift the ARB allowed the maximum landing weight to be increased first to 57,000

lb and in December 1948 to 58,000 lb as an emergency measure.

The Halifax and the Berlin Airlift

From about 1946 relations between the Western Powers and the Soviet Union over the future of Germany had gradually deteriorated, until in June 1948 the Western Powers were confronted with a complete blockade by the Soviet forces of all supply routes to the American, British and French sectors of Berlin. The answer to this could have been the use of force, the withdrawal from Berlin by the Western Powers or the supplying of Berlin by air while diplomatic negotiations continued. The last course was chosen and the Berlin Airlift began, becoming not only the greatest air supply operation in history but also the most successful.

147

Halifax C8 G-ALEF *Red Eagle* of Eagle Aviation being refuelled at Hamburg, Berlin Airlift 1949.
(Author)

Initially, it was estimated that 2000 tons a day were needed immediately, rising to 3000 in August and 5000 tons a day by September 1948, this higher figure to cover the stockpiling necessary for the winter months when weather in that part of Germany would restrict the amount of flying possible. By the end of the Airlift, in early September 1949, 2,325,809 short tons had been flown into Berlin, mainly by the USAF who contributed approximately 76 per cent, the remainder by the RAF, who were forced by a shortage of transport aircraft to bring in civilian operators. Seven of these operators were equipped with Halifax aircraft: British American Air Services, Bond Air Services, Eagle Aviation, Lancashire Aircraft Corporation, Skyflight, Westminster Airways and World Air Freight.

A total of 41 Halifax aircraft from these companies took part in the Airlift and operated from Wunstorf, Hamburg and Schleswigland to Gatow and Tegel airfields in Berlin. By the end of the Lift they had flown 4653 freight sorties and 3509 fuel oil sorties, carrying a total of 52,810.5 tons of cargo, which included coal, oil and food.

The Berlin run was hardly a novelty to the Halifax and certainly not to most of its crews, but the monotony and continuity of the operations was fatiguing to man and machine alike, and it taxed the spares situation and the ground crew in attempting to get 100 per cent serviceability. What was achieved was due to both air and ground crews' determination to stay on the Lift and in the money. When engines failed en route to Berlin or at Berlin, the aircraft were off-loaded and ferried back to base on three engines; aircrew flew 12-hour shifts and ground-crews worked all hours to maintain them in the air. When a shortage of tanker aircraft occurred some of the Halifax aircraft were converted to tankers as described earlier.

A typical freight load for a Halifax on the

Halifax C8 G-AITC (PP320) of World Air Freight at Bovingdon, 1949. (Author)

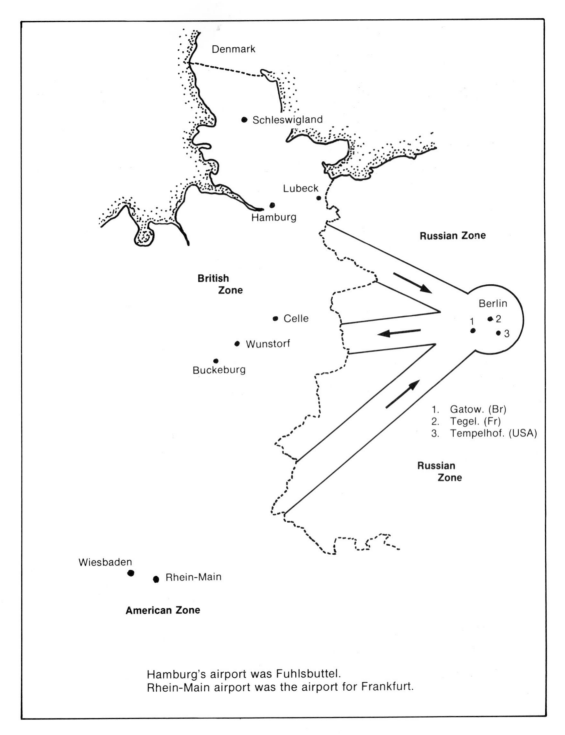

Figure 21 — The air corridors into and out of Berlin, 1948.

Halifax C8 G-AKAC of World Air Freight at Hamburg, Berlin Airlift, 1949. (Author)

Berlin run was $6\frac{1}{2}$ tons, usually of the basic foodstuffs and coal. Most aircraft attempted to do six runs a day, dependent on weather, serviceability and demands. Eagle Aviation, for instance, operated from 26 August 1948 to 15 August 1949 and made over 1000 flights to Berlin, carrying over 7300 tons of supplies and also completing the last flight of the Airlift.

The Halifax C8 on the Airlift was used and abused, yet, operating continually on a short-haul basis for which it was not designed, it responded magnificently. Its Bristol Hercules Mk.100s appeared to relish the continual operation and ignition troubles were less. The aircraft were in general the standard Halifax C8s and were operated usually by a crew of four (some companies used five): pilot, flight engineer, navigator and radio operator.

Access to Berlin was via three corridors (Fig. 21), each one 20 miles wide, with the northern and central corridor approximately 100 miles long and the southern corridor (used by the Americans only) 200 miles long. British aircraft fed into the northern corridor from Fuhlsbuttel (Hamburg), Schweswigland, Lubeck and Wunstorf to Gatow in Berlin. While the USAF relied on DR navigation and radio compass the British aircraft navigated using radio/radar and navigators, with the result that the British were more accurately on their block times into Berlin and approximately at their predetermined position at the specified time in the block. Pilots were given a specified time to arrive at the Fronhau beacon with an allotted track, height and speed; prior to arriving at the beacon instructions were issued over the R/T to do a 90 degree turn for identification purposes on the approach radar, then on to Fronhau beacon and on into Gatow. Initially, British aircraft operated into Gatow, where the RAF ATC and GCA were superb and contributed in no small way to the success of the Airlift. Later, the freighter Halifax aircraft were routed to Tegel, where it was generally conceded that the American GCA was not up to the same standard.

International agreement confined the aircraft of the Western Powers to an area 20 miles in radius around the centre of the city, but ATC and GCA were able to monitor the aircraft on the full approach to Berlin. Pilots had to report their position in the traffic pattern and were then checked through the various points onto the final approach and onto the runway threshold, usually accompanied by calm instructions from RAF ATC or funny remarks from GCA if one's approach was a little below the expected standard. The return to base after the unloading was along the central corridor, to coffee/tea and another load. In the case of the Halifax freighters, loading was done with the pannier up in position and the loading of the fuselage through the normal entrance door.

On 8 October 1948 Halifax C8 G-AKGZ (ex-PP338) of World Air Freight Ltd became the first Halifax casualty. When trying to correct a swing off the runway the undercarriage dug into soft soil and collapsed. To maintain runway clearance for the other Airlift aircraft, bulldozers moved into action and removed G-AKGZ — in two halves! The remarks of World Air Freight ground crew on the parentage of bulldozer drivers cannot be repeated, for a Category A repair was turned into a write-off.

Bond Air Services with their Halifax/Haltons were the major Airlift operator from Hamburg, their chief pilot being Chris Treen. Bond Air Services moved onto the Airlift on 4 August 1948 when one of their C8s was stationed at Wunstorf, but on 14 November along with other freight charter operators they were transferred to Hamburg (Fuhlsbuttel); at the peak of the Airlift Bonds were contributing 12 Halifax aircraft, some being Haltons and Mk.A9s leased from Aviation Traders. The last flight by Bonds on the Lift was made on 15 August 1949 with the company having flown 2577 sorties.

British American Air Services' contribution to the Airlift was two Halifax C8 tankers which operated from Schleswigland. These were unfortunately reduced to one aircraft when G-AKBB was badly damaged when carrying out a cross-wind landing at night at Schleswig'. The company had flown a total of 660 sorties by the time they withdrew from the Airlift on 12 July 1949.

Lancashire Aircraft Corporation was another major operator of Halifax aircraft, even before the Airlift. Originally they supplied six aircraft, later increased to 12. The fleet was originally based at Wunstorf on the freight run but when aircraft were requested for the 'wet' lift Lancashire Aircraft Corporation converted their Halifax aircraft to tankers and moved to Schleswig' on 22 November. Their last aircraft was converted to a tanker in December. The company finished their contract on the Airlift on 12 July 1949 having transported 2,701,440 lb of freight and 3,676,380 gallons of fuel while flying 1,160,000 miles.

Another Halifax operator from Schleswigland on the 'wet' lift was Westminster Airways, who had joined the

Damaged propellers being removed from Halton G-AHDP of Bond Air Services, after wheels-up landing (Schleswigland), Berlin Airlift. (R. R. Aspden).

freight lift while operating Dakotas. Then two Haltons were purchased and converted to tankers; on termination of the Airlift they had flown 544 sorties totalling 1660 hours.

World Air Freight supplied two aircraft for the Airlift, both Halifax C8s, losing one in the first week of their contract. Operating first from Wunstorf and later from Hamburg, the company had by the end of the Lift completed 1200 hours of flying, carrying out 507 sorties. One trying and unusual incident suffered by one of their crews was when G-AITC, after taking off from Hamburg at night and fully loaded, had total electrical failure caused by the cracking through of the main busbar. A safe return and landing was made back at Hamburg with the crew using hand-torch illumination in the cockpit.

Skyflight Ltd, who had taken over three of LAMS Halifax C8s, arrived at Wunstorf on 11 September, carried out their first sortie on 17 September and withdrew on 6 October after carrying out 40 sorties — the shortest period of any operator.

Typical of the spirit shown by the ground crews of the charter operators was the accident that occured to Halton G-AHDP of Bond Air Services. Taking off from Tegel, and during retraction of the undercarriage, the aircraft hit a down-draught from the aircraft in front, smashing the aircraft back to the ground and onto its retracting undercarriage. The jacks were bent and

G-AHDP — new propellers being fitted during repair in the open. (R. R. Aspden).

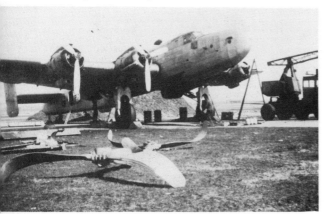

retraction could not be made, but as the aircraft was on its way back to base at Hamburg the situation was accepted. On arrival at Hamburg a dummy landing was attempted, but air traffic control could see the undercarriage folding up, so G-AHDP was diverted to Schleswigland for an emergency landing. The pilot, Captain Leach, made a perfect five-pointer — pannier and four propellers — perfect in the respect that nothing else was damaged. Unfortunately, further damage then occurred when the RAF damaged the inner oil coolers and nacelles while moving the aircraft. The Assistant Engineering Chief of Bonds, Mr. Aspden, having already assessed the damage, called up a repair crew from Hamburg and got on with the job of jacking up and repairing the undercarriage damage, changing the propellers and generally getting G-AHDP in to flyable condition — such a few words to describe a lot of hard work and long hours. Twelve days after the accident the Halton was flight tested and airborne back to Hamburg for another pannier and another load on the Airlift.

Some incidents and accidents were due to lack of experience, while some just happened; some incidents made one chuckle and some could be lived without. Captain G. Mahony of Westminster Airways had one of the latter. Operating with a Halton from Schleswigland into Tegel he suffered loss of brake pressure in the air, so was obliged to return to Schleswigland via Berlin:

> The engineer battled a long time with what he thought was the trouble — a brake relay valve — but eventually a brakeless landing had to be made at Schleswig' and this was quite successful. While the engineer was working on this, I sought to dump the load in order to reduce the landing weight and thus the landing speed required. It could conceivably also be a safety measure in case of accident but I was informed that Derv seemed a very inert and safe load. Jettisoning the load was a tedious business, and while doing this I had

been given a bit of spare sky just north of Schleswig' where I was out of the way. I went round and round in a race-course holding pattern at a constant height, and there I made a mistake; I had not considered that Derv (unlike petrol) is sticky stuff. It emerged at the jettison valve as a spray, and a lot of it must have remained in suspension in the air, so that as I orbitted I managed to coat the windscreen with it. It was a fine night and I remember thinking (looking through the windscreen) that the visibility at ground level was deteriorating and considered the chances of fog. I actually called Schleswig' for an update on the weather — which must have mystified them. Eventually the penny dropped but there was no chance of cleaning the windscreen.

On 21 March 1949 LAC tanker G-AJZZ struck high ground near Schleswigland during a BABs let-down. This was the start of a period of incidents and accidents, for by now the Tegel runway, which had been quickly built of rubble from Berlin covered by a thin layer of tarmac, began to subside and suffer from undulations; this, together with cross-winds and soft ground to the sides of the runway, created further hazards for the heavily laden civil Halifax/Halton aircraft, with the result that undercarriage problems became prevalent. Nevertheless, in March an Eagle Airways freighter had averaged three sorties a day for a month, while Halifax G-AKAC of World Air Freight had averaged two sorties a day for 120 days but unfortunately fatally crashed on 30 April 1949 while doing a low-level turn at night nine miles west of Oranienburg in the Russian Zone. On 1 June LAC tanker G-AKBJ was written off in a landing accident at Tegel, followed by one to LAC tanker G-ALBZ on 12 June.

The Halifax/Halton aircraft were by now obsolete, and normally would have been retired from active flying. The consumption of spare parts (for all types of aircraft) had

Halifax Mk.3 NA684 trials aircraft (nick-named *The Knocker*) operated by Flight Refuelling Ltd. (Flight Refuelling)

risen with the increased intensity of flying, yet by improvisation and superhuman efforts by air and ground crew these problems were kept at bay, and with the possibility of a truce with the Russians, and thus termination of the Airlift, the Halifax aircraft companies and crews battled to get as much freight and oil into Berlin as humanly possible.

On 13 July 1949 the contracts of Lancashire Aircraft Corporation, British American Air Services and Westminster Airways were terminated and civil operations at Schleswigland base came to an end, but the remaining ten freighters at Hamburg continued at full intensity throughout July, uplifting a record 5945 tons in spite of extensive periods of fog and low stratus. The

G-AHDP ready to fly again. (R. R. Aspden).

decision finally to end the civil operation of the Airlift was made at the end of July and the last sortie was on 15 August by Eagle Aviation Halifax G-AIAP flown by Captain Villa, the aircraft carrying 14,400 lb of flour to Tegel.

Most Halifax crews had completed 200-300 sorties each by the end of the Airlift and the Halifax/Halton aircraft had contributed 52,810.5 tons to a grand total by civil operators of 146,980.2 tons — the Halifax aircraft's share being over one third of the total; still second to none.

After the Berlin Airlift many companies felt that to risk the profits they had made on the Airlift so as to remain in civil aviation was too high a price to pay, so crews were paid off, many never to fly again; and aircraft were scrapped as the high cost of conversion to a freighter after carrying Derv was too high. Most companies reduced the number of aircraft they were operating — the charter market was the usual seasonal one of fruit and vegetables, and foreign operators with more modern aircraft had entered the market while the British charter operators were fighting the blockade of Berlin. By the first months of 1950 the charter market was so depressed that a number of major operators decided to cease operations. By the end of 1950 the Lancashire Aircraft Corporation was the only major Halifax operator still in business, carrying textiles, fruit, fish and vegetables. They finally withdrew their Halifax aircraft in June 1952 when the company acquired Yorks.

One Halifax lived on in film, though hardly recognised as such. In 1950 G-AHDM (PP228) was at Westminster Airways (Engineering) at Blackbushe and was converted by the film studio team to become the 'Reindeer' aircraft in the film *No Highway*. The conversion entailed the building-up of the wings, the lengthening of the nose and the fitting of a nose wheel from a Brabazon, changing the shape of the fuselage and tail, and giving it the registration G-AFOH.

The first civil-registered and converted Halifax, PP336, the Maharajah of Baroda's own personal aircraft, was not only a long-distance traveller but had a long life as well. Sold in 1947 to South Africa as ZS-BTA it was purchased by Lancashire Aircraft Corporation in November 1949, with whom it operated until its C of A expired in April 1952. It was scrapped in 1953.

The days of the Halifax were over; the more modern, more economical passenger/freight aircraft were displacing the converted bombers.

Civil-registered Halifax aircraft

Mk.3

NA684	G-AJPG	College of Aeronautics. Scrapped 1949.
NR169	G-AGXA	No.466 Squadron. G. N. Wikner's *Waltzing Matilda*. 16.5.46 flown to Australia. Air Carriers July 1947 as VH-BDT. Scrapped 1948.

Mk.6

RG658	G-AKNG	LAC. To Bovingdon in RAF markings, May 1948.
RG695	G-AKJI	Air Freight. To Doncaster in RAF markings, 1948.
RG698	G-AKJJ	Air Freight. To Doncaster in RAF markings, 1948.
RG700	G-AKNH	LAC. To Bovingdon in RAF markings, May 1948.
RG712	G-AKNK	LAC. To Bovingdon in RAF markings, May 1948.
RG716	G-AKBI	LAC. To Bovingdon in RAF markings, May 1948.
RG717	G-AKNI	LAC. To Bovingdon in RAF markings, May 1948.
RG718	G-ALCY	LAC. To Brough in RAF markings, May 1949.
RG720	G-AJTX	LAC. To Bovingdon in RAF markings, May 1947.
RG722	G-AJSZ	LAC. To Bovingdon in RAF markings, May 1947.
RG736	G-AKUT	LAMS. To Stansted in RAF markings, May 1948 — Air Tech. Pakistan Air Force 1949.
RG756	G-AJTY	LAC. To Bovingdon in RAF markings, May 1947.
RG757	G-AJTZ	LAC. To Bovingdon in RAF markings, May 1947.
RG759	G-AKNJ	LAC. To Bovingdon in RAF markings, May 1948.
RG763	G-AKAP	Air Tech. To Thame in RAF markings, August 1947.
RG774	G-ALCZ	LAC. To Bovingdon in RAF markings, May 1949.
RG779	G-AKLK	LAMS. To Stansted in RAF markings, May 1948 — Air Tech. Pakistan Air Force 1949.
RG781	G-AKLJ	LAMS. To Stansted in RAF markings, May 1948 — Air Tech. Pakistan Air Force 1949.
RG783	G-AKLI	LAMS. To Stansted in RAF markings, May 1948 — Air Tech. Pakistan Air Force 1949.
RG784	G-AKAW	LAMS. To Stansted in RAF markings, May 1947 — Air Tech. Pakistan Air Force 1949.
RG785	G-AJBE	LAMS. To Stansted in RAF markings, May 1948 — Air Tech. Pakistan Air Force 1949.
RG790	G-AIBG	LAMS. To Stansted in RAF markings, May 1948.
RG813	G-AKUU	Air Tech. To Thame in RAF markings, Sept 1948. Pakistan Air Force 1949.
RG822	G-ALDZ	LAC. To Brough in RAF markings, May 1949.
RG824	G-AJUA	LAC. To Bovingdon in RAF markings, May 1947.
RG825	G-AJUB	LAC. To Bovingdon in RAF markings, May 1947.
RG826	G-ALEA	LAC. To Brough in RAF markings, May 1949.

RG827	G-ALEB	LAC. To Brough in RAF markings, May 1949.
RG847	G-ALEC	LAC. To Brough in RAF markings, May 1949.
RG853	G-ALED	LAC. To Brough in RAF markings, May 1949.
RG877	G-ALEE	LAC. To Brough in RAF markings, May 1949.
PP171	G-AKNL	LAC. To Bovingdon in RAF markings, May 1948.
ST801	G-ALOM	Aviation Traders April 1949. Reduced to spares, November 1949.
ST808	G-ALCD	LAC. To Brough in RAF markings, July 1949.

Mk.C8

PP217	G-AKJF	First production C8 — RAF 1945. Sky Taxis Ltd 1947. LAMS 1947. MCA Fire Dept December 1950.
PP218	G-AIWI	LAMS 1948. Skyflight 1948-49. Scrapped 1949.
PP219	G-AKBA	Air Tech 1948 — leased to Alpha. Crashed May 1948.
PP220	G-AKXT	LAC. Scrapped 1950.
PP222	G-AIHU	LAC 1947. Flew into high ground December 1947.
PP223	G-AKGP	Air Tech 1947. To S.A.de N.A. as F-BESE, 1948.
PP224	G-AHDL	Converted to Halton by Shorts (SH23C) — BOAC 1946. Aviation Traders 1948. Westminster Airways 1949. Crashed April 1949.
PP228	G-AHDM	Converted to Halton by Shorts (SH20C) — BOAC 1946. Aviation Traders 1948. Westminster Airways 1948. Scrapped September 1950, used as basis for 'Reindeer' aircraft in film *No Highway*.
PP229	G-ALBS	Hyland Automobiles 1948. Scrapped August 1950.
PP230	G-AHWN	Handley Page 1946. RAF 1947. LAC 1948. WFU July 1949.
PP231	G-AKBK	LAC 1949. Scrapped 1950.
PP233	G-AKBJ	LAC 1948. Crashed on landing June 1949.
PP234	G-AHDN	Converted to Halton by Shorts (SH24C) — BOAC 1947. Aviation Traders 1948. Scrapped November 1950.
PP235	G-AIWN	LAMS 1947. Payloads Ltd 1947. Bond Air Services 1949. WFU May 1950.
PP236	G-AHDO	Converted to Halton by Shorts (SH29C) — BOAC 1947. Aviation Traders 1948. Bond Air Services 1949. Scrapped November 1950.
PP237	G-AKBB	Air Tech 1948. BAAS 1949. DBER February 1949.
PP238	G-AHWM	Handley Page 1946. RAF 1947. Handley Page 1947 as G-AJZY. LAC March 1948. Crashed and burnt out March 1951.
PP239	G-AHZO	LAMS 1946. Skyflight 1949. Dismantled 1949.
PP240	G-AIOH	C. L. Air Surveys 1947. Bond Air Services 1947. Crashed on landing May 1947.
PP241	G-AIHY	LAC 1947. DBER December 1949.
PP242	G-AHZL	LAMS 1946. Dismantled 1949.
PP243	G-AIOI	C. L. Air Surveys 1947. — Bond Air Services 1947. DBER February 1949.

PP244	G-AHZN	LAMS 1946. Ditched September 1946.
PP245	G-AIWR	LAMS 1947. To South Africa as ZS-BUL. Crashed November 1947.
PP246	G-AHZK	LAMS 1946. Skyflight 1949. WFU 1949.
PP247	G-AHZJ	LAMS 1946. DBER August 1947.
PP259	G-AJNT	Payloads Ltd 1947. To France as F-BCQY June 1947.
PP260	G-AHZM	LAMS 1946. Cannibalised September 1946.
PP261	G-AHYH	BOAC 1946. RAF 1947. LAC 1948. Scrapped October 1949.
PP262	G-AIHV	LAC 1947. WFU April 1953.
PP263	G-AJPJ	Chartair 1947. BAAS 1948. Mayfair Air Services 1948. Flown to Israel July 1948.
PP264	G-AJBK	Air Freight Ltd 1947. Sold to France as F-BCJZ 1947. DBER December 1947.
PP265	G-AIWT	LAMS 1947. Payloads Ltd 1947. WFU September 48.
PP266	G-AIWM	LAMS 1947. Scrapped 1949.
PP267	G-AKAC	Payloads Ltd 1948. World Air Freight 1948. Crashed on Berlin Airlift 29 April 1949.
PP268	G-AHDP	Converted to Halton by Shorts (SH25C) — BOAC 1947. Aviation Traders 1948. WFU April 1949.
PP269	G-AHDR	Converted to Halton by Shorts (SH26C) — BOAC 1947. E. M. Sutton 1948. To Breguet Co as F-BECK June 1948.
PP270	G-ALBT	Hylands Automobiles 1948. Scrapped August 1950.
PP271	G-AIAN	BOAC 1946. RAF 1947. Scrapped December 1949.
PP272	G-AIAO	BOAC 1946. RAF 1947. Scrapped December 1949.
PP273	G-AKCT	Payloads Ltd 1947. Air Globe 1947 as HB-AIK. To Egyptian Air Force December 1948.
PP274	G-AGTK	Anglo-French Distributors 1947. Sold as F-BCJX December 1947.
PP275	G-ALBZ	LAC 1949. DBER On Berlin Airlift May 1949.
PP276	G-AJBL	Air Freight 1947. Scrapped July 1949.
PP277	G-AHDS	Converted to Halton by Shorts (SH22C) — BOAC 1946. Aviation Traders 1948. Operated by Bond Air Services on Berlin Airlift. WFU July 1951.
PP278	G-AHVT	Anglo-French Distributors 1947. Sold as F-BCJR September 1947.
PP279	G-AJNU	Payloads Ltd 1947. To Pakistan Airways as AP-ACH May 1948.
PP280	G-AILO	College of Aeronautics 1947. LAC 1949. WFU September 1951.
PP281	G-AIAP	BOAC 1946. RAF 1947. Air Tech 1948. Eagle Aviation 1950. Crashed November 1950.
PP282	G-AKEC	LAC 1948. DBER December 1952.
PP283	G-AKAD	BAAS 1948. DBER May 1948.
PP284	G-AIHW	LAC 1947. DBER on landing LHR June 1947.
PP286	G-AIWJ	LAMS 1947. Dismantled June 1949.
PP287	G-AGPC	Anglo-French Distributors 1947. To Air Cargo as F-BCJS 1947. Crashed December 1948.

PP288	G-AIWP	LAMS 1948. Skyflight on Berlin Air Lift. Sold as scrap March 1950.
PP289	G-AKBP	Payloads Ltd 1947. To Air Globe as HB-AIL 1947. Egyptian Air Force December 1948.
PP290	G-AIWO	LAMS 1946. Reduced to spares 1947.
PP291	G-AIWL	LAMS 1946. Reduced to spares 1949.
PP292	G-AJNV	Payloads Ltd 1947. To Air Globe as HB-AIF 1947. Egyptian Air Force December 1948.
PP293	G-AIZO	Union Air Services 1947. Bond Air Services 1949. Crashed May 1948.
PP294	G-AIHX	LAC 1947. Wrecked September 1948.
PP295	G-AIWK	LAMS 1947. Scrapped after vandalism at Sydney, Australia, December 1947.
PP296	G-AJNW	Payloads Ltd 1949. Westminster Airways 1949. WFU April 1950.
PP308	G-AHDT	Converted to Halton by Shorts (SH27C) — BOAC 1947. Aviation Traders 1948. Operated by Bond Aircraft Services on Berlin Airlift. WFU November 1949.
PP309	G-AHKK	Anglo-French Distributors 1947. Sold as F-BCJV July 1947.
PP310	G-AHDU	Converted to Halton by Shorts (SH18C) — BOAC 1946. Aviation Traders 1948. Operated by Bond Aircraft Services on Berlin Airlift. WFU July 1950.
PP311	G-AHYI	BOAC 1946. RAF 1947. Anglo-French Distributors 1948. Skyflight 1949. Scrapped 1949.
PP312	G-AJNX	Payloads Ltd 1948. Bond Aircraft Services 1948. To Pakistan Airways as AP-ABZ May 1948. Crashed May 1948.
PP313	G-AJPK	LAMS 1947. Payloads Ltd 1947. Hoyes 1947. WFU October 1948.
PP314	G-AHDV	Converted to Halton by Shorts (SH21C) — BOAC 1946. Aviation Traders 1948. Westminster Airways 1949. LAC 1951. DBER on ground December 1952.
PP315	G-AHDW	Converted to Halton by Shorts (SH19C) — BOAC 1946. Aviation Traders 1948. Scrapped November 1950.
PP316	G-AHDX	Converted to Halton by Shorts (SH28C) — BOAC 1947. Aviation Traders 1948. World Air Carriers 1950. Crashed in Alps April 1950.
PP317	G-AIID	BOAC 1946. RAF 1947. Anglo-French Distributors 1948. Skyflight 1949. Scrapped October 1949.
PP319	G-ALBU	Hyland Automobiles 1948. Scrapped August 1950.
PP320	G-AITC	College of Aeronautics 1947. World Air Freight 1949. Crashed 1950.
PP321	G-ALBV	Hyland Automobiles 1948. Scrapped August 1950.
PP322	G-AJNY	Payloads Ltd 1948. Bowmaker Ltd 1948. To Pakistan Airways as AP-ACG May 1948.
PP323	G-AJNZ	Payloads Ltd 1947. World Air Freight 1947. Crashed in Isle of Man September 1948.
PP324	G-AKGO	Air Tech 1947. To Stansted in RAF colours, May 1948.
PP326	G-AIAR	BOAC 1946. RAF 1947. Air Tech 1948. Chartair 1949. BAAS 1949. WFU May 1951.

PP327	G-AIAS	BOAC 1946. RAF 1947. LAMS 1947 as spares.
PP328	G-AJCG	To Norway as LN-OAS. Petair 1947 — cancelled June 1949.
PP329	G-AKBR	Payloads Ltd 1948. Anglo-French Distributors 1948. Skyflight 1948. Eagle Airways 1949. WFU 1950.
PP330	G-AJXD	Anglo-French Distributors 1947. Sold to S.A. de N.A. as F-BCJQ.
PP331	G-AHWL	Anglo-French Distributors 1947. Sold as F-BCJT October 1947.
PP333	G-AKGN	BAAS 1948. Chartair 1949. Scrapped after gale damage December 1949.
PP334	G-AJZZ	LAC 1948. Crashed on Berlin Airlift March 1949.
PP335	G-ALCX	LAC 1948. Scrapped 1952.
PP336	G-AGZP	Reworked to VIP transport for Maharajah of Baroda 1946. BAAS 1946. Sold to Alpha Airways as ZS-BTA 1947. LAC 1949. Scrapped 1953.
PP337	G-ALEF	To Vingtor Airways as LN-OAT 1948. Eagle Aviation 1948. Scrapped 1950.
PP338	G-AKGZ	World Air Freight 1948. Crashed on Berlin Airlift October 1948.

Mk.A9

RT759	G-AMBX	R. A. Short May 1950. Scrapped February 1951.
RT762	G-ALYN	Aviation Traders March 1950. Scrapped May 1951.
RT763	G-ALON	Aviation Traders March 1949. Operated by Bond Air Services on Berlin Airlift. WFU June 1950.
RT772	G-ALYM	Aviation Traders March 1950. Scrapped May 1951.
RT776	G-ALYJ	Aviation Traders March 1950. Scrapped May 1951.
RT785	G-ALYK	Aviation Traders March 1950. Scrapped.
RT787	G-ALOO	Aviation Traders March 1949. To Egyptian Air Force 1950 and numbered 1158.
RT788	G-ALVH	Aviation Traders September 1949. To Egyptian Air Force May 1950 and numbered 1163.
RT791	G-ALIR	Aviation Traders March 1950.
RT793	G-ALVI	Aviation Traders September 1949. To Egyptian Air Force January 1950 and numbered 1156.
RT816	G-AMCG	Aviation Traders June 1950. Reduced to spares.
RT832	G-ALSK	Aviation Traders March 1950.
RT836	G-AMCC	Aviation Traders June 1950. Reduced to spares.
RT837	G-ALYL	Aviation Traders March 1950. Scrapped.
RT846	G-ALOP	Aviation Traders 1949. To Egyptian Air Force February 1950 and numbered 1155.
RT848	G-ALUU	Aviation Traders August 1949. Scrapped November 1950.
RT852	G-ALVJ	Aviation Traders September 1949. To Egyptian Air Force and numbered 1159, February 1950.
RT873	G-ALUV	Aviation Traders August 1949. Scrapped November 1950.

RT879	G-ALSL	Aviation Traders March 1950. Reduced to spares November 1950.
RT884	G-ALYI	Aviation Traders March 1950. Scrapped May 1951.
RT885	G-AKKP	Aviation Traders March 1950. Scrapped.
RT888	G-ALOR	Aviation Traders 1949. To Egyptian Air Force and numbered 1157, February 1950.
RT890	G-AMCE	Aviation Traders June 1950. Reduced to spares.
RT893	G-AMCD	Aviation Traders June 1950. Reduced to spares.
RT895	G-AMCB	Aviation Traders June 1950. Reduced to spares.
RT901	G-ALVK	Aviation Traders September 1949. To Egyptian Air Force and numbered 1160, March 1950.
RT907	G-ALVL	Aviation Traders September 1949. To Egyptian Air Force and numbered 1162, April 1950.
RT924	G-ALUT	Aviation Traders August 1949. Scrapped November 1950.
RT935	G-AMCF	Aviation Traders June 1950. Reduced to spares.
RT937	G-ALOS	Aviation Traders 1949. Operated by Bond Air Services on Berlin Airlift. Reduced to scrap July 1949.
RT938	G-ALVM	Aviation Traders September 1950. To Egyptian Air Force and numbered 1161, March 1950.
RT982	G-AKKU	Aviation Traders March 1950.

Abbreviations:	DBER	Damaged beyond economical repair
	LAC	Lancashire Aircraft Corporation
	LAMS	London Aero & Motor Services
	(SH-C)	Short & Harland conversion serial number
	WFU	Withdrawn from use

Chapter 10
Finale

The post-war role of the Halifax in the Royal Air Force was much reduced by the Air Staff's decision to standardise on certain aircraft in a range of roles, which appears in hindsight to have been carried out in haste without adequate appreciation of each aircraft type's capabilities, the role it was to undertake, or the climate in which it was to operate; for instance, the withdrawal of the Beaufighter in the Far East and its replacement by the Mosquito. The latter was a good aircraft, yet certainly not suited to the high temperatures and humidity encountered there at certain times of the year and in certain areas; during a trial period in 1944 its airframe had already proved to deteriorate quickly in the high humidity, whilst its close-cowled engines were susceptible to overheating.

At home in Bomber Command, immediately after VJ Day the Halifax was withdrawn from service and so left that Command without an aircraft capable of operating under 'hot and high' conditions in the Far East or anywhere else — shown when No.617 Squadron Lancasters tried operating alongside No.298 (Airborne Support) Squadron Halifaxes in India's central provinces in 1946. What is even more surprising about the withdrawal of the Halifax from Bomber Command is that, in August 1945, the MAP requested visits by RAE and Avro representatives to carry out examinations of serious wing defects found on Lancasters, which had rendered large numbers of Bomber Command Lancasters unserviceable.

A classic portrait of an aircraft which was 'Second to None'.

Bomber Command's Halifaxes were despatched to the main graveyards of No.29 MU at High Ercall and Rawcliffe, where large numbers of them were quickly and unceremoniously scrapped, having been flown in for their last touch-down by their veteran crews and in some cases by volunteer ex-Halifax pilots who wanted to have their last feel of the controls of the Halifax.

So, as quickly as possible after the war Bomber Command Halifaxes were consigned to the scrap-heap and, like the Stirling, no official attempt was made to retain one for posterity, as if the authorities were embarrassed by its presence, for in spite of the specification and interference the Halifax and Handley Page had proved them wrong.

Post-war squadrons of No.38 Group Transport Command were still equipped with the Halifax A3, it having proved to be the best aircraft for the heavy duty role of airborne support, while some other units of the same Command were re-equipping with the Marks A7 and C8. Two of the No.38 Group squadrons were Nos 620 and 644, which in 1946 were based in Palestine and operated over the Middle East with their A7s.

No.620 Squadron was stationed at Lydda and No.644 at Qastina, until in 1946 Israeli terrorists carried out organised attacks on Lydda, Petah Tikva and Qastina RAF stations, during which three Halifaxes were destroyed and eight damaged beyond repair by high explosives. Because the defence personnel reacted fairly quickly the raiders withdrew leaving behind gelignite sticks and Molotov Cocktails. After this raid No.644 Squadron withdrew from Qastina to Bilbeis airfield near Cairo (Egypt) while Qastina defences were improved. During September 1946 both Squadrons were renumbered, with No.620 Squadron becoming No.113 Squadron and No.644 becoming No.47 Squadron; No.47 Squadron was then posted back to the UK and was re-equipped with Halifax A9 aircraft, which it operated until 1948, when it again re-equipped with another Handley Page aircraft — the Hastings.

Another squadron of No.38 Group was No.298 Squadron, which had also operated in the airborne support role and in May 1945 had re-equipped from the Halifax A3 to the A7. It was then posted to the Far East to carry out the same role as it had in Europe, moving out via Rennes, Tripoli, Lydda and Shaibah to Karachi. Before the squadron had assembled and organised themselves at their base in India prior to operations, the Japanese had surrendered — or as a squadron wag remarked, 'They knew 298 was on the way'. The squadron and its CO, Wg Cdr Norman, then prepared themselves to undertake any role that HQ India required. The first of these turned out to be the trooping of ex-POWs from various areas to central points in India, and then followed some involvement in paratrooping and Jeep drops, and also flights over the 'Hump' to China — the only British-built bomber to do so. A further duty was the positioning of three fully bombed-up Halifaxes at Bombay when Indian seamen in RN warships in Bombay harbour mutinied against their British officers.

This was followed by a spell in Burma on Operation *Hunger*, when the crews operated the Halifaxes from a dirt strip at Meiktila, each aircraft carrying 12,000 lb of rice and salt to Burmese hill tribes in the Kachin Hills. These tribes had remained loyal to the British Crown throughout the war and were now starving. The run to the DZ was made through the hills with the drop being made at heights at a maximum of 200 ft — and normally less than half of this — as the commodities were carried in burlap sacks and liable to burst if dropped too high. No one needed to worry; the crews knew their Halifaxes — tree-top cutting was on and the sacks were dropped really low. One day a No.617 Squadron Lancaster was sent into Meiktila airstrip on a trial run, but the dirt airstrip proved too short for it; with less than half the Halifax's load its take-off found it clipping the tree tops. No further Lancaster attempts were made; in fact No.617 Squadron and its Lancasters left the Far East shortly afterwards.

It would appear that the powers-that-be still didn't know the Halifax and couldn't —

or wouldn't — believe anything wrong of the Lancaster, for in 1946 the RAE Farnborough sent out an engineer officer to No.298 Squadron to check on the overheating of the Halifax's Hercules engines — no overheating has been experienced or reported! Yet No.617 Squadron had experienced overheating of the Merlins on their Lancasters, but no engineer officer was sent to check on them. At that time both Nos 298 and 617 Squadrons were stationed at Digri airfield (India), and whereas the Halifaxes could carry out their engine checks and taxi out to the runway and 'hold', the Lancasters had to obtain take-off clearance before start-up so as to prevent overheating of their liquid-cooled Merlins.

The Halifax was also used by various units in Flying Training Command; for instance, the Empire Air Navigation School at Shawbury operated modified B3s, such as NA243 *Rigel*, NA276 *Altair*, NA279 *Capella*, and five modified B6s named and numbered PN188 *Leonides*, PN203 *Mars*, PN206 *Fomalhaut*, PN207 *Jupiter*, and RG352 *Pollux*. A Mk.9 ST814 named *Sirius* was also used, but this afterwards went to No.1 Radio School at Cranwell, which also had on its inventory three B6s serial numbered RG874, RG875 and RG876.

The Empire Radio School at Debden had a modified B6, RG815 named *Mercury*, which was left in its normal metal finish; on 19 May 1946 *Mercury* took off from St. Mawgan in Cornwall to make a 25,000 mile liaison flight loaded up with £10,000 of AI radar and navigational equipment, which they demonstrated to the air forces in Palestine, Iraq, India, Burma, New Zealand and Australia.

At the Airborne Forces Experimental Establishment at Beaulieu a number of Halifax aircraft were among the fleet in the wartime and postwar years; some of these were NA644, LL615, TW780, RT758 and PN308. PN308 arrived at AFEE on the 31 July 1945 and had been allocated for the parachuting of heavy equipment; apart from a visit to RAE it spent its life at AFEE until 25 April 1949 when it departed to No.49 MU. An A7, PP350 arrived from High Ercall in 1947

and was used as an experimental test bed for trials of the 8000 lb UFC (Universal Freight Carrier), which was an extra large pannier which could accommodate a Jeep and gun, Jeep and trailer, or any similar load. It fitted into the bomb-bay of the Halifax minus the bomb-doors, was dropped from the aircraft on eight 42 ft parachutes and landed on three pneumatic shock absorbers. Blisters underneath the outer wing of the aircraft housed cameras for filming the test drops.

A further role in the post-war RAF for the Halifax was the continuation of its role of maritime reconnaissance and long-range meteorological flights with Coastal Command. One of the squadrons operating the Halifax was No.518, which operated from Tiree. Early in 1945 it relinquished its white and grey painted Met.5s and re-equipped with GR6s. At the end of 1945 the squadron moved to Aldergrove where it was renumbered 202 Squadron. It continued to operate the GR6 until 1951 when it re-equipped with the Hastings.

Another squadron in Coastal Command was No.224, which formerly operated Lancaster ASR3s from St. Eval, but re-equipped with Halifax GR6s and was then posted to Gibraltar — the change in temperature and aircraft must have been an improvement. The squadron continued to operate from Gibraltar until 1952, when RG841 carried out the last Halifax GR flight on 17 March. Further Coastal Command squadrons that operated the Halifax postwar were Nos 517, 519, 520 and 521, but all had been disbanded by or in 1946.

By the end of 1946 in the Far East No.298 Squadron had been reduced from its original complement of 32 aircraft to about half that number, due partly to crashes but mainly to cannibalisation because of lack of the supply of spares from the UK, and so the squadron was disbanded. The squadron finished its last few months at Risalpur on the North West Frontier of India carrying out photographic duties and helping to maintain the peace.

Meanwhile, No.47 Squadron had moved to the UK, and at Fairford were re-equipped with Halifax A9s. In 1947, in the atrocious weather of the first months of the year, the squadron was called on to help to supply by air villagers and animals marooned in and around the moors in Staffordshire. Unfortunately, on 3 February one aircraft was lost near the the beleaguered village of Butterton. The pilot was Sqn Ldr McIntyre, an experienced wartime flyer who was very popular with the other aircrew. The pilot reported that he had made two unsuccessful attempts at dropping food to the villagers and that the village was temporarily lost in the mist; the next news was from an eye-witness of the crash.

The squadrons of No.38 Group continued their airborne support exercises and demonstrated drops with the Halifax until 1948, when No.47 Squadron was re-equipped with the Hastings and became the trial squadron for that aircraft. They operated it on the Berlin Airlift alongside its predecessor, the Halifax, which was being operated by the civilian charter companies.

The College of Aeronautics at Cranfield operated a C8, PP320, with the civil registration of G-AITC, which was fitted with a comprehensive range of radar equipment including *Loran* and *Gee;* this aircraft was sold in 1949 to World Air Freight, who flew it on the Berlin Airlift. The College also acquired a B3 NA684, which was reputed to have force-landed at Cranfield and never to have been repossessed by the RAF; in any case it was purchased by the College from the Air Ministry and finished its days as a static engine test rig. Also operated by the College was another C8, PP332, which had formerly been operated by No.301 (Polish) Squadron; it was later sold to Pakistan.

Nos 301 and 304 (Polish) Squadrons operated Halifax C8s in Transport Command on transport duties in the period 1945-46. They were the only RAF Squadrons to operate the C8, and the end of these duties came with the repatriation of Polish personnel.

One of the biggest post-war operators of the Halifax was the French Air Force. They had of course operated the aircraft in the RAF in wartime, and the two squadrons concerned, No.346 'Guyenne' and No.347 'Tunisie', had built up a very fine reputation in No.4 Group Bomber Command. On 20 October 1945 these two squadrons took off from their base at Elvington with their battle-scarred B7s and some new B6s and headed for their new base at Bordeaux Merignac and their home country — a country they had proudly represented, a country for which so many Free French airmen had laid down their lives.

Shortly after settling at their new base the two squadrons began their peacetime operations, with No.346 Squadron being reorganised into a transport role, stripping their Halifax aircraft of all military equipment and installing passenger seats and panniers, while No.347 Squadron maintained its aircraft in a military and armed condition and operated air-sea rescue/met., flight/maritime recce flights.

After converting their aircraft to the transport role No.346 Squadron began a regular civil/military passenger service down through West Africa and to South America. The flight from Bordeaux to Dakar was usually accomplished within a day's flight and up to 32 passengers were carried on this portion of the route, the squadron operating six regular return flights every month. When the temperature got a little too high inside the fuselage the escape hatches were opened, which may appear crude but altogether it was a quick and economic way to open a route, for the airframe and engines behaved well and the venture proved satisfactory. Some of the panniers were modified and enlarged at the rear to accommodate a Hercules engine. In 1949 No.346 'Guyenne' Squadron was absorbed by No.347 'Tunisie' Squadron and became Groupe 1/25. The aircraft were in use until 26 October 1951 when they were withdrawn from service, although some were retained as instructional airframes and missile launchers.

The Parachute Test Unit at Henlow operated a Halifax A9, RT936, testing all manner of parachutes and related equipment, until the aircraft was struck off charge in August 1954; prior to this the same unit had

Starboard engine installations for trials of Hastings power-plant on Halifax RG642. Note mix of three- and four-blade props. (RAE).

employed another A9, RT868, on similar duties. Not so far away, at Cardington, in one of the airship sheds there was a cannibalised Halifax, which was still there in 1956.

Three other operators of the Halifax in the experimental role were civilian companies; one was the Bristol Engine Co. who operated a B6 (RG724) on the testing of oil coolers and other engine accessories, another B6 (LV776) on engine cooling experiments and developments, and a modified B6 (NP715) on the development of fire detection and extinguishers. The second company was Airspeed Ltd at Christchurch, who employed an A9 (RT935) as a tug for towing repaired Horsa gliders, but this departed to No.48 MU in February 1950. The third company was General Aircraft Ltd of Feltham, who also used the Halifax as a tug; during the early

post-war years they were developing tailless gliders under the direction of Kronfeld. The Halifaxes used as tugs were an A3 (NA295) and an A9 (RT894).

As mentioned previously, Coastal Command became interested in flight refuelling of their Halifax Met. 6 aircraft and at a meeting in 1946 between Handley Page Ltd, Flight Refuelling Ltd and the M of S, Flight Refuelling were given a contract to carry out a trial installation on one aircraft; if this proved satisfactory then a further nine conversion sets would be manufactured. One Halifax (RG839) was received at Staverton from No.44 MU on the 15 May 1946 for conversion as a 'receiver', but the refuelling trials were abandoned by Coastal Command in late 1946 as they had lost interest in the project. The requirement was cancelled in

1947, the aircraft converted back to standard and returned to No.44 MU on 16 October 1947.

A further contract obtained by Flight Refuelling Ltd was the conversion of Halifax B3 HX246 for mainplane thermal de-icing, the aircraft being modified by Handley Page's with electrically de-iced propellers. Flight Refuelling then removed the mainplane armoured edge and installed an unarmoured heated leading edge and also installed thermal de-icing equipment. The aircraft arrived at Staverton for conversion on 5 November 1943, but due to shortage of the required equipment and unserviceability of equipment the aircraft was not ready for testing at the RAE until 1945. By June 1950 both the RAE and Boscombe Down had completed their tests and the aircraft was put up for disposal.

Another contract for Flight Refuelling Ltd was from the Directorate of Engine Research & Development (DERD) of the MoS, and was for a study of the detonation characteristics of aviation fuels in flight. The Bristol Hercules 16 power-plants of the Halifax Mk.3 selected, NA684, together with their modified carburettors were prepared and calibrated by the Bristol Aeroplane Co. and Messrs Hobson Ltd, and the special equipment installation and preparation of the aircraft was completed by F.R.L. Each test engine was fitted with flight test dynamometers and detonation detection equipment with the fuel system altered to allow test fuels to be carried separately. The testing equipment was very comprehensive and included gas sampling analysis cells and means for determining dynamic ignition timing. To monitor the equipment and the automatic recorders four flight test observers were carried, the flight detonation trials being carried out both in the UK and in the Sudan.

As mentioned in previous chapters, Airtech Ltd was one of the companies which, soon after the war, were involved in the overhaul, conversion and maintenance of Halifax aircraft. For instance, in 1946 eight Halifax B6 aircraft were flown from Stansted to Thame airfield for overhaul by the company; one or more of these were modified so that a mounting in the bomb-bay could provide carriage of spare Hercules engines. These eight aircraft (RG736, RG779, RG781, RG782, RG783, RG784, RG785 and RG813) were sold to the Pakistan Air Force and by the middle of 1949 British American Air Service crews had ferried the aircraft out to Pakistan, where the Service used them for reconnaissance, freighting and training, being operated by No.12 Squadron PAF until they were phased out of service in 1955.

On the civil side in Pakistan, three Halifax C8s were acquired from Airtech by Pakistan Airways. After overhaul by Airtech they were registered as follows:-

G-AJNU   ex-PP279, re-registered as
AP-ACH
G-AJNX   ex-PP312, re-registered as
AP-ABZ
G-AJNY   ex-PP322, re-registered as
AP-ACG

After withdrawal from airline service these aircraft were transferred to the Pakistan Air Force as instructional airframes, and a number of British instructors were employed on them.

In 1948 the Egyptian Air Force became another customer for the Halifax. They purchased nine A9 aircraft from the MoS, which were overhauled by Aviation Traders. Work commenced on the aircraft in November 1948 and the first one was delivered to Egypt via Malta in January 1949. One of the nine was RT938 and was the last Halifax produced, while two more had been operated by No.113 Squadron in the Middle East in 1947, so were more or less on home ground! The serial numbers of these nine aircraft were: RT787, RT788, RT793, RT846, RT852, RT888, RT901, RT907 and RT938.

RAE Farnborough employed two Halifax aircraft on engine flight test work during the post-war years. One of these was a B6 (RG642) which arrived from Preston on 16 April 1945 and was allocated for installation of the Hercules 100 RAE low drag power-plant. Work had been carried on at RAE for quite a time to develop a cowling and an installation in which the cooling would be adequate, entry drag reduced and external drag minimal. The engine installation developed was bench-tested first, but as the installation was destined for the Hastings/Hermes aircraft it was decided to flight test the whole installation in the starboard inner engine position on RG642, to check the correlation between bench tests and flight tests. Results indicated that the improvements on the flight tests were less than those found on the bench tests. Eventually the tests were completed and on 29 July 1947 RG642 departed Farnborough for No.44 MU and retirement.

The second Halifax was a Mk.7 (NP748), which was used to check correlation of flight tests with bench tests of the standard Hercules 100 power-plant. This indicated that the pressure and velocity distributions were different in flight from those on the bench. However, the conclusion of the test report was that the determination of the cooling drag was such that it would serve as a standard for comparison with any future power-plant that might be introduced.

Two other test beds still in use after the war were operated by the De Havilland Propeller Co. One was a B6 (RG820) while the other was an A7 (PP389). Both arrived at Hatfield in 1946 and were used for propeller testing, although PP389 was also used as a tug for towing the Horsa glider, which had been modified with a nose similar in shape to the one for the Comet airliner. At least one of these aircraft, and maybe both at some time or other, flew with a spray frame fitted to the fuselage on the starboard side ahead of the starboard inner engine. RG820 was also in 1946 flying with four-blade inner and three-blade outer propellers. PP389 finished its stint of test and tug flying on 29 October 1947 and departed to No.45 MU, while RG820 was in use until it departed by road to RAF Hednesford for instructional use on 29 September 1951.

A B3 (LV999/G) was in use after the war for trials with a 'D' Type rear turret and was also fitted with 'Village Inn' AGL (T) radar, while some A7 aircraft of No.38 Group were also fitted with the 'D' turret, but this was not standard.

One aircraft that had more ground history than flying was A7 PN323, which had been produced by Fairey Aviation under MoS contract and had its first flight on 13 September 1945. After about 10 hours' flying it was delivered to No.29 MU at High Ercall for storage. In 1948 the decision was made to reduce the aircraft to components but it was then acquired by Standard Telephone and Cable for use as a static test bed for radio aerials and resided at Park Street from 1948 to 1951. It appeared as an engineless hulk with a crude metal nose fairing and a single central fin. It was then acquired by a preservation group but, because they were unable to obtain suitable accommodation for the airframe, the aircraft deteriorated until the point was reached when the preservation group removed the nose section and gave it to the Skyframe Museum. After this museum disbanded, the nose section was transported to the Imperial War Museum in London, who renovated it and displayed it for exhibition there and subsequently at Duxford. The starboard main undercarriage leg casting was also kept by the group and is now on exhibition in the RAF Museum at Hendon.

Neither the RAF nor any civilian organisation had retained any mark of the Halifax for posterity, and the fact that there is one is due solely to the efforts of volunteers/members of the Norwegian Aviation Historical Society and the RAF Sub-Aqua Team. This sole representative of 6176 Halifaxes built is a B2, W1048, which was located in 90 feet of water in Lake Hoklingen in Norway. On 30 June 1973 at 14.10 hours W1048 broke the surface again and was found to be in a quite fair condition though minus the outer starboard mainplane, which was salvaged later. It was then the lot of W/O J. Davis and his team from No.71 MU to dismantle and transport the last Halifax back to its homeland. Today it is on exhibition, only partly restored, in the RAF Museum.

Meanwhile, in 1984 the Yorkshire Air

Museum at Elvington near York — a wartime Halifax base — was instrumental in recovering the major portion of the fuselage of Halifax HR792 from Stornoway, where it had crashed during the war, and are in the process of assembling a complete aircraft with parts gathered from many sources.

Throughout this volume the author has used the Lancaster as a comparison. If this should puzzle the reader, then he or she should remember that the media have, in general, portrayed the Lancaster in many scenes and roles, making it all things to all men. Thus myth and fact become intermingled. In fact the Lancaster was a specialised bomb carrier, with problems and faults like any other aircraft. Writing of the Halifax, the author has described it 'warts and all', and so the Lancaster, as a comparison, must be treated in the same way.

Who is to decide which was the greatest heavy aircraft of WW2? Certainly not the Air Staff or an AOC, but only the crews. For example, the Wellington was not only built in greater numbers than either the Halifax or Lancaster but soldiered on throughout the war, the B17 fought through fighters and flak to bomb Germany in daylight, and the Halifax operated in many roles and scenarios. Protagonists of each may argue their case — but no one should doubt that, to her crews, the *Halifax was Second to None.*

To us, though our numbers may dwindle, she will always remain a tough lady — capable of tackling any job, anywhere.

Appendix: Halifax Data

General Data: Mks 1, 2 and 5

	Mk.1 Srs 2	Mk.2 Srs 1A	Mk.5 Srs 1A
Wingspan	98 ft 8 ins	98 ft 8 ins	98 ft 8 ins
Length (tail up)	70 ft 1 in	71 ft 7 ins[1]	71 ft 7 ins[1]
M/plane aerofoil section, C-Section	NACA 23021	NACA 23021	NACA 23021
M/plane aerofoil section, outboard	NACA 23009	NACA 23009	NACA 23009
Mainplane chord at root	16 ft	16 ft	16 ft
Mainplane chord at tip	6 ft 6 ins	6 ft 6 ins	6 ft 6 ins
Mainplane total area	1250 sq ft	1250 sq ft	1250 sq ft
Tailplane span (overall)	30 ft 4 ins	30 ft 4 ins	30 ft 4 ins
Tailplane aerofoil section	Symmetric	Symmetric	Symmetric
Tailplane maximum chord	8 ft 6 ins	8 ft 6 ins	8 ft 6 ins
Tailplane area plus elevators	223.4 sq ft	223.4 sq ft	223.4 sq ft
Fin and rudder total area	117.6 sq ft	117.6 sq ft	117.6 sq ft[2]
Undercarriage type	Messier	Messier	Dowty
Undercarriage track	24 ft 8 ins	24 ft 8 ins	24 ft 8 ins
Hydraulic system	Messier	Messier	Dowty
Fuel capacity, normal	1552 IG	1882 IG	1882 IG
Fuel capacity, long-range	2442 IG	2572 IG	2572 IG
Fuel capacity, extra long-range	—	2732 IG	2732 IG
Oil capacity	112 IG	112 IG	112 IG
Tare weight	33,700 lb	34,800 lb	36,400 lb
All-up weight at take-off	55,000 lb	60,000 lb	60,000 lb
Armament, nose	2 Mgs	2 Mgs	1 Mg
mid-upper	—	4 Mgs	4 Mgs
tail	4 Mgs	4 Mgs	4 Mgs
Bomb-load	13,000 lb	13,000 lb	13,000 lb
Maximum power/engine at take-off	1075 hp	1280 hp	1280 hp[3]
Maximum speed and altitude (mph and ft)	262 at 18,000	264 at 18,000	261 at 19,500
Maximum cruising speed, MS gear	198 mph at FTH[4]	228 at 14,000	228 at 14,500
FS gear	204 at 18,000	216 at 18,000	218 at 15,000
Service ceiling	18,000 ft	21,000 ft	21,000 ft
Time to service ceiling	41 mins	43.5 mins	45 mins
Average rate of climb	439 ft/min	482 ft/min	466 ft/min

[1] Without mod. 452 nose; then length is 70 ft 1 ins.
[2] With introduction of 'D' fin and rudder the area increased to 145.4 sq ft.
[3] With Merlin 20 engines.
[4] Full Throttle Height.

General Data: Mks 3, 6 and 7

	Mk. 3	*Mk. 6*	*Mk. 7*
Wingspan	[1]98 ft 8 ins	103 ft 8 ins	103 ft 8 ins
Length (tail up)	71 ft 7 ins	71 ft 7 ins	71 ft 7 ins
M/plane aerofoil section, C/section	NACA 23021	NACA 23021	NACA 23021
M/plane aerofoil section, outboard	NACA 23009	NACA 23009	NACA 23009
Mainplane chord at root	16 ft	16 ft	16 ft
Mainplane chord at tip	6 ft 6 ins	6 ft 6 ins	6 ft 6 ins
Mainplane total area	[2]1250 sq ft	1275 sq ft	1275 sq ft
Tailplane span (overall)	30 ft 4 ins	30 ft 4 ins	30 ft 4 ins
Tailplane aerofoil section	Symmetric	Symmetric	Symmetric
Tailplane maximum chord	8 ft 6 ins	8 ft 6 ins	8 ft 6 ins
Tailplane area plus elevator	223.4 sq ft	223.4 sq ft	223.4 sq ft
Fin and rudder total area	145.4 sq ft.	145.4 sq ft.	145.4 sq ft.
Undercarriage type	Messier	Messier	Messier
Undercarriage track	24 ft 8 ins	24 ft 8 ins	24 ft 8 ins
Hydraulic system	Messier	Messier	Messier
Fuel capacity, normal	1806 IG	1882 IG	1882 IG
Fuel capacity, long range	2496 IG	2880 IG	2880 IG
Fuel capacity, extra long range	2656 IG	—	—
Oil capacity	128 IG	128 IG	128 IG
Tare weight	37,630 lb	39,000 lb	38,500 lb
All-up weight at take-off	65,000 lb	68,000 lb	65,000 lb
Armament, [3]nose	1 Mg	1 Mg	1 Mg
mid-upper	4 Mgs	4 Mgs	4 Mgs
tail	4 Mgs	4 Mgs	4 Mgs
Bomb-load	13,000 lb	12,000 lb	12,000 lb
Maximum power/engine at take-off	1580 hp	1675 hp	1580 hp
Maximum speed and altitude (mph and ft)	281 at 13,500	309 at 19,500	281 at 13,500
Maximum cruising speed MS gear	242 at 10,000	256 at 13,500	242 at 10,000
FS gear	228 at 20,000	272 at 22,500	227 at 20,000
Service ceiling	20,000 ft	24,000 ft	20,000 ft
Time to service ceiling	45 mins	31 mins	45 mins
Average rate of climb		774 ft/min	

[1]This was 103 ft 8 ins with extended wingtips on later production aircraft.
[2]This was 1275 sq ft with extended wingtips on later production aircraft.
[3]Some aircraft had either FN64 underturret or 0.5 mg under-blister.

Note: the A3 and A7 aircraft's tare weights were less at 37,300 and 37,450 lb respectively.

General Data: Mks C8 and A9

	Mk. C8	*Mk. A9*
Wingspan	103 ft 8 ins	103 ft 8 ins
Length (tail up)	73 ft 7 ins	71 ft 7 ins
M/Plane aerofoil section, C/Section	NACA 23021	NACA 23021
M/Plane aerofoil section, outboard	NACA 23009	NACA 23009
Mainplane chord at root	16 ft	16 ft
Mainplane chord at tip	8 ft 6 ins	8 ft 6 ins
Mainplane total area	1275 sq ft	1275 sq ft
Tailplane span (overall)	30 ft 4 ins	30 ft 4 ins
Tailplane aerofoil section	Symmetric	Symmetric
Tailplane maximum chord	8 ft 6 ins	8 ft 6 ins
Tailplane area plus elevator	223.4 sq ft	223.4 sq ft
Fin and rudder total area	145.4 sq ft	145.4 sq ft
Undercarriage type	Messier	Messier
Undercarriage track	24 ft 8ins	24 ft 8 ins
Hydraulic system	Messier	Messier
Fuel capacity, normal	2190 IG	2070 IG
Fuel capacity, long-range	2880 IG	2760 IG
Oil capacity	128 IG	128 IG
Tare weight	37,760 lb	37,800 lb
All-up weight at take-off	68,000 lb	65,000 lb
Armament, nose	N/A	1 Mg
mid-upper	N/A	Nil
tail	N/A	2 Mgs[1]
Bomb-load	Nil	12,000[2]
Maximum power/engine at take-off	1675 hp	1580 hp
Maximum speed and altitude (mph and ft)	320 at 19,500	289 at 13,500
Maximum crusing speed MS gear	260 at 10,000	242 at 10,000
FS gear	270 at 15,000	—
Service ceiling	25,000 ft	21,000 ft
Time to 10,000 ft	10 mins	12 mins
Average rate of climb	1,000 ft min	833 ft min

[1]'D' type turret with 0.5 in. Brownings.
[2]Bombs could be carried on the A9 carriers, but these were normally for containers, or the gun and Jeep combination with the heavy beam.

Gun Turret Data

Type A mid-upper turret

Operation	Electro-hydraulic
Diameter of ring	43 ins
Weight	630 lb with guns and ammunition
Guns	4 × multi-Browning 0.303 in. with 1000 rounds/gun
Speed of rotation	Normal: 24 degrees per second
	High speed 48 degrees per second
Quantity of fluid	6 pints type 'A' anti-freeze oil
Field of fire	Azimuth 360 degrees
	Elevation 74 degrees
	Depression $2\frac{1}{2}$ degrees
Ammunition feed	Direct from ammunition box
Gunsight	Reflector Type Mk.3 or 3A
Working pressure	1200 psi rotation
	750 psi rotation

Type C nose turret

Operation	Electro-hydraulic
Diameter of ring	38.3 ins
Weight	499 lb with ammunition and guns
Guns	2 × multi-Browning 0.303 in. with 1000 rounds/gun
Speed of rotation	Normal: 24 degrees per second
	High speed: 48 degrees per second
Quantity of fluid	6 pints type 'A' anti-freeze oil
Field of fire	Azimuth 100 degrees each side of a/c centreline
	Elevation 60 degrees
	Depression 45 degrees
Ammunition feed	Direct from ammunition box
Gunsight	Reflector Type Mk.3 or 3A

Type C mid-upper turret

Operation	Electro-hydraulic
Diameter of ring	38.3 ins
Weight	547 lb with guns and ammunition
Guns	2 × multi-Browning 0.303 in. with 1000 rounds/gun
Speed of rotation	Normal: 24 degrees per second
	High speed: 48 degrees per second
Quantity of fluid	6 pints type 'A' anti-freeze oil
Working pressure	1200 psi rotation
	750 psi elevation
Field of fire	Azimuth 360 degrees continuous
	Elevation 60 degrees
	Depression 45 degrees
Ammunition feed	Direct from ammunition box
Gunsight	Reflector Type Mk.3 or 3A

Type E rear turret

Operation	Electro-hydraulic
Diameter of ring	36.95 ins
Weight	674 lb with guns and air gunner
Guns	4 × multi-Browning 0.303 in. with 2500 rounds/gun
Speed of rotation	Normal: 36 degrees per second
Quantity of fluid	7 pints type 'A' anti-freeze oil
Field of fire	Azimuth 90 degrees each side of a/c centreline
	Elevation 60 degrees
	Depression 50 degrees
Ammunition feed	Electrically driven assister
Gunsight	Reflector Type Mk.3 or 3A

Type D rear turret

Operation	Electro-hydraulic
Diameter of ring	36.95 ins
Weight	405 lb (less guns and ammunition)
Guns	2 × multi-Browning 0.5 in. with 2300 rounds
Speed of rotation	36 degrees per second
Quantity of fluid	5 pints type 'A' anti-freeze oil
Field of fire	Azimuth 90 degrees each way
	Elevation 45 degrees
	Depression 45 degrees
Ammunition feed	Electric feed assister
Gunsight	GGS Mk.2C or reflector Type 3A
Max working pressure	Rotation 1750 psi
	Elevation/depression 1250 psi

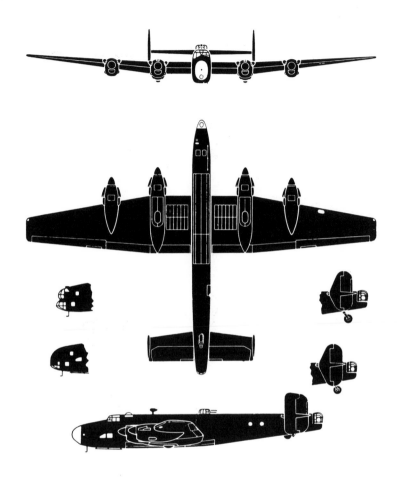

HALIFAX I, II and V (4-Merlin)
Bomber

Span 98 feet 8 inches   Length 71 feet 7 inches

May be seen with any of the noses or tails shown.

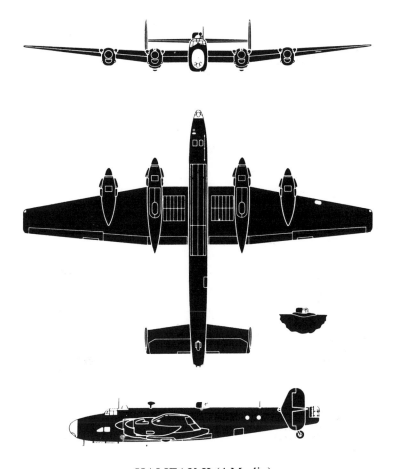

HALIFAX II (4-Merlin)
(Modified)
Bomber

Span 99 feet 0 inches   Length 71 feet 7 inches

Recognition Features: Mid wing: in-line engines: long nose: wings have dihedral from inboard engines and in plan rectangular centre section and almost equal taper to square-cut tips: inboard engine nacelles project beyond trailing edge: deep fuselage with dorsal and rear gun turrets: square cut tail plane: large characteristic twin fins and rudders outrigged.
May be seen with fairing round dorsal turret.

175

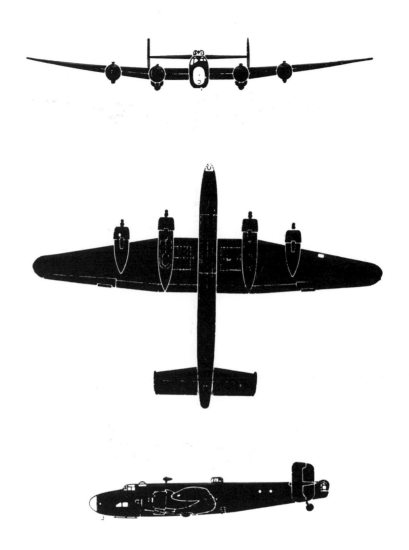

HALIFAX III (4-Hercules)
Bomber

Span 104 feet 0 inches   Length 71 feet 7 inches

May be seen with square-cut wing-tips and span 98 feet 8 inches as HALIFAX II.

Recognition Features: Halifax A.VII and A.IX similar to but without dorsal turret and with nose similar Halifax VIII (A.L.122). Halifax B.VI and B.VII also similar and with or without radar bulge below fuselage.

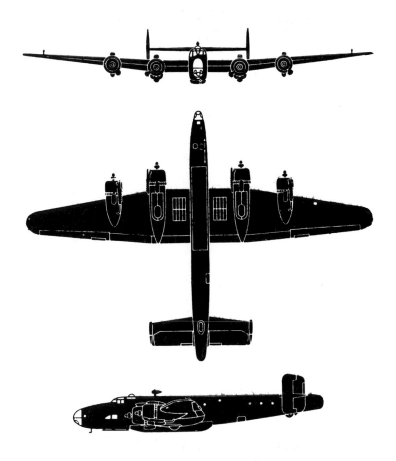

HALIFAX VIII (4-Hercules)
Transport

Span 103 feet 8 inches   Length 73 feet 7 inches

May be seen without bulge below fuselage.

Index

Glossary of abbreviations and code names

A&AEE	Aeroplane and Armament Experimental Establishment
A&AEE 760	Test reports covering Halifax
A&AEE 766	Test reports covering Lancaster
AFEE	Airborne Forces Experimental Establishment
AGL (T)	Airborne gun laying (turret) (Air gunner's radar)
AI	Airborne Interception (Radar)
AID	Aeronautical Inspection Directorate
AM	Air Ministry
AOC	Air Officer Commanding
AP970	Air Publication covering design
AP	Armour piercing (also Air Publication)
ARB	Air Registration Board
AS	Anti-submarine
ATA	Air Transport Auxiliary
ASI	Air speed indicator
ASV	Air-to-Surface Vessel (Radar)
AUW	All-up weight
BHP	Brake horsepower
BOAC	British Overseas Airways Corporation
CO	Commanding Officer
C of A	Certificate of Airworthiness
C of G	Centre of Gravity
C of P	Centre of Pressure
CHT	Cylinder head temperatures
D.Armt.D.	Directorate of Armament Development
DBER	Damaged beyond economic repair
DERD	Directorate of Engine Research and Development
Derv	Diesel fuel
DOR	Direction of rotation (also Directorate of Operational Requirements)
DR	Dead reckoning navigation
DTD	Directorate of Technical Development
DV	Direct vision window (window opened to allow vision forward)
Eureka	Ground radar beacon for homing
FN	Fraser-Nash
FRL	Flight Refuelling Ltd
FS	Supercharger gearing — fully supercharged
G	Gravity
GCA	Ground controlled approach (ground radar)
Gee	Navigational aid
GA Dwg	General-arrangement drawing
GP	General purpose
HC	Heavy capacity (blast effect bomb)
HCU	Heavy Conversion Unit
HE	High explosive
'HP'	Sir Frederick Handley Page
HP	Handley Page Ltd
H2S	Code name for radar navigation and bombing device

IAS	Indicated airspeed
ITP	Instructions to Proceed
Jostle	Code name for airborne device to interfere with German transmissions
LAC	Lancashire Aircraft Corporation
LAPG	London Aircraft Production Group
LAMS	London Aero and Motor Services
Loran	Acronym for long-range navigation system
LPTB	London Passenger Transport Board
MAP	Ministry of Aircraft Production
MC	Medium capacity (also mixture control on carburettor)
Met	Meteorology
'Milk Run'	Flights between Ulster and Northern Britain carrying milk
Mod	Modification
MoD	Ministry of Defence
MoS	Minstry of Supply
MS	Supercharger gearing — medium supercharged
MU	Maintenance Unit
OAT	Outside air temperature
OR	Operational Requirement
OTU	Operational Training Unit
PV12	Private Venture 12 — R-R engine that was developed into the Merlin
PoW	Prisoner of war
RAE	Royal Aircraft Establishment
Rebecca	Airborne receiver of Eureka ground transmissions
R of C	Rate of climb
R-R	Rolls-Royce
RTO	Resident technical officer
R/T	Radio telephony
SAP	Semi-armour-piercing
SAMM	Société d'Applications des Machines Mortrices
SBAC	Society of British Aircraft (now Aerospace) Constructors
SBC	Small bomb container
SL	Sea level
SOC	Shut-off cock
SOE	Special Operations Executive
STC	Standard Telephone & Cable Co
TAF(2nd)	Second Tactical Air Force
TAS	True air speed
TCDU	Transport Command Development Unit
TO	Take-off
TRE	Telecommunications Research Establishment
U/c	Undercarriage
'Wet Lift'	The carriage of liquid fuels on the Berlin Airlift
WFU	Withdrawn from use
W/T	Wireless telegraphy
YARD	York Aircraft Repair Depot

HP 61, HALIFAX V1